Housing, Markets and Policy

In many ways we are better housed than we were in the 1970s but the traditional housing problems of shortage and affordability are back on the agenda, along with newer concerns such as sustainability and social exclusion. The new orthodoxy of privatisation and deregulation has also been severely challenged by the current global economic crisis, compounding other housing issues such as the capacity of the building industry to meet future needs.

Exploring the transformation of the housing system since the pivotal decade of the 1970s, this collection of specially commissioned essays by distinguished specialists addresses the big issues in housing and housing policy in the UK. This distinctive and coherent analysis locates housing debates in their wider economic, social and policy contexts, steering a course between accounts that focus on economic theory and those that emphasise policy.

This approach provides students, researchers, practitioners and policy makers with a deeper understanding of the present housing system and its problems. It therefore establishes a basis for developing better solutions to those problems into the twenty-first century.

Peter Malpass is Professor of Housing and Urban Studies at the University of the West of England, UK.

Rob Rowlands is Lecturer at the Centre for Urban and Regional Studies, School of Public Policy, University of Birmingham, UK.

Housing and society series
Edited by Ray Forrest,
School for Policy Studies, University of Bristol

This series aims to situate housing within its wider social, political and economic context at both national and international level. In doing so it will draw on the full range of social science disciplines and on mainstream debate on the nature of contemporary social change. The ebooks are intended to appeal to an international academic audience as well as to practitioners and policymakers – to be theoretically informed and policy-relevant.

Housing, Markets and Policy
Edited by Peter Malpass and Rob Rowlands

Housing and Health in Europe
Edited by David Ormandy

The Hidden Millions
Graham Tipple and Suzanne Speak

Housing, Care and Inheritance
Misa Izuhara

Housing and Social Transition in Japan
Edited by Yosuke Hirayama and Richard Ronald

Housing Transformations
Shaping the space of twenty-first century living
Bridget Franklin

Housing and Social Policy
Contemporary themes and critical perspectives
Edited by Peter Somerville with Nigel Sprigings

Housing and Social Change
East–West perspectives
Edited by Ray Forrest and James Lee

Urban Poverty, Housing and Social Change in China
Ya Ping Wang

Gentrification in a Global Context
Edited by Rowland Atkinson and Gary Bridge

Housing, Markets and Policy

Edited by
Peter Malpass and
Rob Rowlands

Routledge
Taylor & Francis Group

LONDON AND NEW YORK

E·S·R·C
ECONOMIC
& SOCIAL
RESEARCH
COUNCIL

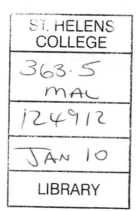
First published 2010
by Routledge
2 Park Square, Milton Park, Abingdon, Oxon OX14 4RN

Simultaneously published in the USA and Canada
by Routledge
270 Madison Avenue, New York, NY 10016, USA

Routledge is an imprint of the Taylor & Francis Group, an informa business

Typeset in Times and Frutiger by
Keyword Group Ltd,
Printed and bound in Great Britain by
TJ International Ltd, Padstow, Cornwall

British Library Cataloguing in Publication Data
A catalogue record for this book is available from the British Library

Library of Congress Cataloging-in-Publication Data
   Housing, markets, and policy / edited by Peter Malpass and
      Rob Rowlands.—1st ed.
      p. cm.— (Housing and society series)
   1. Housing policy. 2. Real property—Ownership. 3. Real estate business.
I. Malpass, Peter. II. Rowlands, Robert.
   HD7287.3.H687 2009
   333.33'8—dc22   2009001428

ISBN13: 978-0-415-47778-9 (hbk)
ISBN13: 978-0-415-47779-6 (pbk)
ISBN13: 978-0-203-87281-9 (ebk)

ISBN10: 0-415-47778-6 (hbk)
ISBN10: 0-415-47779-4 (pbk)
ISBN10: 0-203-87281-9 (ebk)

Contents

Contents

Illustrations

Contributors

Peter Malpass is professor of housing and urban studies at UWE, Bristol

Rob Rowlands is a lecturer at the Centre for Urban & Regional Studies (CURS), University of Birmingham

Chris Watson is an honorary senior lecturer at CURS

Pat Niner is an honorary senior lecturer at CURS

Ray Forrest is professor of urban studies at the University of Bristol

Colin Jones is professor of estate management at Heriot-Watt University, Edinburgh

David Mullins is professor of housing policy at CURS

Hal Pawson is professor of housing at Heriot-Watt University, Edinburgh

Peter Kemp is professor of social policy at the University of Oxford

Peter Williams is an independent consultant

Glen Bramley is professor of urban studies at Heriot-Watt University, Edinburgh

Peter Lee is director of CURS

Alan Murie is emeritus professor of urban and regional studies at CURS

Chris Paris is emeritus professor of housing studies at the University of Ulster

Preface

This book was prompted by a wish among colleagues and friends of Professor Alan Murie to mark his retirement from the University of Birmingham in July 2008. For more than thirty years Alan has made, and, as his chapter in this book demonstrates, continues to make, important, insightful and trenchant contributions to housing scholarship. Through his research and writing, and as the founding editor of *Housing Studies*, Alan has had a substantial influence on the development of housing studies as a distinct field of academic endeavour, both in the UK and overseas. Governments have not always liked or accepted the implications of Alan's analyses of housing policy and the housing system in the UK, but among the academic community his work has been universally recognised for its rigour, humanity and integrity.

Acknowledgments

We would like to express our gratitude to the Council of Mortgage Lenders, and to Steve Wilcox for data from the *UK Housing Review*.

Crown Copyright material is reproduced under the terms of the Click-use Licence by permission of the Office of Public Sector Information (OPSI).

Peter Malpass and Rob Rowlands

Authors (front row, from left): Chris Paris, Ray Forrest, Alan Murie, Glen Bramley and Pat Niner; (at the back) Hal Pawson, Peter Malpass, Colin Jones, Rob Rowlands, David Mullins, Peter Williams, Chris Watson, Peter Kemp and Peter Lee.

1 Introduction

Transformation and change in housing

Peter Malpass and Rob Rowlands

In Britain it is the run on the Northern Rock Bank, one of the country's top five mortgage lenders, in August 2007 that symbolises the start of what turned out to be a global financial crisis of epic proportions. But in reality Northern Rock was just a little local casualty of a gathering storm that had begun when the boom in the American housing market peaked in 2006 and began a rapid slide towards slump. The bursting of the American housing market bubble, inflated by aggressive lending to sub-prime (i.e. unusually risky) borrowers, quickly brought the entire world banking system to the brink of collapse. The nationalisation of Northern Rock was ultimately overshadowed by the sheer scale of the international crisis, the demise of much bigger and apparently stronger institutions and the size of the rescue packages hastily assembled by governments around the world in 2008. But Northern Rock remains important as a reminder of how much the British housing market has changed, how significant housing has become in the economy and how interconnected national economies are in the present period.

The credit crunch and its aftermath have changed the political and economic landscape, undermining the hegemonic position of the theory that deregulated markets produce the best outcomes, and challenging policy-makers to rein in the excesses of the free market. The crisis has raised the profile of housing in a number of ways, implicating mortgage-lenders, bringing mortgage-lending to a virtual halt, and as a result lowering output of much-needed new homes. This in turn has raised questions about the achievement of government's housing production targets and about what other policy options might need to be considered. On a wider perspective it raises questions about the wisdom of an economic policy that relies so heavily on rising house prices to sustain credit-based consumer spending, and on the accumulation of wealth through home ownership as an alternative to adequate public services.

The aim of this book is not to focus exclusively or even mainly on the post-2007 crisis, but it is intended to explore and analyse the big issues in contemporary debates about housing and housing policy in the UK. The crisis may have changed the way we think about these issues, but it did not manufacture them from nothing: the housing system as we know it today has been a long time in the making. The theme linking the various contributions is that the 1970s was a pivotal decade in the second half of the twentieth century, and that since that time there has been a profound transformation in the housing system and housing policy in the UK. In the period up to the late 1960s UK housing policy enjoyed a period of political priority and administrative coherence. The problem facing the country was understood in terms of two main dimensions: a serious gross shortage (compounded by the Second World War); and a problem of poor-quality housing – also partly due to the impact of the war, but mostly a product of a much longer-term failure to maintain, modernise and improve houses in line with changing expectations. For 25 years policy was primarily focused on addressing these two problems through high levels of house-building, and replacement of worn-out dwellings. The 1970s saw the weakening or abandonment of assumptions previously taken for granted and marked the boundary between postwar housing policy and the emergence of a period of privatisation and deregulation (Murie, forthcoming), leading to the establishment of a new orthodoxy by the end of the twentieth century. Subsequent chapters describe, analyse and explain aspects of the transformation of housing and housing policy, as a basis for understanding the present and thinking about the future. The purpose of this opening chapter is first to show how and why the 1970s were so important, to identify the dimensions of change and transformation since that time, and then to outline the scope and structure of the book as a whole.

The 1970s: 'Crisis, what crisis?'

'Crisis, what crisis?' was a newspaper headline-writer's interpretation of the British prime minister's attempt to play down the severity of the situation facing the country in the so-called 'winter of discontent' of 1978–9. The word 'crisis' is too easily applied to situations that are merely difficult, and there were certainly plenty of those during the 1970s. But if the word is applied in a stricter sense, to mean a genuine turning-point, then there are good grounds for arguing that the decade as a whole deserves to be seen in this way. It was a tumultuous decade of political and economic turmoil, both domestically and internationally, the outcomes of which included tectonic shifts in politics and in economic and social policies. Two events of global significance were: first, the collapse in 1971 of the Bretton Woods agreement of 1944 governing international exchange rates, allowing inflation to rise and exposing the weak British currency to speculative attack; and second, in 1973, a brief Arab–Israeli war that was followed by a quadrupling of world oil prices as the producing countries flexed their economic muscles. This alone was enough to send shock waves through the world economy, but oil prices doubled again between 1978 and 1981. Keynesian policies of economic demand management that had underpinned the long postwar boom in much of Europe, Japan and the United States were abandoned, with inevitable consequences for unemployment, which in Britain rose to levels not seen since the 1930s. The postwar ascendancy of liberal and social-democratic ideas began to be effectively challenged by a resurgent conservative ideology, and a global crisis of capitalism became also a 'fiscal crisis for the state' (O'Connor, 1973). In particular, the expanded volumes of state expenditure on various welfare services since 1945 were blamed for at least part of the economic crisis, with severe consequences for future spending and service provision. The era of welfare capitalism (sometimes referred to as 'Fordism'), which had lasted since 1945, came to an end in the global economic crisis of the mid-1970s. In the years that followed a new phase – post-industrial, post-Fordist, post-welfare – was established, in which governments became less confident of their ability to manage national economies in the face of globalisation. Market forces were given freer rein generally and state welfare provisions developed in the previous era were cut back or modified, in ways that often mimic the market, placing emphasis on consumer choice and responsibility rather than on collective provision for individual needs, prompting references to 'post-welfare states'. The retreat from the high point of collectivist social policy in the postwar era and the rise of choice-based personalised welfare is a defining feature of the period since the 1970s. Housing has played a key role in this process, as subsequent chapters reveal.

In the UK the decade began with the election of a Conservative government, which confronted problems of rising inflation and unemployment, industrial unrest and a resurgence of nationalist rhetoric in Scotland and Wales. The Northern Ireland Troubles, which had begun in the late 1960s, were in a particularly florid and violent phase. These were times of increasing political polarisation, with conflicts centred on controversial legislation such as the Industrial Relations Act of 1971. Polarisation became explicit in early 1974 when the prime minister, Edward Heath, in the midst of an industrial dispute with the miners, called an election on the theme of 'Who governs Britain?' In view of the way that British political debate has been recast in more recent times, it is important to recall that in those days the conflict between capital and labour was still prominent.

The UK economy seemed to be particularly adversely affected by the consequences of the oil price rises, and inflation rose to 25 per cent in 1975. This, together with a falling pound and vanishing reserves, led to a humiliating request for assistance from the International Monetary Fund, whose rescue package of loans came with conditions demanding cuts in public expenditure. 'It was the economic crisis of 1976 that finally broke the continuity in the social policies of the postwar era' (Glennerster, 1995: 167). Arguments that the welfare state was a burden that the economy could no longer carry gained ground, and debate shifted from expansion to retrenchment. The crisis of the welfare state did not necessarily imply its destruction, but it did imply that it should be something smaller and different. Housing, as the most market-based of the main welfare state services, was in the forefront of change.

In housing the 1970s was a time of change for reasons going beyond the immediate crises affecting the economy and the welfare state. These crises intersected with other processes of change that were already in train within the housing system. A long-term perspective on the housing market and housing policy suggests that a process of market modernisation had been under way since the early part of the century, shifting from the predominance of private renting in 1900 to individual home ownership as the modernised form of housing provision (Harloe, 1985; Malpass and Murie, 1999). It was at the start of the 1970s that the proportion of households that were home owners passed 50 per cent. This was a fact not lost on politicians aware of what it meant in terms of votes and electoral politics.

Overlying this deep process was the impact of the two world wars: by 1970 the UK housing system had been affected by the direct impact of war or recovery from it for more than half a century. The wars had short-term impacts in terms of very low levels of new building, equally low levels of repair and maintenance activity, and, in the Second World War, substantial losses and damage due to bombing. Making good the accumulated shortages took many years, and it is arguable that at least some of the clearance and redevelopment activity in the 1930s and from the mid-1950s onwards, together with physical modernisation of the remaining pre-1914 stock, would have been dealt with by normal market processes had it not been for the effects of the wars. Moreover, the wars had considerable implications for the politics of housing, initially in the form of demands for rent controls (which had the unintended consequence of providing landlords with an excuse for not maintaining and improving their properties). And the knock on effect of rent control was that the state became heavily involved in subsidising the production of council houses.

It is interesting that the two world wars had a greater disruptive impact on the house building industry than did either of the full-blown economic crises in the early 1930s or the mid-1970s. The consequence was that by 1970 local authorities had built nearly 6 million houses and flats, mostly aimed at reducing the overall shortage and not targeted on the least well off. It was at this point that a number of things came together to precipitate change: the growing pressure on welfare state expenditure coincided with ministers arguing that the end of the overall housing shortage was within sight, and the housing market restructuring process was reaching a stage where some difficult strategic decisions were implicitly (if not explicitly) required. One of these concerned council rents policy and another was the question of the sale of council houses. It has been shown (Malpass, 1990) that the system for setting council rents and subsidies was losing coherence and effectiveness by the late 1960s. Kemeny (1995) has referred to this as a maturation crisis – as councils accumulated stocks of houses over many years so the average cost of debt repayment per dwelling fell, especially in inflationary conditions, with the effect that those councils with older stocks could charge low rents and still cover costs. As governments began to argue for less new building by local councils this would have the effect of increasing the number of localities where rents at well below market levels became feasible, without Exchequer subsidy, making council housing increasingly attractive to tenants as compared with other tenures. What made this into a maturation crisis rather than a boon was that there was a powerful coalition of interests supporting the private market, especially the further growth of home ownership. On this view council housing could not be permitted to emerge as a viable competitor, offering good quality accommodation at below market rates. The response of the Labour government in the late 1960s had been to carry out a review of rents and subsidy policy, but to take no action. The incoming Conservative government pressed ahead with controversial and mould-breaking legislation to facilitate the withdrawal of subsidies and to force council rents to rise substantially, beyond what would be required to cover costs (Malpass, 1990).

The question of the sale of council houses came onto the agenda in the 1970s partly for party political reasons. Council estates were seen as enclaves of Labour voters, and the Conservatives reasoned that the opportunity to buy their homes (at discounted prices) might make them more likely to vote Conservative. Margaret Thatcher was later to claim that the promise of the right to buy at the 1979 general election did indeed persuade thousands of council tenants to vote Conservative for the first time (Malpass and Murie, 1990: 88). But the sale of council houses was also partly a response to pressures that had been building up over many years in the context of the modernisation of the housing market. Harloe (1985) has argued that public housing is only likely to embrace the better-off fraction of the working class in times of political and economic disruption, especially in the aftermath of major wars. The long-term role of public housing in normal times, he argued, was likely to be residual, accommodating the least well off and others who could not find or afford suitable homes on the open market.

As Britain, and in particular the housing market, continued to recover from the Second World War two factors came into play to suggest a smaller council sector. First, living standards were rising throughout the 1950s and 1960s, creating a kind of golden age for home ownership and making it more affordable for a wider proportion of the population. So home ownership was brought within the financial reach of many of precisely that group of better-off workers who had benefited most from both the postwar economic boom and the opportunity to rent a good-quality council house at a subsidised rent. To some extent it was the success of postwar full-employment policies and increased affluence that undermined council housing as a broadly based tenure.

The second factor at work by the 1970s was that, although the growth of home ownership, which had been an increasingly important objective of housing policy since the early 1950s, had been boosted by transfers from private renting, the supply of attractive dwellings from this pool was declining. Council housing therefore represented a second source of additional supply, ideally suited to deliver suitable and affordable homes to the better-off working class, the group most likely to aspire to buying a home of their own. They were also precisely the group that needed to be drawn into home ownership if it was to spread to increasing proportions of people on lower incomes. It is important to remember that British housing policy has always been based on the assumption that the market would provide for most people most of the time. From that point of view, a public sector of over 30 per cent could easily appear to be overgrown, especially when there was a demonstrable overlap between the incomes of many first-time buyers and those of better-off council tenants. Higher rents and discounted sales, therefore, can be seen as two linked parts of a strategic response to this situation.

Before leaving the 1970s there are two further points to make. First, it was a decade when there was a decisive shift in the relationship between central and local government, as illustrated by both rents and sales policies. Hitherto, local authorities had enjoyed considerable freedom to determine their own policies on both these issues, but the Housing Finance Act, 1972, was a major assault on local autonomy in the area of rent-setting, and by 1980 the right to buy had removed local discretion in that area too. Meanwhile, actions initiated by the Labour government of 1974–9 had begun to reduce local authorities' freedom to determine their own capital expenditure programmes. Second, the really radical housing policy measures were associated with the Conservative governments in power at either end of the decade (council rents and subsidies in 1972 and the right to buy, and then rents and subsidies again in 1980). The mid-70s Labour government initiated a fundamental review of housing finance in 1974 but the eventual outcome was certainly not the radical reform that had been anticipated at the start (Malpass, 2008a). The review endorsed the existing arrangements for assisting home owners, and proposed a new system for paying subsidies to local authorities in a way which allowed a subsequent Conservative government to impose large rent increases in the early 1980s (DoE, 1977; Holmans, 1991). Labour's position on housing in the 1970s lacked the simple clarity of the Conservatives, and it was certainly less willing to offend the local authorities, which made it difficult to move housing policy forward in the way that the forces discussed above implied it should go.

Housing in an era of privatisation and deregulation

Changes in housing since the 1970s need to be seen in relation to a rapidly changing social, economic and political context. The economy experienced deep recessions in the early 1980s and again a decade later, before a prolonged period of growth from 1996 to 2007. An increasingly market-based housing system has been directly and significantly affected by these ups and downs (Bramley *et al.*, 2004). The economy lost large numbers of manufacturing and coal-mining jobs in the 1980s and the size of the manufacturing sector of the economy has continued to shrink, with implications for housing demand, especially in the former industrial heartlands of the Midlands and the north of England, south Wales and west central Scotland. Equally, the growth of a service-based economy, particularly in London, has had very different consequences for housing demand in the south-east.

In the period 1945 to 1978 inequality of income and wealth in the UK was on a downwards trajectory, but subsequently the direction of change was reversed, particularly during the 1980s. The incomes of the highest earners have continued to rise faster than those on lower pay, and as income differences tend to be mapped onto the housing market these sorts of trends have implications for who lives where, and who gets access to spatially distributed scarce urban resources, such as good schools and health care. Not surprisingly, increased socio-spatial segregation has become a theme in the academic literature in recent years.

One of the most important social trends of the period since the 1970s has been the decline of collectivism in both the workplace and in social policy. The Conservative governments of the 1980s conducted a prolonged assault on the powers and freedoms of trade unions, and in social policy the modernisation project of recent years has emphasised the need to continue the move away from a provider orientation to a customer focus. People have been encouraged to see themselves primarily as consumers, exercising choices that are, by their nature, individual and self-centred. Of course, along with choice goes responsibility, and a characteristic of the reform of public services, most obviously in pensions and housing, has been the move from collective means of provision to individual, risk-bearing mechanisms provided by the private market. Great importance is attached to people taking responsibility for their own well-being, and making choices in their own best interest.

The governance of the United Kingdom provides another dimension of change. Foster (2005) has suggested that the country became less well governed under Margaret Thatcher: although ministers had been persistently overstretched in the 1970s, she began a revolution – the virtual collapse of cabinet government, subsequently carried on under Tony Blair. On a different scale, it was under Blair in the late 1990s that Scotland and Wales finally obtained a degree of control over domestic matters, including housing. Northern Ireland is a special case, which has been in and out of direct rule from Westminster since the early 1970s. The logic of devolution is that policies and outcomes will tend to diverge as decisions are made in the light of circumstances and politics within the various jurisdictions. There are already signs of divergence in the different parts of the UK, although it is arguable that the direction of travel in Northern Ireland has been towards the English situation. At the local level the erosion of the position of local authorities has been progressively reduced by both Conservative and Labour governments since the 1970s. Local authorities have been losing housing stock since 1980 and they have been encouraged to think of themselves as strategic enablers rather than providers of housing (and other services). More recently there has been an attempt to build up regional-level strategic planning in England.

The transformation of housing can be measured in different ways. Table 1.1 provides information on the growth of the housing stock since the 1970s, showing that there has been a net increase of 28 per cent, in an era when, for much of the time, house-building was not a high priority of governments.

The graph in Figure 1.1 draws attention to the different components of housing production over a longer period, highlighting the sharp decline in new building by local authorities and the failure of private builders and housing associations to make up the loss. Figure 1.1 also highlights the relatively stable levels

Table 1.1 Housing stock in different parts of the UK, 1976–2006 (millions)

	1976	1986	1996	2006
England	17.1	18.9	20.4	22.0
Wales	1.0	1.1	1.2	1.3
Scotland	1.9	2.0	2.2	2.4
Northern Ireland	0.4	0.5	0.6	0.7
UK	20.6	22.6	24.5	26.4

Source: Wilcox, 2007

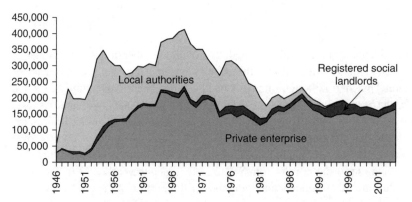

1.1 Housebuilding: permanent dwelling completions by tenure, Great Britain.
Source: Crown Copyright, DCLG live tables 244–7 (last updated Nov–Dec 2008).

of private house-building over a long run of years. A curious feature of the UK housing system in this period has been the unresponsiveness of supply to demand, indicated by rising prices and growing concerns about affordability, culminating in the government commissioning a review of the problem (Barker, 2003, 2004).

Turning from production to consumption, housing research in the UK has routinely employed the concept of tenure as a key analytical tool, and much attention has been paid to tenure growth and decline as part of a longer-term transition from a predominantly private rented system to a predominantly owner-occupied system.

In this context the changing size and role of public housing has attracted the interest of researchers in a number of disciplines. From the late 1970s debate began to focus on the implications of the privatisation of public housing and of its 'residualisation' – its drift towards a residual, or safety-net, role for the least well off. The decline of public housing has been linked to changes in the welfare state, with housing being seen as the service most vulnerable to cuts and residualisation. More recently, since the late 1980s, another trend has run alongside residualisation: demunicipalisation through the large-scale transfer of the ownership of local authority housing stocks to new owners, principally newly formed not-for-profit housing associations. This process has gone furthest in England, but transfers have taken place in Wales and Scotland, the largest of all being the transfer of the Glasgow municipal stock. (In the case of Northern Ireland all municipal housing was transferred to the Northern Ireland Housing Executive in the midst of the troubles in 1971.)

The outcome of these ongoing processes is that social housing in the present period is very different from how it looked in 1970: a smaller sector, both numerically and proportionally, socially narrower and with a different pattern of ownership. The total UK stock of social housing units fell by more than 1.6 million between 1971 and 2006. Council dwellings fell by 57 per cent between 1976 and 2006, and by that date councils owned only 54 per cent of all social housing in Great Britain, compared with 91 per cent in 1986 (Wilcox, 2007). This clearly suggests that the future of social housing lies in the housing association sub-sector.

Meanwhile, as Figure 1.2 shows, home ownership has continued to grow, from just 50 per cent at the start of the 1970s to more than 70 per cent today. The sale of houses to sitting tenants by local authorities, other public-sector bodies (including the Northern Ireland Housing Executive and the former new town corporations) and housing associations contributed to that growth, as well as bringing in many new working-class owners and creating mixed-tenure neighbourhoods where the term 'council estate' had previously applied. Another, and less predictable, sign of the vitality of the housing market is the revival of private renting, which had seemed in terminal decline in 1970. Both home ownership and private

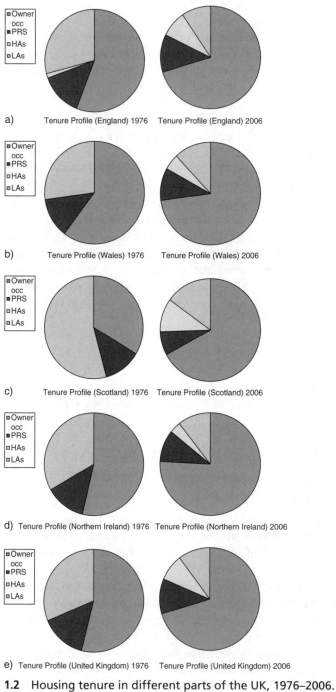

a) Tenure Profile (England) 1976   Tenure Profile (England) 2006

b) Tenure Profile (Wales) 1976   Tenure Profile (Wales) 2006

c) Tenure Profile (Scotland) 1976   Tenure Profile (Scotland) 2006

d) Tenure Profile (Northern Ireland) 1976   Tenure Profile (Northern Ireland) 2006

e) Tenure Profile (United Kingdom) 1976   Tenure Profile (United Kingdom) 2006

1.2 Housing tenure in different parts of the UK, 1976–2006.
Source: Wilcox, 2007.
Key: *Owner occ:* Owner-occupied; *PRS:* Private rented sector; *HAs:*
Housing associations; *LAs:* Local authority-owned.

renting benefited from deregulation in the 1980s. Deregulation of the lending industry and the subsequent conversion of most mutual building societies into commercial banks led to a considerable increase in the supply and accessibility of mortgage funds. And in the case of private renting, it was the deregulation of tenancy agreements and rents after the Housing Act, 1988, that facilitated the first measurable revival of investment in this sector for several generations.

Accompanying tenure restructuring is a set of other indicators of transformation. First, tenure restructuring implies a different pattern of opportunities and outcomes for individuals, and a different set of suppliers and other supply-side actors, reflecting the growth and liberalisation of the market. In this context it is necessary to say that growth has been fuelled by important changes in both the lending policies and practices of the mortgage providers and in the ways that they raise their supplies of money for lending. Previously overwhelmingly reliant on retail savings deposited by individual customers they have begun to raise significant amounts of money from wholesale money markets, and to indulge in the practice of securitisation. This is essentially a way of inflating the volume of lending by selling the rights to future income streams. Purchasers of these rights effectively allow the lenders to recover a substantial proportion of any loan very much more quickly than through traditional repayment methods, realising cash that can be lent to more home-buyers, leading to a new round of securitisation.

Second, the state has drawn back, relying to a greater extent on private enterprise to meet housing needs and demands. Implicit in this is a more relaxed stance on the implications of more pervasive market forces in terms of the distribution of costs and benefits. Third, transformation can be measured in terms of greater socio-spatial segregation and wider inequality as the housing market reflects and amplifies inequalities generated elsewhere. Fourth, transformation also means greater complexity, both because of the fragmentation of governance and the difficulty of achieving desired policy goals through reliance on actors and institutions primarily motivated by market forces and considerations of profit and loss. Fifth, complexity is further increased by the growing importance of housing wealth and its potential to be realised in order to pay for welfare. This refers to the possibility that housing policy decisions may be influenced by non-housing considerations involving individuals' capacity to provide for their own welfare needs. Finally, transformation has brought new problems, and revived some old ones in different forms. Traditional housing problems of shortage and affordability are back on the agenda, along with newer concerns such as sustainability and social exclusion.

Finally in this section we come to housing policy. In the period up to the end of the 1970s all governments had relied on local authorities to play a significant role in tackling housing problems that were seen to lie predominantly in the private market. The great transformation in policy thinking has been to reverse that perception, despite all the evidence that has accumulated in recent years about problems of supply and affordability in the market. Local authority housing has come to be seen as part of the problem to be tackled, and the answers apparently lie in the market and with market-driven agencies. Despite the lack of fundamental reform emerging from the housing finance review in the mid-1970s there has subsequently been considerable, piecemeal, change. Among the most significant measures have been the elimination of mortgage interest tax relief during the 1990s and the introduction of housing benefit (HB) in 1982–3. The introduction of HB (or something like it) was a necessary precondition of the deregulation of private renting and the withdrawal of bricks-and-mortar subsidies in the social rented sector. However, it remains an area in need of further reform, not least to embrace low-income home owners.

Housing remained a good issue for the Conservatives at general elections in the 1980s as they pressed ahead with the privatisation and deregulation agenda. After 1997 there was no great change of direction, and overall the Labour governments of Tony Blair and Gordon Brown have pursued policies characterised by continuity with trajectories set up under the Tories. They have not been willing to return to a more central role for local authorities, and have actively resisted demands that they should assist authorities to retain their council houses. No government has been prepared to adopt policies to reverse the residualisation of social housing, preferring instead to increase the rhetorical emphasis on mixed communities (Hills, 2007). In that sense housing remains the wobbly pillar under the welfare state, but looking at housing and the welfare state from a different direction it can be argued that housing, specifically the owner-occupier sector, has become increasingly important in the context of the modernisation project. The more that people are expected to take responsibility for their own well-being, especially in old age in an era when company pension schemes are of diminishing value, the more that housing wealth comes into focus as a potential source of spending power (Groves et al., 2007; Malpass, 2008b).

Scope and structure of the book

This book is concerned with the questions that arise from the transformation of housing and housing policy. How much is the process driven by policy and how much by other factors? How are tenures changing their meanings and roles in the overall housing system? How far will residualisation proceed, or has it begun to level out? Is tenure becoming less important than locality in some parts of the housing system? How are people affected by when and where they enter housing, and are some cohorts significantly advantaged or disadvantaged? What lessons can be learned from the past, and what do they imply for the future?

It is difficult within one volume to cover all aspects of contemporary housing debates, and there are some obvious gaps in this book. Questions of 'race' and gender, for example, are not directly addressed; nor is the controversial question of antisocial behaviour and what to do about it (Flint, 2006). Omission does not imply lack of importance, just lack of space. The scope of the book is confined to the UK, again for similar reasons. This national focus may be justified in terms of the degree of dynamism displayed by UK housing and housing policy in the last 30–35 years, and by the suggestion that in some respects the UK has travelled further in the same general direction as a number of its neighbours in continental Europe, particularly in terms of privatisation and deregulation. The book is about housing in the UK as a whole, and does not aim to provide a detailed survey of trends and differences among the four constituent nations. Differences and variations between England, Scotland, Wales and Northern Ireland are mentioned and acknowledged as and when they have a bearing on particular topics and debates. In this sense the scope of the book is wider than the government review of English housing policy 1975–2000 (ODPM, 2005). That project was confined to England and to a review of five policy themes over the period to 2000.

The chapters follow a logical and chronological progression: Chapter 2 concentrates on the housing system and housing policy in the 1970s, providing a baseline position for understanding the subsequent transformation. This chapter sets the scene for the remainder of the book, reviewing some of the key issues of the period: for example, the Cullingworth reports on housing need and the role of council housing; the debates on housing finance, the Review of Housing Finance, which became the Housing Policy Review; the growing emphasis on housing renewal; the new role for the Housing Corporation; and the first signs of the growing importance of partnership working.

The next four chapters look at aspects of the ongoing restructuring of the social rented sector. In Chapter 3 Ray Forrest provides a retrospective assessment of British council housing, that also engages with current debates around social cohesion, social mix and social and environmental sustainability. The pervasive image of direct state housing provision in Britain, and in most countries, is now one of failure, inefficiency and poverty. However, the role of housing tenures is not a given but is contingent on a wide range of contextual and institutional factors. This chapter revisits the role of British council housing as a form of provision which was for certain sections of the working class aspirational and popular, and which represented a key element in social mobility and enhanced life chances. Linking to Colin Jones's Chapter 4 on the right to buy, it also shows that the success of this policy was critically dependent upon the prior success of council housing in providing homes that people wanted to buy. Jones assesses the extent to which the right to buy has been the principal agent and the cause of the changes to the housing system. The analysis encompasses the ramifications of the right to buy across tenures and neighbourhoods, its significance in the cascading of wealth, and its consequences in terms of complexity and fragmentation for housing policy, affordability problems and housing markets. The chapter therefore sets the right to buy within the wider perspective of other fundamental influences on the housing system and regional variations.

David Mullins and Hal Pawson then look in Chapter 5 at the way in which the remaining social housing has been gradually moved from municipal ownership into the not-for-profit sector. Over the last 20 years more than a million council homes have been transferred to a variety of housing associations, mostly newly created bodies set up for the purpose. The chapter reflects on the emergence and evolution of stock transfer, showing how it became a mainstream policy, and how it has been turned to meet different purposes over time. A key issue here is the extent to which stock transfer represents a form of privatisation. Twenty years on from the first large-scale transfer it is also appropriate to look at how the new organisations have bedded down, and what impact they have made on the wider housing association sector. In Chapter 6 Peter Malpass provides a critical assessment of the rise of housing associations and their contribution to the transformation of social renting in the UK. From their position on the margins of both housing policy and the housing system in the early 1970s they have progressed to the point where they seem certain to become the second-largest sector after owner occupation. The chapter discusses the changes that have occurred within what was the 'voluntary housing movement', and assesses the extent to which growth and change reflect the hand of government and its agents.

Chapters 7 to 9 consider developments in housing market activity. In Chapter 7, Peter Kemp discusses the transformation of private renting since the early 1970s. He shows how the size, nature and role of this sector within the housing market have changed in that period and the factors that have influenced that transformation. He also examines how public policy towards private renting has changed and explores the emergence and growth of 'buy to let' investment in private rental housing in the period since the mid-1990s. Kemp concludes that after decades of decline private renting now faces a more secure future. The current turmoil in the owner-occupier market, on the other hand, raises important questions about this most dominant part of the UK housing system, examined by Peter Williams in Chapter 8. He identifies the ways in which the owner-occupied sector has not only grown but fundamentally changed since the 1970s, before running into its worst crisis in living memory. Williams provides a valuable account of the way the housing market crisis has developed since the summer of 2007. Further change, going beyond a 'market correction', seems inevitable, with potentially profound implications for home owners, for builders and lenders, and for government policy. One of the features of the housing market in recent years has been the apparent unresponsiveness of supply to demand, a topic taken up in Chapter 9. Here Glen Bramley considers the rediscovery of housing supply as a policy issue in the early 2000s after 25 years of neglect by successive governments. He looks at the complex economic, political and environmental challenges involved in meeting plans for significantly increased volumes of house-building.

Chapters 10 and 11 also look at a highly topical set of issues around regeneration and the sustainability of communities. In Chapter 10 Peter Lee emphasises how housing policy and, more specifically, the spatial aspects of housing strategy development have evolved in response to changes in the discourse affecting housing. Central to this changing discourse are issues of distribution and access to housing and how this has altered over the past 20 to 30 years. In Chapter 11 Rob Rowlands considers the meaning of the role of community and housing in delivering sustainable communities. Implementing a concept which incorporates disputed terminology is difficult and the role and place of housing in this aim is unclear. He concludes by arguing for a more integrated approach that focuses on the neighbourhood as the crux of delivery.

In Chapter 12 Alan Murie reflects on the way that housing policy seemed to go into decline from the late 1970s, only to be rediscovered in the present decade. He looks at some of the key dimensions of this shift in status and the discourses around it, initially considering the changing importance of the policy area and then referring in more detail to key elements in the recent discussion of policy: affordability, the future of social rented housing, housing and life chances. Finally he considers alternative futures for housing policy and especially the social rented sector. In the final chapter Chris Paris sums up and draws some conclusions from the book as a whole.

References

Barker, K. (2003) *Review of Housing Supply: securing our future needs. An interim report*, London: Treasury and ODPM.

—— (2004) *Review of Housing Supply: delivering stability: securing our housing needs, Final report*, London: HMSO.

Bramley, G., Munro, M. and Pawson, H. (2004) *Key Issues in Housing Policy: policies and markets in 21st-century Britain*, Basingstoke: Palgrave Macmillan.

DoE (Department of the Environment) (1977) *Housing Policy: a consultative document,* London: HMSO, Cmnd 6851.

Flint, J. (ed.) (2006) *Housing, Urban Governance and Antisocial Behaviour: Perspectives, Policies and Practice*, Bristol: Policy Press.

Foster, C. (2005) *British Government in Crisis,* Oxford: Hart.

Glennerster, H. (1995) *British Social Policy Since 1945,* Oxford: Blackwell.

Groves, R., Murie, A. and Watson, C. (2007) *Housing and the New Welfare State,* Aldershot: Ashgate.

Harloe, M. (1985) *Private Rented Housing in the United States and Europe,* Beckenham: Croom Helm.

Hills, J. (2007) *Ends and Means: the future roles of social housing in England,* CASE Report 34, Centre for the Analysis of Social Exclusion & London School of Economics.

Holmans, A. (1991) 'The 1977 National Housing Policy Review in Retrospect', *Housing Studies*, 6(3), 206–19.

Kemeny, J. (1995) *From Public Housing to the Social Market*, London: Routledge.

Malpass, P. (1990) *Reshaping Housing Policy: subsidies, rents and residualisation*, London: Routledge.

—— (2008a) 'Policy making in interesting times: the Housing Finance and Policy Review, 1975–77,' *People, Places and Policy Online*, 2(2), 65–75.

—— (2008b) 'Housing and the New Welfare State: wobbly pillar or cornerstone?' *Housing Studies*, 23(1), 1–19.

Malpass, P. and Murie, M. (1990) *Housing Policy and Practice*, Basingstoke: Macmillan, 3rd edition.

—— (1999) *Housing Policy and Practice,* Basingstoke: Macmillan, 5th edition.

Murie, A. (forthcoming) 'Modernisation of Housing in England: Welfare States, Rationing, Affordability and Competition', in *Tijdschrift voor Sociale en Economische Geografie.*

O'Connor, J. (1973) *The Fiscal Crisis of the State,* New York: St Martin's Press.

ODPM (Office of the Deputy Prime Minister) (2005) *Lessons from the past, challenges for the future for housing policy: an evaluation of English housing policy, 1975–2000*, London: ODPM.

Wilcox, S. (2007) *UK Housing Review 2007/2008*, London: CML/CIH.

2 Housing policy and the housing system in the 1970s

Christopher Watson and Pat Niner

As established in Chapter 1, the 1970s may be seen as a turning point in the development of British housing policy; a decade in which the postwar consensus on the objectives and general direction of policy began to be challenged by new perspectives, some of which took hold from the 1980s onwards. How was housing perceived in the 1970s? What was the nature of the housing system and how was it analysed? What were the main issues of the day and the debates to which they gave rise? This chapter will examine these and other questions as a background to the chapters that follow.

It can be argued that the basis of the housing situation in the 1970s reflected issues and concerns that had dominated the political agenda since the Second World War. Housing shortage, bad housing conditions, including the problem of the slums and the effects of overcrowding, major and continuing changes in the pattern of tenure, and concerns about the rising costs of the public-sector housing programme were dominant themes in the 1950s and 1960s and continued to be so, to varying degrees, throughout the 1970s.

Understanding housing in the 1970s

For policy-makers and the relatively small but growing band of housing researchers, the 1960s and 1970s were marked by a broadening range of information and advice from national, regional and in some cases local surveys and studies. Some came from government, for example, with the commissioning of a variety of housing surveys, such as *Scottish Housing in 1965* (Cullingworth, 1967) and the *West Midlands Conurbation Housing Survey 1966* (Welch, 1971); while important statistical series were started, such as *Social Trends* in 1970, the *General Household Survey* in 1971 and the *English House Condition Survey*, also in 1971.

Researchers in both government and the academic world were also contributing independently to information and analysis: for example, through the work of Cullingworth on private renting (1963); Donnison on household movement (1961) and the government of housing (1967); and Rex and Moore on housing classes (1967). In government, the work of the Social Research Unit in the Department of the Environment and of the Building Research Establishment included studies directed at the improvement of housing design but spread into a much wider range of social research on housing, including commissioned research from research institutes and universities (Hole, 1979).

Compared with the 1950s, the growth of research and information gave a much sounder basis for policy in the 1960s and 1970s, and contributed to an interest in monitoring and evaluating policies and their effects. However, many issues were decided on the basis of political standpoints, exemplified by the long-running debate on the sale of council houses (Murie, 1975) and the failure of the 1957 Rent Act to achieve its objective of liberating 'economic man' so that the supply of private rented housing would be increased and its management improved.

These experiences began to give rise to an understanding that housing is highly complex and that housing policy can often be characterised by conflict and contradictions. Some of the basic characteristics of housing in Britain, which are now seen as axiomatic, were enunciated in ways that made sense: for example, that social policy and the distribution of the goods and services to which it relates is based on an assessment of social need rather than on demand; that in the case of housing a large private sector operates, in contrast to some other areas of policy such as education and health, which are dominated by public provision; and that housing is characterised fundamentally by its high cost, its long life and its fixed location. The dynamic nature of housing was also recognised. Change was attributable not only, for example, to programmes of new building, clearance and improvement but also to change *in situ*, such as family formation and ageing, and to residential mobility, both of which could be seen as a process of adjustment in the relationships between households and their dwellings. Even if no new building or other programmes were to take place, housing would still be affected by the process of change.

Such considerations gave rise to the concept of the British housing system as a complex of housing sectors, subsystems or submarkets, with different locations, physical and social characteristics, tenures and costs (Murie *et al.*, 1976). The role of government was seen to be important in housing, particularly in relation to policy, but the housing system also contained a variety of institutions, including local authorities and private-sector organisations, all of which could influence and be influenced by the system.

Other perspectives included the notion of housing classes, put forward by Rex and Moore (1967); urban managerialism (Pahl, 1970), which saw inequalities in housing as a consequence of the activities of 'gatekeepers' who controlled access to housing, especially in the owner-occupied and council-housing sectors; and Marxist accounts, with their emphasis on production and consumption, and the role of 'exchange professionals', such as estate agents (Bassett and Short, 1980).

All these approaches, however, tended to use tenure as an organising framework and thus, 'the most effective framework for understanding the way the housing market operated in Britain began to be based on an understanding of the role of state intervention and the partitioning of housing finance between different tenures' (Murie, 2006: 16).

Into the 1970s

One of the priorities of the Labour governments elected in 1964 and 1966 was the public-sector house-building programme. Housing was an important election issue, both nationally and locally, and Labour came to power in 1964 committed to a promise that 500,000 dwellings a year would be completed within the lifetime of a Parliament – a target almost achieved with 480,000 completions in 1968. The emphasis of the programme was on council housing and much of what was provided was in multi-storey or other forms of industrialised building. The expectation was that with 'one last heave' the main problems of postwar housing shortage would be overcome; and that rates of council building could then be reduced. Indeed, by the end of the 1960s it was being said that, since the number of dwellings now exceeded the number of households (with a suitable allowance for vacancies), the nature of the housing problem was changing. Denis Howell, Minister of State in the Ministry of Housing and Local Government, said in 1969 that 'dwellings already outnumber households in Great Britain' and that a surplus of about one million dwellings should be expected by 1973 (HC Deb 16 December 1969 vol. 793 cc 1114–5). This sat oddly, however, with public concern about access to housing and the criticism aroused most memorably by the 1966 television film *Cathy Come Home*, with its dramatic depiction of the problems of homelessness and the failures of bureaucratic housing management.

Part of the desire to 'talk up' the end of housing shortage stemmed from the economic difficulties of the late 1960s: the devaluation of the pound in 1967, the need to cut public expenditure and the consequent need to review a range of housing and other policies. Linked to the decline in house-building was a decline in rates of slum clearance and a new emphasis on the retention and improvement of older housing, foreshadowed in the 1968 White Paper *Old Houses into New Homes* (Great Britain, 1968a), which led to the passing of the Housing Act, 1969. The White Paper saw a change in the balance of need between new house-building and improvement, requiring 'a corresponding change in the emphasis of local authority housing programmes' (p. 1).

The proportion of public-authority tenants was at a peak in the late 1960s and early 1970s. In Great Britain in 1971, 50 per cent of households were

19

owner-occupiers, 31 per cent were public-authority tenants and 19 per cent were in the private rented sector. A continuing concern of public policy, at least at national government level, was with the principles and outcomes of allocation policies for housing in the public sector, especially the local-authority sector. An important report by the Central Housing Advisory Committee, *Council Housing: Purposes, Procedures and Priorities* (Great Britain, 1969), widely referred to as the Cullingworth Report, discussed the changing context of council housing and emphasised that the 'huge decline in the privately rented sector' had greatly reduced the alternatives to a council house facing a household wishing to rent (or unable to buy); and concluded that local authorities 'must take a wider responsibility for people who at one time would have been housed in the private sector' (pp. 5–6). This meant a change in the allocation policies and practices of local authorities, based on a 'clearer, deeper and more detailed understanding of the changing housing situation in their areas', and on a recognition that

> . . . we do not have a single 'national' housing problem: we have a large number of local housing problems of great variety. National housing policies, slum-clearance campaigns and new building drives are no longer adequate to meet this new situation. Local and regional policies need to be forged to deal appropriately with particular problems. And these must be based on an understanding of these problems and the context in which they arise. (p. 12)

This and the earlier Seebohm Report on local authority social services (Great Britain, 1968b) gave credence to the idea of a comprehensive housing service and a new role for local authorities in assessing and planning, across all tenures, for housing needs in their areas.

A further topical issue was that of housing finance, especially in the aftermath of the economic crisis associated with the devaluation of sterling in 1967. A review of housing finance was instituted by the Labour government but abandoned before the 1970 election. The Conservative victory in that year enabled new proposals to be brought forward that led to the Housing Finance Act, 1972, which, among many provisions, introduced 'fair rents' in the council sector in a bid to reduce the extent of rent subsidisation. One striking feature was the introduction for the first time of a national rent rebate scheme: until 1972, local authorities could provide rebates if they wished but many chose not to, preferring instead to subsidise rents for all their tenants, rather than revert to the 'means testing' associated with the distribution of benefits in the depression of the 1920s and 1930s. However, the linking of rents to tenants' ability to pay and a radical change in the subsidy system marked the beginning of a new system of personal subsidy (where needed) in place of the 'bricks and mortar' (construction) subsidies for council housing, first put in place in the Housing and Town Planning etc. Act, 1919. In making this change, Britain followed a path already established in many neighbouring countries of Western Europe.

At the same time, the Conservative government took steps to further promote owner-occupation, or, as they preferred to call it, 'home ownership . . . the most rewarding form of house tenure' (Great Britain, 1971: 4). The importance of tax relief on mortgage interest payments was reaffirmed; and steps were taken to make more flexible the Option Mortgage Scheme, introduced by the Labour government in 1967, which provided a subsidy towards the mortgage costs of low-income borrowers whose incomes were too low for them to benefit from tax relief on their mortgage interest repayments.

By the end of the 1960s and into the early 1970s, a number of features were evident in the British housing situation. First, local authorities played a very important role in the provision of council housing and seemed likely to increase their involvement in future, partly through a redefinition of responsibilities (the comprehensive housing service) and the acquisition of new aspects of the national housing programme (house and area improvement).

Second, relations between central and local government were much more evenly balanced than they are today. Local authorities had a good deal of freedom and a great deal of responsibility for local housing matters. Central government depended on the local authorities to deliver the housing programme and to meet the targets that formed part of their promises at the time of national elections. In some cases, targets could be achieved only by the government offering higher subsidies, as was the case for high-rise building under the Housing Subsidies Act, 1967.

Third, the private sector in housing was growing in importance all the time. This was due partly to rising demand, made effective by the availability of mortgage finance and the favourable tax treatment of owner-occupation; and partly to a climate of encouragement for home ownership that was supported by all main political parties, and associated most strongly with the Conservatives. In fact, the Labour Party was concerned that a reputation for being 'against' home ownership (even if not supported by the facts) could be damaging to them at election time.

Finally, the continuing decline of the private rented sector came to be seen as inevitable, after the failure of the 1957 Rent Act to revive it, the scandal of Rachmanism, and the work of the Milner Holland Committee (Great Britain, 1965) on the private rented sector in London. The combined effects of lack of investment, slum clearance, sales into owner-occupation – either to sitting tenants or with vacant possession – and, in some cases, municipal or housing association acquisitions seemed to be sounding a death knell for a form of tenure that was considered outdated and inappropriate in a modern world. This was fertile ground for the supporters of housing associations, the 'voluntary' housing sector, to expand their role in the acquisition and improvement of older private rented housing and in new building as a source of good-quality rented housing for people in need. The Housing Act, 1974, in effect planned by the Conservative government and enacted by the Labour government elected in 1974, created very favourable conditions for the future growth of a generously subsidised, and what would now be termed a 'reformed' and 'modernised', voluntary housing movement.

Tenure was important as a framework for housing policy and, despite the official encouragement of local authorities to take a comprehensive approach to the formulation and implementation of housing policies at local level, this advice, though emanating from central government, was generally not followed at national level. Different legal and financial regimes applied to each of the three main tenures; standards for both existing and new housing differed between tenures; levels of council-house building were often determined as a residual of what was being built for owner-occupation; and notwithstanding the adoption of 'fair rents' as a principle to be applied to the council sector from 1972 (a system introduced by Labour in 1965 for the independent determination of rents in the private rented sector), the suggestion that this would provide 'a fairer choice between owning a home and renting one' or 'fairness between one citizen and another in giving and receiving help towards housing costs' (Great Britain, 1971: 1) was plainly wrong. For example, the more tenants earned, the less they received in rent rebate; while the more owner-occupiers earned, the more they received in mortgage interest tax relief (Murie *et al.*, 1976: 105).

The oil shock, the International Monetary Fund and the Housing Policy Review

The middle and latter years of the 1970s were characterised by a combination of events that had a profound impact on the economy and on housing policy. They included the oil shock of late 1973 and the sterling crisis of 1976, which forced the government to borrow from the International Monetary Fund. Inflationary pressures continued to build up in the early 1970s, including significant inflation in house prices. The average purchase price of a house in the United Kingdom in 1968 was £4,300, rising to £7,300 in 1972 and £9,600 by mid-1973. The average value of mortgages granted rose from £3,200 in 1968 to £6,000 in mid-1973 (Great Britain, 1973a: 45).

The Labour government embarked in 1974 on what the then Secretary of State for the Environment, Anthony Crosland, declared would be a fundamental review of housing finance, designed to get back to the basics and not to spare any of the 'sacred cows' that he believed reflected the shortcomings of the existing system. This ambitious aim was soon tempered by the realities of the prevailing economic and political climate, and the promised fundamental review was transmuted to the worthy but disappointing Green Paper *Housing Policy: a consultative document* (Great Britain, 1977a). This formed the basis for a Housing Bill presented to Parliament in early 1979, but the Bill was lost with the government's defeat in the May 1979 election.

Typical of the disappointment engendered by the Review was its defence of the system of tax relief on mortgage interest payments: a sure sign of nervousness about the consequences of interfering with a policy that was thought to encourage new building, as well as being an important element in the household budgets of the growing number of home owners. Labour still felt on the defensive about its perceived attitude towards home ownership, yet it is estimated that public spending on mortgage interest relief (at 1999–2000 prices) increased from £2.18 billion in 1975–6 to £4.19 billion in 1980–1 (Stephens *et al.*, 2005: 20), reflecting the inflation in house prices and mortgage interest rates during this time. Holmans (2005: 6) argues, however, that the value of the Housing Policy Review lay in

> . . . demonstrating that there was no set of reforms to be had that would deliver better housing to more households at lower cost to the public purse without there being a large number of losers; and that no simple local authority subsidy system could be devised which would cope inexpensively with economic conditions [such as] those experienced in the first half of the 1970s.

In contrast to the fortress mentality that affected the beleaguered Labour government in the late 1970s, the surprisingly uncontroversial gradual withdrawal of mortgage interest relief in the 1990s has since been described as one of the biggest and most successfully implemented policy changes in the restructuring of housing subsidies (Stephens *et al.*, 2005: 22).

Some key issues

The institutional framework and research on private-sector institutions

During the 1970s, attention began to turn to the institutional framework for housing and in particular the role of the private sector. As Cullingworth (1979) observed,

> like it or not, governments have to have regard for market behaviour to a far greater extent than is the case with other social services. (p. 144)

This needed to be reflected in the research agenda. The inter-relatedness and sometimes conflicting nature of policy, coupled with the independent actions of the private sector, made the goal of 'comprehensive' housing policies elusive. For example,

> considering the very important role of private-sector developers – building over half of all the houses completed in England and Wales between 1968 and 1972, and a quarter of those in Scotland – surprisingly little is known about the way decisions are made in individual firms, or the effect these may have on opportunities for owner-occupation.
>
> (Murie *et al.*, 1976: 148–9)

Perhaps more was known about the operation of the building societies, and to some people their image was a negative one, with the rationing of mortgage funds, the insistence on being a saver before being allowed to become a borrower, and the practice of 'red-lining' certain areas as too risky to lend in, thus sometimes thwarting the ambitions of improvement programmes in areas of older housing. In some cases the response by local authorities was to 'municipalise' housing in such areas, by taking it into public ownership. Some authorities, using a power introduced in the Housing Act, 1923, were also active in mortgage-lending in areas and to people that the building societies regarded as marginal. This was seen by government as a positive contribution to the needs of lower-income households and other groups, such as single women, who could experience discrimination when applying for a building-society loan. Local government also developed the 'option lease', better known as the 'half-and-half mortgage' or 'equity sharing' and the 1977 Housing Policy Review suggested this could be a permanent tenure arrangement or a stepping-stone to owner-occupation. It was the forerunner of the present system of shared ownership.

These interventions were considered necessary as a means of extending home ownership to a wider range of households and were, in effect, a corollary to the financial imperative, or the perceived need (or both), to limit further growth of the public rented sector. Research interest in the private sector developed in the 1970s (for example, Harloe *et al.*, 1974; Murie *et al.*, 1976), and a research programme at the Birmingham University Centre for Urban and Regional Studies made a number of in-depth studies of private-sector institutions in housing, including private builders, building societies and 'exchange professionals,' such as estate agents (for example, Housing Monitoring Team, 1978, 1981, 1982).

The consolidation of housing improvement policy

In contrast to the tensions in the 1970s between the Labour Party and Conservative Party on the subject of council housing and particularly the bad feeling aroused by the Housing Finance Act, 1972, which removed the power of local authorities to set their own rents (later repealed by a Labour government in 1975), there was considerable unanimity, as noted previously, on the subject of housing renewal. Both main parties were committed to housing improvement as an important element in housing policy and both favoured an area approach to the treatment of substandard housing considered suitable for improvement. The scale of the problem was large. The second national house condition survey in England, carried out in 1971, estimated that there were about 1.25 million unfit dwellings, amounting to 7 per cent of the total housing stock (Great Britain, 1973b). In Scotland, some 190,000 dwellings, or 10 per cent of the housing stock, were below the statutory tolerable standard (Great Britain, 1973c). Yet in England in 1972, the Conservative Minister for Housing and Construction, Julian Amery, launching a new slum clearance drive, said that

> If we . . . really set our hands to it, we can beat the problem of slums and unsatisfactory housing within a measurable time. . . . For the first time, there is light at the end of the tunnel. We must strike out for it. There are times when the mere size of the problem seems so daunting that some may feel it is not in our power to solve it, at any rate in our time. Well, this is not true. (Great Britain, 1972a)

Six years later, the publication of the 1976 English house condition survey showed a less rosy picture. Nearly 800,000 dwellings were estimated to be unfit and 2.2 million required repairs costing over £1,000 each. More than 3 million dwellings were estimated to be in need of attention, representing almost 20 per cent of the housing stock. At the time, about 170,000 substandard houses a year were being improved and even without further deterioration of the stock, it was estimated that, even at an improvement and clearance rate of 200,000 dwellings a year, it would take fifteen 15 years to tackle the three million dwellings requiring attention (Thomas, 1979: 53–4).

Despite the relatively slow progress in dealing with slums and other older housing, government support for housing improvement and the process of 'gradual renewal' continued throughout the 1970s and beyond. The area approach, however, although appealing to governments wishing to concentrate resources where needs are presumed to be greatest, often cannot respond adequately to needs arising elsewhere, and this concern about policies of spatial targeting remains an issue to the present day.

Another reason for the relatively slow progress of house improvement was the essentially voluntary nature of the process. Slum clearance had been imposed on residents, while renewal policies in the 1970s tried to respect residents' wishes and to work with local communities. The importance of 'participation' was beginning to be recognised: experience was gained and much was learned from the process. However, the emphasis on the physical improvement of dwellings and their surrounding environment lacked the holistic approach that became a feature of subsequent policies and was an important lesson from the experiences of the 1970s.

Other policies that had a bearing on older housing in the 1970s included the Community Development Programmes (CDPs) and the Inner Area Studies (Kyung and Watson, 2008). The Home Office created twelve CDPs in the period between 1969 and 1972, while the Department of the Environment in 1972 set up six Inner Area Studies (IASs) in Oldham, Rotherham and Sunderland and parts of Liverpool, Birmingham and Lambeth. The tasks of the CDPs and IASs were to help deprived communities to help themselves by overcoming what was seen as apathy (Cameron and Davoudi, 1998: 235–52). But in IASs there was less emphasis on community involvement and more on local-authority management. The project teams of CDPs and IASs concluded that, in contrast to the assumptions that had given rise to the projects in the first place, residents in these areas were not inadequate or deficient; they suffered from the same kinds of problems as people in other localities. These problems revolved essentially around issues of economic decline, a contraction in employment opportunities and diminishing individual and community wealth (Lawless, 1989: 9). The Inner Area Studies, published between 1974 and 1977, led to the Labour Government's Inner Urban Areas Act, 1978, which gave local authorities, in partnership with central government, extensive powers to pursue economic development and job creation.

Housing allocation policies and alternative thinking on the future of council housing

With around 30 per cent of housing rented from local authorities, the allocation and management of council housing in the 1970s had a great impact not only on the six million households that were council tenants but also on those who were waiting for the allocation of a suitable property. Local authorities were free to determine their own allocation policies, although under the Housing Act, 1957, they had a duty to provide housing 'to meet the needs of the district', particularly to relieve overcrowding and to provide alternative accommodation for those displaced by public action, such as slum clearance. In selecting tenants, they were required under Section 113 of the Act to give 'reasonable preference' to 'persons who are occupying insanitary or over-crowded houses, have large families or are living under unsatisfactory housing conditions'. Further guidance on the selection of tenants and allocation priorities and procedures was given by Ministry circular and by a succession of reports from the Central Housing Advisory Committee (CHAC) Housing Management Sub-Committee (Niner, 1975: 20). The Housing (Homeless Persons) Act, 1977, placed a further duty on local authorities to provide accommodation for certain categories of homeless people.

The Cullingworth Report (Great Britain, 1969) was critical of the allocation policies used by many local authorities, in particular the reliance on residential qualifications in allocating housing. The Report favoured the use of points schemes based on housing need. But local authorities were not required to follow this advice and many did not do so. Significant groups in the population were thereby excluded from consideration for a council house – for example, on grounds of age, single-person status, or lack of a residential qualification. Some councils operated 'merit' schemes, which involved councillors in the allocation of housing to individual households.

The Labour governments in the 1970s, perhaps sensing a weakness in the stance of many local authorities towards a wider definition of housing need, not only facilitated the passage of the Housing (Homeless Persons) Bill, which was enacted in 1977, but also in the Housing Policy Review of the same year reiterated the need for local authorities to widen their allocation criteria to include people affected by the continued decline of the private rented sector, or unable to become owner-occupiers. In a sense this can be seen as an acknowledgement of public concern about some of the shortcomings of council housing, influenced partly by the poor quality of the system-built housing of the 1960s and early 1970s, partly by the inadequacies of housing management and the position of housing as a 'Cinderella' service in local government, and partly by the emerging problem of 'difficult-to-let' estates, all of which were giving council housing a bad reputation and making it harder for its political and professional supporters to champion. Council housing, which for many years had provided a solution to the housing needs of working people, was beginning to be seen as a problem. The lack of resources to improve standards of housing management and to repair and maintain properties adequately provided fertile ground for alternative thinking about the future of council housing.

Among the main alternatives that gained currency in the 1970s was the policy of council-house sales. It was not a new policy. The power for local authorities to sell council housing was first given to local authorities in 1936; some did and some did not use it and there was a polarisation of views, both political and administrative, at both central and local government levels (Murie, 1975). In the election campaign of October 1974, however, the Conservatives proposed a Bill to enforce the sale of council houses, allowing tenants of three or more years' standing the right to buy at one third less than market values, with a five-year pre-emption clause (ibid.: 32). In 1978 Peter Walker, a former Secretary of State for the Environment in the Conservative government of 1970–4, suggested that tenants of 30 years' or more standing should be given their council housing, while others of 20 or even five years' standing should be granted mortgages to enable them to buy their homes. The Labour government continued to resist this and similar thinking but ultimately was not successful in doing so.

On allocation policies, the possibility of allowing market forces to determine the allocation of council housing was discussed by a subcommittee of the Scottish Housing Advisory Committee (SHAC), appointed in 1978 to consider allocation and transfer policies (Great Britain, 1980):

> We have considered the view that there is no longer any need for the same degree of bureaucratic management of the allocation process as in the past because of the elimination of the crude housing shortage and that, given the introduction in 1972 of a national rent rebate scheme, there would be a balance of advantage in allowing cost to the consumer to become the basis of the allocation process in the public sector as it is in the owner-occupied and (to a lesser extent) in the private rented sector. Such an approach would involve allowing applicants and existing tenants to choose freely among the stock of vacant housing according to their willingness and ability to pay rents. These would require considerable differentiation, compared to present practices, to reflect the desirability of the house. (pp. 6–7)

The subcommittee decided not to follow this approach, but the fact that it was considered reflected thinking that was current at the time. A Postscript to the Report contained a prescient warning. After expressing the hope that its recommendations would 'receive a more ready acceptance than did those of our predecessors', it went on to say:

> Already government dissatisfaction with the present use of council housing has led to the introduction of legislation to remove residential qualifications from allocation processes. It would, in our view, be regrettable if authorities failed to adapt their policies to changing needs. This could lead to further moves to reduce or remove the degree of local independence and diversity that currently exists. (p. 91)

Housing needs and housing investment

One of the main issues for housing policy and practice in the 1970s was the assessment of housing needs. The definition of housing need as 'the extent to which the quality and quantity of existing housing falls short of that required to provide each household or person in the population, irrespective of ability to pay, or particular personal preferences, with accommodation of a specified minimum standard or above' (Needleman, 1965: 18) was widely recognised and was distinguished from housing 'demand' and housing 'desires': what today might be referred to as housing 'aspirations'. The obligation of local authorities to respond to 'housing need' in its widest sense was a key theme of the 1969 Cullingworth Report (Great Britain, 1969) and was developed further in a later report, this time for the Scottish

Housing Advisory Committee, *Planning for Housing Needs: pointers towards a comprehensive approach* (Great Britain, 1972b), prepared by the SHAC Working Party on Housing Needs, also chaired by Barry Cullingworth.

The SHAC Report argued the importance of a comprehensive assessment of housing needs. Waiting lists for local authority housing could no longer be seen as 'adequate as a sole means for determining new housing programmes' (ibid.: 23). Trends in the private rented and owner-occupied sectors also had to be examined, as did many other aspects of the local housing situation, including house condition and the need for clearance and improvement. It was recommended that the Scottish Development Department (one of the departments of the Scottish Office) should prepare a manual outlining techniques of measuring housing needs, to be published for the guidance of local authorities; and that the Department should publish annually the detailed Census-based household projections that were now available for all regions and sub-divisions of Scotland.

These recommendations were followed, and resulted in the publication of extensive and detailed guidance in *Local Housing Needs and Strategies: a case study of the Dundee sub-region* (Great Britain, 1976) and *Assessing Housing Needs: a manual of guidance* (Great Britain, 1977b). The recommended approach formed the basis for the introduction in Scotland in 1977 of Housing Plans, a scheme under which it was intended that local authorities should eventually be given a single block allocation for all their capital expenditure on housing; and that investment should be allocated according to the relative needs of authorities as contained in their Housing Plans. Similar measures were introduced in England and Wales as Housing Strategies and Investment Programmes. The intention was that the new systems would give local authorities greater freedom to determine their own housing expenditure and priorities, based on a comprehensive and regularly updated assessment of local housing needs, using methodologies recommended by central government. However, the introduction of Housing Plans and Housing Strategies and Investment Programmes took place at a time when cuts in public expenditure were beginning to become very severe, and the system of housing plans was one of the main victims. A policy approach, and a stream of work developed over more than ten years that had been intended to give local authorities greater freedom was used, in practice, as a means of exerting greater central control of and restrictions on housing expenditure: a 'freedom to spend less', as it was sometimes put, although the appropriateness of the word 'freedom' might be questioned in this context, especially following the election of the Conservative government in 1979.

The Conservatives criticised the housing plan system, seeing it as a means by which councils could bid up their demands for housing investment. In both 1979–80 and 1980–1, the Conservative government reduced already committed HIP allocations, leading to an expected overspend of £180 million on local authority housing programmes in 1980–1 (HC Deb 27 October 1980 vol. 991 cc 28–32).

In a statement to Parliament in February 1980, Michael Heseltine, Secretary of State for the Environment, spoke of a reassessment of housing policy, which had to recognise the 'significant general improvement of housing conditions in the last 30 years'. He went on:

> Needs and problems have become increasingly specific and local. The emphasis of public-sector housing policy now must be to meet particular needs, such as those of the elderly and the handicapped. We have to concentrate on modernising, improving and making better use of the existing housing stock, rather than on the general provision of new houses. We must encourage home ownership and the private sector. (HC Deb 21 February 1980 vol. 979 cc 666–82)

In future, therefore, levels of public expenditure were not to be based on assessments of need but would be set 'at levels which the nation can afford'.

The beginnings of 'partnership' in housing

In and before the 1970s, especially before the local-government reorganisations of 1974 in England and Wales and 1975 in Scotland, local authority housing departments were normally responsible for the provision and management of council housing. Responsibilities for owner-occupied housing, the private rented sector, and housing renewal were normally the responsibility of other departments; and in the case of private housing built for sale, this was usually the planning department, with its responsibilities for land-use planning and development control. This departmental division of responsibilities was often reflected in an authority's committee structure, so there was nowhere, other than the full Council, at which local housing matters might be looked at 'in the round', if indeed they ever were. This was part of the background to the call for a comprehensive approach to housing by local authorities.

Another reason, however, was the relative lack of communication between local authorities and private-sector housing organisations in their areas, perhaps more so in Labour-controlled than in Conservative-controlled areas. An obvious requirement of the comprehensive approach, therefore, was that communication and interaction should be improved on all fronts, both within local government and between local government and external organisations. Internal issues were addressed to some extent through the 'corporate' approach to local authority management, recommended by both the Bains Report in England and Wales (Great Britain, 1972c) and the Paterson Report in Scotland (Great Britain, 1973e). External relations remained problematic but the need to improve them became all the more evident with the requirements of the Housing Plans and Housing

Strategies and Investment Programme systems. The 1977 Housing Policy Review said that

> . . . local authorities will need to develop their existing working relationship with all other bodies – the Housing Corporation, registered housing associations, local house-builders, building societies, new town corporations, county councils and tenants' and community organisations concerned with housing in their areas. (Great Britain, 1977a: 43)

In an attempt to put this advice into practice, the Centre for Urban and Regional Studies at Birmingham University, as part of a research programme on 'Monitoring the Housing System', convened in 1978 a 'Public–Private Sector Housing Forum' for representatives of Dudley Metropolitan Borough, the Housing Corporation, the Regional Water Authority and twelve private sector organisations working in the Borough. The purpose was to discuss Housing Investment Programmes and resources for house-building; it was an innovative event for its time, an early attempt to develop what would now be termed a 'partnership' approach involving many of the key local 'stakeholders' (Watson et al., 1979: 41–52).

Perhaps surprisingly, 'partnership' had already entered the public-policy vocabulary in the 1970s. For example, the 1973 White Paper *Widening the Choice; the next steps in housing* (Great Britain, 1973d: 6), under the heading 'Local Authority/Private Enterprise Partnership Schemes' referred to a Working Party comprising representatives of local planning authorities, landowners, house-builders and the Department of the Environment, which had examined the scope for 'new forms of partnership' between local authorities and private enterprise in undertaking large-scale residential development in the South-East of England.

As a final example, the 1977 White Paper *Policy for the Inner Cities* (Great Britain, 1977c) saw an expanded role for the public sector at local level as a means of overcoming urban decline. The Labour government decided in favour of local authorities as the natural agencies to tackle inner-city problems at the head of partnerships encompassing all public-sector agencies working at a local level. But there were not enough public-sector resources to compensate for the level of private-sector disinvestment facing inner cities. This early and rather public-sector-oriented attempt at 'partnership' was not successful. Moreover, the concept of partnership was new and perhaps more suited to the changed political environment of the 1980s and beyond.

Seeds of change

This chapter concludes with some brief reflections on the experiences of the 1970s, seen from the perspective of the early twenty-first century. What 'seeds of change' were there in the 1970s that have proved significant in influencing the directions of future policy and the nature of the housing system?

From the end of the Second World War to the early 1970s, local authorities had a major and largely unchallenged role in the housing system. But they did not dominate it and it was not generally suggested that they should. Already there were signs, however, that the growth in the supply of local authority housing could not continue, partly for financial reasons, partly because of concerns about the quality of new public-sector housing, especially in the 1960s and 1970s (itself partly a function of lack of resources); and partly because of the realisation that many housing needs were not being met by the public sector, when it was evident that they should be.

The seemingly recurrent financial crises of the late 1960s and 1970s also caused a loss of faith in the ability of governments to deal with the country's problems. Today it is recognised that 'external events', 'international markets', 'globalisation' and the poor social and political accountability of many multinational corporations are often beyond the ability of national governments to control or even influence. This was not recognised in the same way in the 1970s, though the 1973 oil shock and its aftermath brought home to many people the vulnerability of the national economy to external forces. The regular growth of the economy that many had taken for granted could no longer be assumed and this had its effects on housing, local-government services and many other aspects of everyday life.

The history of housing policy is full of good intentions. Interventions were going to be 'temporary', until conditions could be brought back to 'normal' (for example, the Housing and Town Planning etc. Act, 1919); problems were going to be 'solved' within a measurable time – problems such as slum clearance and overcrowding in the 1930s, housing shortage in 1969, and slums and unsatisfactory housing (again) in 1972. Politicians and others liked to see 'light at the end of the tunnel', but the 1970s was a time when it became more realistic to view many housing problems as more of a moving target than problems capable of outright solution. Possibly learning from the experience, the Conservative government for a long time in the 1980s steadfastly refused to produce forecasts of housing need, and thus could not be challenged that it was failing to meet them.

Changes in the pattern of tenure continued throughout the 1970s and the kid-glove handling of mortgage-interest tax relief in the 1977 Housing Policy Review provides a good example of the sensitivities of the time. The debate on council-house sales, and the arguments put forward by the Conservatives, especially in the election campaigns of 1974 and, more spectacularly, 1979, led to profound changes in the direction of housing policy that are still being played out today.

Had circumstances in the 1970s been different, had local authority housing (especially recently built housing) been better designed, built, maintained and managed, and had local authorities paid more heed to the exhortations to look more comprehensively at their housing responsibilities, the appeal to many tenants in 1979 of getting out of the council-housing sector might not have been so strong. Moreover, if there had been stronger champions for council housing its position might have been perceived differently, both within and outside government circles. The problems of public-sector housing finance from the mid-1960s throughout the 1970s are symbolised most clearly by the two attempts at housing finance reviews, one of which was suspended while the other became a review of housing policy.

In the 1970s also, the role of local authority housing began to change. Needs other than 'general needs' were gradually acknowledged, including to some extent the needs of the homeless; and the phenomenon of the difficult-to-let estate emerged. Residualisation and polarisation began to be recognised; and all of these became major issues in the decades that followed.

At the same time, the first steps were taken to create and develop better working relationships between the public and private sectors in housing, through what would now be termed as 'partnership' working between a range of stakeholders, who now would also include local residents and community groups, the 'customers' of the 'services' that are being provided. This, too, has become a central feature of the present-day approach in housing policy.

There were four general elections in the 1970s: one in 1970, two in 1974 and one in 1979. During that time, Labour and the Conservatives had roughly the same number of years in power. Housing was a major issue in each of the elections, in a way that it has not seemed to be in any election since 1979. Paradoxically, perhaps, the most radical innovations of the 1970s were introduced by Conservative governments, in the Housing Finance Act, 1972 and the Housing Act, 1979; while the main area of consensus was in the approach to the treatment of older housing, where there was more or less all-party agreement. Yet housing policy issues were not resolved by the change of government in 1979; problems still remain and are just as difficult to deal with. But housing has become a more individual and a more personal matter than it was and the seeds of that change were among the most important to have been planted in the 1970s.

References

Bassett, K. and Short, J. (1980) *Housing and Residential Structure: alternative approaches*, London: Routledge & Kegan Paul.

Cameron, S. and Davoudi, S. (1998) 'Combating social exclusion: looking in or looking out?', in Madanipour, A., Cars, G. and Allen, J. (eds) *Social Exclusion in European Cities: processes, experiences and responses*, London: Jessica Kingsley Publishers.

Cullingworth, J.B. (1963) *Housing in Transition: a case study in the city of Lancaster 1958–1962,* London: Heinemann.

Cullingworth, J.B. (1967) *Scottish Housing in 1965*, Edinburgh: Scottish Development Department.

Cullingworth, J.B. (1979) *Essays on Housing Policy: the British scene*, London: George Allen and Unwin.

Donnison, D.V. (1961) 'The movement of households in England', *Journal of the Royal Statistical Society*, Series A, Part 1, 60–80.

Donnison, D.V. (1967) *The Government of Housing*, Harmondsworth: Penguin Books.

Great Britain (1965) *Report of the Committee on Housing in Greater London,* London: Her Majesty's Stationery Office, Cmnd. 2605.

Great Britain (1968a) *Old Houses into New Homes,* Ministry of Housing and Local Government and Welsh Office, London: Her Majesty's Stationery Office, Cmnd. 3602.

Great Britain (1968b) *Report of the Committee on Local Authority and Allied Personal Social Services*, London: Her Majesty's Stationery Office, Cmnd. 3703.

Great Britain (1969) *Council Housing Purposes, Procedures and Priorities,* Ninth Report of the Housing Management Sub-Committee of the Central Housing Advisory Committee, Ministry of Housing and Local Government and Welsh Office, London: Her Majesty's Stationery Office.

Great Britain (1971) *Fair Deal for Housing*, London: Her Majesty's Stationery Office, Cmnd. 4728.

Great Britain (1972a) *Slums and Older Housing: an overall strategy. Circular 50/72*, London: Department of the Environment.

Great Britain (1972b) *Planning for Housing Needs: pointers towards a comprehensive approach*, Report of the Working Party on Housing Needs of the Scottish Housing Advisory Committee, Edinburgh: Her Majesty's Stationery Office.

Great Britain (1972c) *The New Local Authorities: management and structures*, London: Her Majesty's Stationery Office.

Great Britain (1973a) *Housing and Construction Statistics*, London: Her Majesty's Stationery Office.

Great Britain (1973b) *House Condition Survey 1971, England and Wales*, London: Department of the Environment.

Great Britain (1973c) *Towards Better Homes: proposals for dealing with Scotland's older housing*, Edinburgh: Her Majesty's Stationery Office, Cmnd. 5338.

Great Britain (1973d) *Widening the Choice: the next steps in housing*, London: Her Majesty's Stationery Office, Cmnd. 5280.

Great Britain (1973e) *The New Scottish Local Authorities: organisation and management structures*, Edinburgh: Her Majesty's Stationery Office.

Great Britain (1976) *Local Housing Needs and Strategies: a case study of the Dundee sub-region*, Scottish Development Department, Edinburgh: Her Majesty's Stationery Office.

Great Britain (1977a) *Housing Policy: a consultative document*, London: Her Majesty's Stationery Office, Cmnd 6851.

Great Britain (1977b) *Assessing Housing Needs: a manual of guidance*, Scottish Housing Handbook 1, Scottish Development Department, Edinburgh: Her Majesty's Stationery Office.

Great Britain (1977c) *Policy for the Inner Cities*, London: Her Majesty's Stationery Office, Cmnd 6845.

Great Britain (1980) *Allocation and Transfer of Council Housing*, Report by a Subcommittee of the Scottish Housing Advisory Committee, Scottish Development Department, Edinburgh: Her Majesty's Stationery Office.

Griffith, J.A.G. (1966) *Central Departments and Local Authorities*, London: George Allen & Unwin.

Harloe, M., Issacharoff, R. and Minns, R. (1974) *The Organisation of Housing: public and private enterprise in London*, London: Heinemann.

Hole, W.V. (1979) 'Social Research in Housing – A Review of Progress in Britain since World War II', *Local Government Studies*, 5(6), 23–40.

Holmans, A. (2005) *Housing and Housing Policy in England 1975–2002: chronology and commentary*, Office of the Deputy Prime Minister, London: Her Majesty's Stationery Office.

Housing Monitoring Team (1978) *The Structure and Functioning of Building Societies*, Birmingham: Centre for Urban and Regional Studies, Research Memorandum 64.

Housing Monitoring Team (1981) *The Housebuilding Industry and Changes in the Market for Housebuilding Work: a review of the British experience*, Birmingham: Centre for Urban and Regional Studies, Occasional Paper 87.

Housing Monitoring Team (1982) *Building Societies and the Local Housing Market*, Birmingham: Centre for Urban and Regional Studies, Occasional Paper 90.

Kyung, S. and Watson, C. (2008) *The Evolution of Housing Renewal and Urban Regeneration Policies in the United Kingdom*, Birmingham: Centre for Urban and Regional Studies, University of Birmingham.

Lawless, P. (1989) *Britain's Inner Cities*, London: Paul Chapman Publishing Ltd.

Murie, A. (1975) *The Sale of Council Houses: a study in social policy*, Birmingham: Centre for Urban and Regional Studies, Occasional Paper 35.

Murie, A. (2006) 'Moving with the times: changing frameworks for housing research and policy' in Malpass, P. and Cairncross, L. (eds) *Building On The Past: visions of housing futures*, Bristol: The Policy Press.

Murie, A., Niner, P. and Watson, C. (1976) *Housing Policy and the Housing System*, London: George Allen & Unwin.

Needleman, L. (1965) *The Economics of Housing*, London: Staples.

Niner, P. (1975) *Local Authority Housing Policy and Practice: a case-study approach*, Birmingham: Centre for Urban and Regional Studies, Occasional Paper 31.

Pahl, R.E. (1970) *Whose City? And Other Essays on Sociology and Planning*, Harlow: Longmans.

Rex, J. and Moore, R. (1967) *Race, Community and Conflict: a study of Sparkbrook*, Oxford: Oxford University Press.

Stephens, M., Whitehead, C. and Munro, M. (2005) *Lessons From The Past, Challenges For The Future For Housing Policy: an evaluation of English Housing Policy 1975–2000*, Office of the Deputy Prime Minister, London: Her Majesty's Stationery Office.

Thomas, A.D. (1979) 'Area Based House Improvement', *Local Government Studies*, 5(6), 53–68.

Watson, C., Forrest, R., Groves, R., Jarman, R. and Williams, P. (1979) 'Housing Investment Programmes and the Private Sector', *Local Government Studies*, 5(6), 41–52.

Welch, R. (1971) *West Midlands Conurbation Housing Survey 1966*, London: Department of the Environment.

3 A privileged state?

Council housing as social escalator

Ray Forrest

Let us first consider the current state of home ownership. At the time of writing this chapter, in the summer of 2008, the discourse is all negative – negative equity, credit crunch, repossessions and mortgage arrears. 'Sub-prime', a financial-sector euphemism for low-income households that are bad credit risks, has entered the popular lexicon. Has the world finally changed? The health of the global economy has been seriously undermined partly through irresponsible lending for house purchase. Are we entering a post-home-ownership world in which households and institutions will approach borrowing and lending for house purchase with a new caution? Has home ownership reached its limit in its present form? Will the proportion of households in the tenure decline, at least in some countries? Perhaps more households will turn to private renting or new hybrid tenures and choose priorities other than feeding the mortgage monster, to paraphrase Bootle (1997).

Well, possibly, but I doubt it. We have been here before, or certainly somewhere like it. In the UK, in the late 1980s, the last major jolt to the housing market provoked similar rhetoric and predictions of a new regime in which properties would be valued for their use value rather than their investment potential (Forrest *et al.*, 1999). A few years later it was business as usual, at least in the sense that people were borrowing more than they should from lenders who should have known better.

However, whether the future of home ownership will be fundamentally changed by the present crisis is not the point of this initial digression. The point is that the role and image of housing tenures are not givens but are contingent on a wide range of contextual and institutional factors. Thus, we should not judge or understand British council housing simply by where we are now but also by where we were and, indeed, by where we could have been.

The pervasive image of direct state housing provision for rental in Britain, as in most countries, is now one of inefficiency, poverty and entrapment. The tenure is generally perceived as posing problems for poor people. Young people entering the housing market today could be forgiven for thinking that the history of British council housing was one of unmitigated failure and stigma. In policy debate it has become the tenure that dare not speak its name, with any references to low-income housing provision usually couched in terms of 'affordable housing'. This is partly the triumph of two or more decades of a neo-liberal ideology in which direct state provision has been effectively marginalised and castigated for contributing to, if not being centrally responsible for, fiscal crisis, cultures of dependency, low productivity and a host of other social and economic evils attributed to postwar welfare statism.

However, a recent analysis charts a changing relationship between different birth cohorts, life chances and council housing (Feinstein *et al.*, 2008). The postwar cohort entered a 'growing sector with new, relatively high-quality housing and little stigma', whereas later cohorts experienced a 'shrinking, ageing sector with a poor reputation' (p. 8). The study found *inter alia* that 'the negative correlations now commonly associated with social housing are not inevitable or inherent to provision of housing by the public sector' (p. 8). For later cohorts, being a council tenant became increasingly associated with negative outcomes. That is, however, not the same as arguing that council housing causes those outcomes. As the report acknowledges, even when controlling for a range of socio-economic factors, there are so many intervening variables that cause and effect are almost impossible to disentangle. The social and economic context in which British council housing now sits is fundamentally different from the earlier postwar period and the impact of council-house sales complicates any conclusions we can draw about the life chances of later cohorts who remained as council tenants. The simple message from this study returns us to where we came in – namely, that the characteristics and role of any form of housing provision are contingent on a range of factors.

It also has to be stressed, however, that the current image of direct state housing provision in general and British council housing in particular derives in part from the mistakes and problems of the past. These include insensitive and often inefficient management, a 'command economy' approach to tenants and their desires, and problems of mobility, design and location. Some of these problems are not, however, inherent to a tenure form of this kind but relate to structurally induced and policy-driven factors. Suffice to say that the calculus of what is affordable in terms of state investment in housing provision has inevitably changed according to shifting economic conditions, political priorities and the relationship between the market and the state sectors (Berry, 1974). Moreover, if we were seeking to condemn flawed forms of housing provision, the experiences of postwar private landlordism would have consigned that particular mode of provision to the dustbin well ahead of council housing.

British council housing was then essentially working-class housing and, with some exceptions, it did represent a social divide between an expanding, white-collar middle class of postwar Britain and their blue-collar counterparts. But it also represented a divide between the working class and some sections of the poor. It developed as general needs housing for what were once referred to as the labour aristocracy rather than the lumpenproletariat. In this context, critiques of council housing are to be found not only among those championing the supremacy of the market but also among those who bemoaned the market's exclusion of the poorest. Many of these were left to languish in low-quality and insecure parts of the private rented sector.

These and other related issues will be returned to as the chapter progresses. However, against this general background the primary aim of this chapter is to explore some of the positive features of council housing in the context of a contemporary literature which is generally and understandably preoccupied with the negative. The central aim will be to highlight the positive contribution council housing made to enhancing the life chances of sections of the British working class. In doing so, it will focus on how tenants in the past regarded council housing, the experience of the more popular, high-quality estates, council housing's role in a rural context and its contribution to the growth of home ownership.

What was council housing for?

It is appropriate at this point to remind ourselves briefly what council housing was for, not so much in relation to its specific institutional British form, but in terms of its general role and function in the housing system. At the most basic level, social rented housing breaks the link between ability to pay and housing opportunities. Left to itself, the market will simply produce either housing that is beyond the reach of many households or housing that is affordable only through overcrowding or bad condition. State rental housing can intervene directly in the relationship in a way that less direct subsidies often cannot. Thus, direct provision can achieve an immediate and significant improvement in the housing conditions and housing opportunities of lower-income households. Given the links between decent housing and improvements in health and general life chances, the link between council housing and social mobility may be indirect but nonetheless extremely significant. Simon (1929), in his treatise on *How to Abolish the Slums*, captures these essentials rather well in describing the progress of the council-house building programme which followed the end of World War I:

> The outstanding feature of our postwar housing campaign has been to set a
> new standard of working-class housing. A family of children growing up in
> any of the million new houses has, so far as the house is concerned, as good

a chance of health and strength as the child of a millionaire. That is a great achievement. And the challenging task now before us is to go on, consistently and steadily, building to this standard, until every family in the country is living in a really good house: a house in which the parents can live and bring up their children in full health of mind and body. (p. 2)

Simon's aspirations were soon thwarted by shifting economic conditions and changing political realities in which council housing was reduced to a more residual role in terms of standards and scale of building. And here crude parallels can be drawn with the way council housing developed in the post-1945 period. As Ravetz (2001: 4) observes, 'The original and daring goals of council housing were quickly lost to sight after its two most "utopian" phases, in the 1920s and after 1945, so that it moved forward with a mounting sense of public failure, but without any counterbalancing indices of success'.

There are a variety of perspectives on the structural role of council housing in British society, some of which represent it as a decommodification of housing which pacified, incorporated and fragmented the working class and effectively reproduced a healthier, more productive capitalist workforce. From this viewpoint it was the state rental sector which prior to the 1970s functioned to reproduce the skilled fraction of the British working class. The right to buy then created a state-subsidised transition to the market for that same fraction. Those without the skills or necessary bargaining power in the labour market were excluded in the pre-1970 period and then offered a second-rate public sector when the privileged section of the working class had moved on.

Whatever one's perspective, as Ravetz emphasises, council housing was a major part of the history of the British working class in the twentieth century, rooted in a genuine concern with, and revulsion from, slum housing conditions, as well as more utopian socialist visions of a better life. Reformist zeal in relation to the slum problem, and the associated health problems, were key drivers in the post-World War 1 phase, whereas pragmatic concerns about a severe numerical housing shortage were the essential elements of the post-World War 2 expansion of council housing. More high-minded aspirations were evident in both phases – a belief among some that there were other, superior, ways of producing housing and better planned, healthier neighbourhoods than relying on market forces. In this respect, Ravetz suggest that the indices of success were at the more micro-level, in the countless improvements in the domestic situations of innumerable working-class households. The more fundamental social transformations did not occur and grander visions soon faded. However, she observes that the failures of council housing were perhaps 'not so much failures in performance as rather, failures to realise ideals and intentions which were in the last resort unrealisable' (p. 4).

A view from the past

In September 2001 the headline on the front page of the *Bristol Weekend Post* was 'HOME IS WHERE THE HEART IS'. It was subheaded 'Millionaire's parents turn down offer of luxury life anywhere in the world – to stay in former council house'. It went on to describe the couple, who had spent their entire married life in the same three-bedroomed semi. Their son had offered to buy them a new luxury apartment anywhere in the world but they said they were happy where they were. It is perhaps remarkable that this story should make the front page – perhaps there was little other local news that day. However, it also reflects a contemporary England where the image of council housing, and former council-owned estates, has declined, so that it is surprising that anyone would choose to stay when something better was on offer. Of course, as households age, local friends, neighbours and other factors become more important considerations. But the story would have been a lot less likely to make the front page if the dwelling had not been a former council house.

If we look back only a few decades there were rather different views of council housing. For example, in the foreword to *The Organisation of Housing* (Harloe *et al.*, 1974), Ray Pahl observed that

> To a large extent Britain has got a more humane and generous approach to housing than other, ostensibly richer, societies. This is largely due to the size and quality of its local-authority housing, which, despite what its critics would say, is probably the best-managed, publicly owned stock in the world. It is an enormous asset to our society and should not lightly be allowed to diminish. (p. x)

Or take this excerpt from Tony Parker's *The People of Providence* (1983), in which Linda and Alan are describing the GLC flat they managed to get in a tower block after enduring two years renting 'two horrible rooms at the back of an old house in Wandsworth'.

> What we've got is first this big sitting room with the floor-to-ceiling windows opening out onto the balcony: then through that door there's the big kitchen, then that door there leads out to the hall. Off one side of that there's the large bedroom which is ours; then opposite that there's the smaller bedroom which is Cindy's; then along toward the front door there's the bathroom and separate toilet on one side, and a little sort of walk-in cupboard opposite that. The hall's wide, that's one of the best things in the flat; it gives you the feeling of airiness and space as soon as you come in. The other thing I like is the balcony which runs from outside here along as far as our bedroom; and the easiness of

keeping it clean; and the friendly neighbours; and the built-in cupboards round the kitchen walls . . . well, I could go for hours about all the good things, so you'd better tell me to stop. (p. 22)

These are, of course, the views of only one sociologist and one couple living on a GLC estate and we could no doubt easily find contrasting observations from the same periods. But they at least establish that there is a more positive narrative about council housing which is somewhat at variance with contemporary perceptions. Moreover, from the vantage point of the early twenty-first century it is easy to forget that even in the early 1970s a substantial minority of households were living in wholly unsatisfactory conditions with many lacking basic amenities. It was estimated, for example, that in 1971 there were some 2.8 million dwellings that were unfit or, if fit, were lacking one or more amenities such as a fixed bath or piped hot water (Department of the Environment, 1977: 36).

These views therefore have to be set in a context in which a move into council housing could often represent a step change in housing circumstances. While there had been substantial improvements in housing conditions throughout the 1950s and 1960s through demolition, new building and refurbishment, the rump of a declining privately rented sector concentrated in the major towns contained a high proportion of households in overcrowded conditions and often sharing kitchens, hot-water supply or lavatories. It is hardly surprising therefore that for many, council housing was a positive experience – more space, key amenities and all at a very reasonable rent.

Council housing in the 1960s was overwhelmingly family housing, with relatively few young or elderly tenants. The legacy of the war and national service also meant that ex-servicemen were heavily represented (Donnison, 1964) – it was still 'homes for heroes'. And at this point in council housing's history, council tenants were viewed by some as feather-bedded and over-subsidised. Writing in the early 1960s, Donnison observed that 'In recent years there have been increasing attacks on the 'privileged' position of council tenants and it has often been urged that their rents be increased' (p. 24). Donnison went on to argue that rents in council housing had increased at the same rate as in the private sector, and in any case those in the council sector tended to have larger families and thus there was less space per person. More tellingly, he argued that wealthy council tenants were a 'rarity' although multiple-earner households were becoming more common as children grew up.

Donnison's reference to wealthy council tenants reflected an increasingly common view in the 1960s and 1970s that the state was subsidising large numbers of households which were on relatively high incomes and paying low rents. Part of this perception derived from the growing numbers of multiple-earner households referred to by Donnison. But it also reflected growing general affluence and social mobility among sections of the working class which had entered council

"It's up to you, Alf—but we feel that you'd help the cause more if you walked"

3.1 An image of council housing in 1969.
Source: *Evening Standard*, 25 July 1969.

housing in the decade or so after the Second World War. The 'Jaguar-driving council tenant' became shorthand for a view that council housing was no longer sufficiently targeted on those most in need of direct state housing provision. A cartoon by Cookson from 1969 captures this image: a 'wealthy' tenant is shown, about to depart his two-car family drive to join the campaign against rent increases.

Relatively high-quality council housing offering secure tenancies at low rents, overlaid on a rapidly changing British society, led inevitably to a greater diversity of social and economic circumstances among households. In that sense there *was* a growing social mix in the council sector in the 1960s and 1970s, which was precisely the reason that a growing number of commentators were calling for higher or differentiated rent levels, such as a charge for additional earners. Fast-forward to today and it seems somewhat ironic that the Housing Minister now bemoans the loss of this very different council housing sector. 'Council housing was originally somewhere which brought together people from different social backgrounds and professions, but this has declined. We need to think radically and start a national debate about whether we can reverse this trend, and have strong, diverse estates with a mix of people' (Fabian Society, 2008).

Tenants' attitudes towards council housing

We shall say more about the right to buy later in this chapter, but it is necessary at this point to touch upon that moment in the history of council housing, because the late 1970s do represent a significant turning-point – albeit rooted in debates and developments which had been gathering momentum for some time. Specifically, it was represented by many analysts as the moment when almost all council tenants were given the opportunity to escape from an unpopular tenure. The evident desire among council tenants to buy their dwelling was presented by some as indicative of a more pervasive dissatisfaction with statist modes of provision. But was council housing so unpopular? This question is of some importance because of the very different vantage point we now have in which perceptions of state housing provision are strongly affected by what council housing has become.

In 1987, Saunders and Harris presented a conference paper entitled *Biting the Nipple? Consumers, Preferences and State Welfare*. Many of the arguments contained in this paper were further developed in Saunders' more substantial book, *A Nation of Home Owners* (1990). Essentially, Saunders and Harris argued that survey data showed that around two-thirds of council tenants were dissatisfied with their landlords, specifically in relation to councils being unresponsive, and that the demand to buy their dwellings was highest among this group. They went on to argue more generally that 'What all this amounts to is that there is a high degree of dissatisfaction among tenants, and it is this rather than any ideological factor which lies at the root of their strong but often frustrated desire to "exit" from the state sector. To adopt Barnett's metaphor, they may be hanging on the nipple of state maternalism, but the experience is far from satisfying' (p. 15).

The question is, however, more complex than this rather one-dimensional statement suggests, and this particular debate also has to be situated in the politically charged context of the 1980s. Council housing found itself at the forefront of the first phase of Thatcherite neoliberalism, a highly visible symbol of direct state intervention and supposedly misguided socialist ideals. In a pervasive attack on statist perspectives evidence was selectively appropriated and debatable connections made between cause and effect. At the core of this argument were data on tenure preferences which had been collected by a variety of surveys over a number of years and which showed a dominant desire for home ownership. But to what extent did the evidence available actually convey a deep-seated frustration and dissatisfaction among council tenants? First, and to return to the opening discussion on the contingent nature of housing-tenure roles and images, the data on tenure preferences clearly showed that attitudes had shifted over time. Neither council housing nor home ownership had inherent or immutable qualities and characteristics that delivered a certain level of preference or satisfaction among the population. Between 1975 and 1989, preference for home ownership rose from 69 to 81 per cent and preference for council housing declined from 21 to 12 per cent. What these kinds of data show is that 'Preferences are not formed in a vacuum and reflect judgements about the quality and type of property available at any time in any tenure' (Forrest and Murie, 1990: 618). We could also add that they reflect shifts in policy which may favour one tenure over another through changes in tax and subsidy regimes. All this seems self-evident and would not be worth emphasising if it were not for a myriad of claims by some politicians, policymakers and academics that the preference for home ownership has some natural, inherent or cultural foundation.

Second, it is reasonable to assume that if there had been such a high level of dissatisfaction among council tenants, then those who could have afforded to would simply have moved out and bought a property elsewhere. There would certainly not be an expectation that they would move out to the privately rented sector and experience worse housing conditions, less security and probably higher rents. It is worth emphasising that it is only recently that private renting has experienced something of a rehabilitation from being perceived as the least desirable tenure and as in terminal decline. A survey carried out in 1989, for example, showed that among council tenants only 2 per cent would prefer private landlordism. But the more telling point is that there was substantial evidence in the early days of the right to buy showing that a significant proportion of purchasers could have afforded to buy elsewhere in the market but had chosen not do so. Most tenants liked the house they lived in and the neighbourhood in which it was located. It was wrong therefore to imply that 'negative' factors dominated preferences. While council tenants may have felt that there were some aspects of the service which needed to be improved they certainly did not feel strongly enough about it to exit the sector, or indeed that it needed a remedy at all.

Moreover, the crude data on housing satisfaction were unambiguous. The vast majority (77 per cent) of council tenants questioned in a 1986 survey were either very satisfied (32 per cent) or fairly satisfied with their housing (BMRB, 1986). Similarly, the 1986 British Social Attitudes Survey found that only 17 per cent of council tenants were dissatisfied with their present accommodation and 24 per cent said they would prefer to buy (Jowell *et al.*, 1986) and a Welsh survey carried out two years later found that 84 per cent of council tenants were either very satisfied (42 per cent) or fairly satisfied with their dwelling. Rather than labour the point with other similar evidence, the general picture over the period which coincided with the introduction and development of the right to buy was one in which most council tenants appeared reasonably happy. The evidence certainly does not convey high levels of discontent. Moreover, tenants were also aware of the wider context in which local authorities operated. For example, less than a third of council tenants believed that their landlord had adequate resources.

The reality of council housing in the 1970s was that a high proportion of tenants were living in dwellings they liked in what they regarded as attractive neighbourhoods, and their point of past reference was often of overcrowded, low-amenity private renting or living with parents. Council housing had provided a higher-quality, more spacious and modern home, a key ingredient of social advancement. Over time, however, expectations changed and home ownership became a more widespread and realisable goal. Thus, while tenants showed a preference for home ownership, they did not necessarily wish to move to realise that desire. They were generally satisfied with local councils and had little enthusiasm for other forms of landlordism. When it came to selling council housing in the early 1980s it was precisely its desirability among many tenants which lay at the root of the enthusiastic take-up.

High-quality estates

Some council dwellings and estates were, of course, considerably more desirable than others and it is perhaps inevitable that most attention has been devoted to the unpopular, the problematic and the disadvantaged parts of the sector (see for example, Cole and Furbey, 1994; Power, 1997; Power and Tunstall, 1995). There is limited interest, or research funding, for investigations of good housing and good estates. If they have received attention it has been part of the kinds of community studies which have rather gone out of fashion in recent decades. Research has become more instrumental and policy-driven and this has tended to marginalise housing and neighbourhood studies which are exploring social change in more general terms. Today we know a lot about poor communities and problem areas. But we do not know very much about residential areas which jog along quite happily and are off the problem-seeking policy radar – some of the better and popular estates which were built in the immediate postwar period. It was these estates which symbolised council housing at its peak, which offered the most privileged state provision and which were the most desirable assets on offer when the era of privatisation emerged in the late 1970s.

Drawing on research undertaken in the late 1990s (see Kennett and Forrest, 2003, for more detail), we can explore some of the experiences and attitudes of residents of two estates built in the immediate postwar period – one by a local authority and one by a New Town corporation. The Three Oaks estate in Eastleigh was completed in 1947 and celebrated its 50th birthday in 1997. Harlow, the fourth New Town to be designated in March 1947, also celebrated its 50th birthday in 1997, and its Grassmore estate was one of the first neighbourhoods completed, in the early 1950s. These two estates represent some of the best examples of postwar public housing in terms of space and design. They were and remain estates which people wish to move into rather than move from. Moreover, in the late 1990s they had not been affected by any major regeneration activities other than the usual kinds of improvements carried out by owners and tenants. In physical terms, therefore, they still expressed a particular vision of social housing in a specific period.

The early New Towns, in particular, were not only major interventions in social and spatial planning but had explicit Utopian aspirations for the postwar working classes. Thus, the design and planning of many New Town estates in this period reflected grander designs about living conditions and lifestyles.

The social aspirations behind the housing programme and legislation of the postwar British Labour Government have been a matter of some debate (Berry, 1974; Cole and Furbey, 1994; Harloe, 1995; Malpass, 1990). Some see postwar British housing policy as embodying a set of ideals which became compromised by economic pressures. Others emphasise a built-in residualism and a neglect of those in greatest need. As has already been stressed, it was in part this active exclusion of the poorest or those deemed to be less deserving which gave the social housing of the early postwar period its social status. While the high point of state intervention in housing *is* about design, space standards and quality (albeit compromised by postwar shortages), it is also about what we would now refer to as active social exclusion. These were heavily planned communities developed in highly interventionist times. And translating visionary ideas into practice involved not only a high degree of planning intervention but also substantial scrutiny and vetting of potential tenants and often explicit social engineering.

The Three Oaks estate in Eastleigh was completed in 1947, with an attractive layout and low densities, and with a clear identity. The approach to the Three Oaks estate was through a large public park, creating a landscape of green, open space. The main road running through the estate was lined on either side by substantial houses with roads running off to squares and culs-de-sac with greens of varying sizes. These greens created different nuclei within the estate. Around each green there were two, three and four-bedroomed houses facing one another. There were small groups of bungalows in one corner, or in the centre of the green itself. These were built originally for small families but were now used mainly for elderly persons. On the main road there was a row of shops built with the estate, two churches (one converted into a museum), a community centre and a secondary school set back slightly beyond a large green. The gardens were substantial, especially those on corner sites.

Grassmore was smaller, about half the size of Three Oaks, with 250 dwellings ranging from small bedsits to large, detached houses. As was common in the New Towns, architectural styles were less traditional. There were two blocks of low-rise flats in the centre and modernist, flat-roofed, four-bedroomed houses opposite. The gardens were generally smaller than in Three Oaks but the feeling of space and greenery was no less strong. Mature trees now shaded some of the terraced houses which faced across the meadow-like green as you entered the estate. There was a small community centre and a public house, both designed originally to be the focus of neighbourly interaction. In the late 1940s, in both Eastleigh and Harlow, this was the countryside. Residents of Three Oaks remembered the thatched cottages nearby and cows straying into their gardens.

For the new-towners of Harlow, most typically moving from London's blitzed East End, the contrast was even greater. Beyond the mud and unmade gardens of their new estate were fields stretching into the distance. As one original resident recalled:

> It was beautiful because it was country. Across the road it was potato fields, toward the Old Town were sage fields and it was really beautiful. We was pioneers really. There was no street lights, no pavements, we had black cinders and we used to walk about when it was dark with torches.

In both estates the front gardens were designed as open-fronted. The openness and condition of the front gardens were important design features of both estates and reflected normative assumptions about social interaction in the new housing areas. They were designed as quasi-public spaces, with social life spilling out into the greens beyond. And the architect's vision was to be policed and regulated, and covenants and rules applied to the upkeep of gardens. For example, on the Grassmore estate the development corporation of the New Town required tenants to 'mow or keep in good order and condition and not alter, fence or plant (otherwise than with turf or grass seed) the front garden . . .'. Pride in one's garden was encouraged with officially organised competitions. One resident of Grassmore was informed by the Housing Manager in 1954 that, 'The Final Judging of the competition has now been completed and I have very much pleasure in notifying you that you have been awarded fifth place in the above group' (letters to tenants from Area Housing Manager). Another visitor's report on a prospective Harlow tenant had under the heading General Comments, 'Good standard of cleanliness and would no doubt prove to be excellent tenants'. In another it simply said, 'suitable for new property'.

The social grading for Harlow was more explicit than in Eastleigh and aimed for that elusive goal of social balance. With a strong resonance with contemporary policy debates, it reflected what for Heraud (1968) was an attempt to 'change the whole character of urban class relationships' (p. 33). 'Social mix' and 'cross-cutting alliances' (Heraud, 1968: 38) were to be encouraged through the development of neighbourhood units, each with a variety of housing provision and a range of facilities such as the local pub and the community centre, in an attempt to avoid the creation of one-class neighbourhoods.

The routes of access to the estates in Eastleigh and Harlow were rather different. Three Oaks served an essentially local population in dire need of housing after five years of war. People registered on the waiting list for housing, accumulated points and waited in a queue. Family size and circumstances determined the dwelling offered and how long they had to wait. Various covert and informal processes operated to influence allocation policies from time to time but for most people it was a matter of waiting their turn. On Grassmore the same bureaucratic processes operated, but in the context of a New Town where employers relocating from London and elsewhere played a critical role in allocation and access. Many of the jobs in Harlow were filled by employees moving with their firms. These key workers were the most privileged in housing terms and were offered the greatest choice. Mr H., an original tenant, had been working as a draughtsman in a London firm:

> I'd only been there about 3 months, and suddenly the notice came round, the fact that he was going to move to Harlow, because there was a new town developing. The employees who went with him would get a house! . . . The second time we come down [to Harlow] the Housing Office gave us a map to look at, a site map, and you picked your number. You sort of came down and more or less picked it from a group of houses. We had a three-bedroomed house.

In both Eastleigh and Harlow it was a period of severe housing shortages and for those fortunate enough to gain access to these estates there was a dramatic change in housing conditions and space standards. The typical experience had been of overcrowded, low-quality accommodation in the privately rented sector. The early years of marriage had usually involved sharing with parents or relatives or renting a room with shared amenities. Looking back from the late 1990s, when the research was carried out, the most striking changes on these estates related to the life course, car ownership, the general maturation of the physical environment and tenure. In contrast to the churning and turnover we associate with contemporary social housing, these two areas had been relatively settled neighbourhoods since their construction. Families had grown up, children had left home and many of the original residents remained.

For this cohort their life trajectories had been influenced by a period of employment and neighbourhood stability, good-quality housing and a generally benign period of social policy. These estates were popular when they were built and they remain popular and desirable places to live. In both Grassmore and Three Oaks, the tenants who moved there in the early 1950s experienced a dramatic change in their housing conditions. Particularly for the original and longstanding residents of these areas, it was that aspect of their housing histories which dominated, rather than issues of tenure or the associated material gains. And perhaps surprisingly, although by the late 1990s these estates had become predominantly owner-occupied, the residents still regarded them as council or corporation estates. However, they were perceived as council estates to a *lesser* degree than other areas. The social housing for the poor, the residual social housing, the housing for those with no choice was clearly seen as somewhere else. It was a label that was applied to the estates objectively in terms of building form and historical origins but also *relatively* in terms of contemporary images and roles.

Sustaining the rural community

There is a substantial and rather separate set of debates and literature on the role of council housing in rural areas (e.g. Shucksmith, 1981; Dunn *et al.*, 1981). As regards the central theme of this chapter, the role of rural council housing is perhaps better captured in terms of social sustainability rather than as a platform for social and spatial mobility Also, critiques of urban council housing as providing for a privileged, skilled elite of the working class to the neglect of the poorest, rarely applied in a rural context. The rural setting for council housing has been one of low-income families, highly polarised income structures and a housing market where tied accommodation, seasonal lettings and seasonal employment, and decaying cottages have been and remain important features. In that sense, while the high-quality postwar council housing in cities offered a significant step up for a particular section of the working class, council housing in rural areas intervened in a starker class division – between, on the one hand, a traditional rural gentry and an affluent professional middle class (of locals and newcomers) and, on the other, a poor working class. The escalator analogy in this context is thus less of an indication of the potential role played by council housing in aiding a wider upward trajectory in terms of life chances and social status (although it may have done so). Rural council housing could, however, provide a rapid ascent from typically low-quality, insecure accommodation to housing of a much higher standard for a group of households which would have remained excluded from any market-based affordable alternatives of an acceptable quality.

Various studies in the 1980s and 1990s had highlighted the extent of rural poverty (Cloke and Milbourne, 1992). While the scale of the problem and the severity of the poverty was generally less severe than for urban areas, it was the polarised nature of the incomes structure in rural areas which was important and had particular implications for housing opportunities. Indeed, in 1981 Shucksmith observed that it was the housing market rather than the labour market which had become the key component of social change in many parts of rural Britain (Shucksmith, 1981). This relates to a major theme in the rural-housing literature, namely that of 'locals versus incomers', in which a lower-income rural working class is priced out of the market by an incumbent and immigrant middle class. This conjures up the classic image of the rural commuter village in which house prices are forced up as urban elites seek the positional status of rural life-styles and rural retreats, with a low-income group of local people living in parental homes, caravans or winter lets, or hidden from view in the small council estate on the edge of the village. Newby (1980) described the contrast in many villages between a group living there by choice with 'the resources to overcome the problems of distance and access to essential services' and another group 'trapped by lack of access to alternative employment, housing and the full range of amenities which the remainder of the population take for granted' (pp. 273–4). And Cloke and Thrift (1990) referred to the role of farmers as 'scene-changers' for sections of the urban middle class seeking 'the ambience of the countryside'. Properties are improved, sold or rented as holiday homes and land-use changes are made to accommodate the changing consumption requirements of the new service class, and generally to the detriment of the poorer sections of the local population.

The 1970s and 1980s saw increasing pressures on housing in rural areas as decades of rural depopulation went into reverse, associated with processes of demographic ageing and shifting aspirations, a new gentrification and 'geriatrification' of rural areas (Redclift and Whatmore, 1990). Council housing played a vitally important role in these transformations which affected the British country-side in the second part of the twentieth century. The basic problem was that there was insufficient provision. Some rural councils had taken the view that it was an employer's responsibility to provide housing (Dunn et al., 1981) and Newby points to the power of sectional interests as the primary explanation for relatively low investment in rural council housing. Describing the situation prior to 1974, he referred to the dominance of farmers and landowners on rural councils and suggested that 'as ratepayers or as employers the farmers who ran the majority of rural councils found it more advantageous to provide tied housing for farm work-ers and to build the minimum of local authority houses' (p. 184). But council housing was built and it provided an escape from often thoroughly inadequate, substandard accommodation and was central to sustaining village communities. The importance of this role is now all too apparent as many low-income households find themselves unable to remain near their work and families and have to com-mute because of unaffordable house prices.

We can demonstrate the contribution council housing made to rural life through an unusual small-scale study carried out in the early 1990s on an estate on the edge of a Cornish village (Forrest and Murie, 1992). The estate consisted of 28 dwellings which were constructed in five phases over a 50-year period. The first dwellings, built in 1927, were three-bedroom terraces, followed by two- and three-bedroom semi-detached houses in the early 1950s. Four more three-bed semis were added in the early 1960s – the last phase of family housing. In the early 1960s six one-bedroom bungalows were added, with a further six two-bedroom bungalows in 1978, which were the final addition. The analysis in 1992 of the histories of dwelling occupancies showed that a total of 79 households had occupied 27 dwellings (no information was available on one of the properties). There had been 27 allocations to the newly built dwellings and the properties had been re-let on 52 occasions. Some of this turnover had involved households exchanging properties or moving into vacated properties elsewhere on the estate. Seven of the dwellings on the estate were connected by kinship ties of some kind. Over time ageing tenants transferred to the smaller bungalows and released the larger houses for growing local families.

Because of local housing pressures some young couples and families were allocated initially to the bungalows earmarked for elderly tenants. In some cases they were able to exchange with more established ageing households whose children had left home. What is evident is that the development of the estate allowed some families to stay together or come together. The variety of dwelling types enabled a process of housing adjustment in relation to family growth and decline. To some degree, it was therefore possible to move through the system, over the life course, but remain on the estate. Housing pressures were greater at some times than at others and correspondence with the local Housing Department showed that it was sometimes difficult to respond to requests to allow kinship links to be maintained or re-established, or to enable people to remain in their own locality. Nevertheless, the overall impression is of a housing department coping sensitively with often difficult demands, sometimes difficult people and often complex household arrangements.

These housing system dynamics in microcosm illustrate the way in which a small rural council estate operated to maintain the social cement of the local community. Needless to say, as the occupancy histories move into the 1980s there is an increasing impression of the estate taking on the character of council housing in general and becoming more residual in nature. There is less flexibility in the allocation process and more of the allocations are of the 'last resort'.

It would be wrong to paint too rosy a picture of this local rural council estate or to suggest that we can generalise to all rural council housing from this small case study. It is true, for example, that the management and allocation process conformed to the image of the paternalistic local authority so out of fashion today. Officers had a high degree of personal knowledge of individual and family circumstances and were likely to have been born and brought up in the local area. Ideas of 'choice' and 'tenants as customers' would have had little resonance. But, of course, by the time these ideas take hold in the 1990s, because of the impact of privatisation policies on the estate (involving in the main the sale of the larger family houses) there is little choice to exercise.

The key point to emphasise is that while the analysis of the history of the estate is strongly imbued with paternalism, the tenants' experience until we move into the latter period does not appear to be one of alienated serfdom or entrapment. And it was clearly a step up a ladder if not onto a moving escalator. The overall narrative is certainly one of escape – from appalling conditions in the tied or privately rented sectors, from often hostile domestic situations, and in some cases from decaying owner-occupied dwellings. Moreover, although there were frustrations and complaints, they derived in the main from the shortage of affordable housing to rent or buy for the lower-income sections of the rural working class. They had no necessary connection with council housing as a form of provision. Indeed, these frustrations have to be set against the behaviour of an elderly couple who sent a Christmas card and a gift to the Housing Department – presumably because they were so pleased with the service they had received. The gift was, of course, returned.

Social mobility and the right to buy

When the right to buy was introduced in 1980, it represented a national and more generous version of local policies which had been around in varied forms since the 1920s. At the core of the controversy over the statutory sales programme were two issues. First, that a sitting-tenant sales policy imposed on local municipalities would undermine significantly the discretion of local councils to shape and prioritise housing policies in relation to local circumstances. Second, the right to buy would be essentially an asset-stripping exercise in which the best properties would be sold, thus depriving future cohorts of the benefits enjoyed by a current generation of council tenants. This effect would be exacerbated if there were limited replacement of the dwellings lost or if the replacements were of lower quality and in less desirable locations. One response to this latter concern was that those buying their council dwellings were generally older, settled households, which were unlikely to move, at least in the short term. Thus, few vacancies would have been created had they remained in the council sector. Of course, as was pointed out, over time moves and vacancies would inevitably occur.

Leaving aside these wider considerations, however, the fact is that many former council tenants did move – and many moved fairly soon after any discount restrictions lapsed. However, many council-house purchasers had little desire to leave a dwelling they might have lived in for most of their adult life. It is, however, this first phase of the right to buy in the early 1980s which can be viewed as the next stage of the social escalator narrative (see Forrest *et al.*, 1995, for an extended analysis). A cohort which had experienced a profound change in living conditions and living standards in the early postwar period were the main beneficiaries when council dwellings were offered for sale at large discounts. It was those older tenants occupying the most desirable dwellings in the most desirable locations who had most on offer, and were in the main most able to take advantage of the offer. This is well documented and the intention is not to tread old ground. However, some aspects of this part of the story are worth reviewing.

There are two related issues. First, when council housing was essentially monetised, was purchase a good investment? Secondly, when sitting-tenant purchasers moved, where did they move to? Were they in a position to trade up in the owner-occupied sector? The first question is relatively straightforward to answer. The first wave of council-house sales coincided with a sustained house-price boom from the mid- to the late 1980s. In line with the general price trends, a council house purchased in the early 1980s would probably have doubled in value by 1989 – before discount. It also has to be borne in mind that the valuable assets on offer were not just prime properties on prime locations on the best estates. The expansion of council housing had involved various acquisitions from the private market. They might be flats or houses in desirable parts of London. There might be a limited number of unusually desirable properties, including thatched cottages or gatehouses in attractive rural enclaves. There might also be flats in stand-alone tower blocks in high-priced parts of London. Although a first postwar generation of tenants had often been fortunate enough to benefit from the high-quality housing on offer, sifting and sorting through the bureaucratic allocation process had also tended to benefit those best able to wait for the most popular vacancies which arose. Thus, there was an inevitable degree of correspondence between those tenants in the best circumstances to buy and the better dwellings. This has been the familiar experience internationally when similar privatisation programmes are introduced. A privileged cohort of one era ends up as the prime beneficiaries of the next. So, while there were some exceptions (and these exceptions increased as the right to buy recruited a wider range of households and properties in later years), generally the combination of discounts, desirable properties and general price trends meant that the first wave of purchasers made a very sound investment.

The difference between the initial purchase price of council houses in the early 1980s and their value by 1989 was also affected by the difficulties of valuing such properties. What was a council house worth on the market? This was not an easy question for valuers in 1980, reliant as they are on comparable market transactions. At that time there were none. Essentially, valuation at that time involved a rough guess using price data for similar property types in the local area, and then reducing it to take account of an assumed 'stigma' factor. This meant that many early purchasers may have benefited from unduly low valuations. When the crunch came in the late 1980s and prices fell, the combination of discounts and low initial valuations also meant that council-house purchasers typically had a much larger equity cushion available to absorb the price deflation than many other first-time buyers purchasing through normal market processes.

There is little doubt, therefore, that in terms of building an asset base as one measure of enhanced social mobility, the right to buy delivered on its promise. For those wishing to sell subsequently, however, did the right to buy also deliver an easily resellable property, enabling a move up the housing ladder? A key indication of the relative desirability in terms of location and dwelling quality of certainly the early tranche of sales, and thus of early resales, was that the market was not confined to first-time buyers. State housing built for the working classes did not create a new bottom end of the market. More than half the purchasers of ex-council dwellings were actually trading up within the owner-occupied sector, typically moving from flats or older terraced housing. And some 25 per cent of those purchasing former council homes in the early 1990s had heads of household in professional or managerial employment.

What about the more general pattern of mobility for those who resold? There may be stories of dramatic moves up the owner-occupied housing ladder for those able to buy the higher-value properties in prime locations – and there has been no research on the longer-term housing destinations and housing wealth trajectories of the early purchasers – but the evidence points to more modest social and economic gains. This is hardly surprising, since few home-owners find themselves able to make substantial price leaps unless they receive some windfall monies through inheritance or some chance event. The picture was generally one of local, short-distance moves and a modest degree of trading up – in line with the general pattern of residential mobility. Given that many first-wave purchasers were mature households with adult children, subsequent movement out also had strong associations with empty nests. Buying their council home opened up the possibility for longer-distance retirement migration for some or for a smaller dwelling in a more desirable neighbourhood for others. The more socially diverse nature of council tenancy in the early 1980s compared to the present day was also reflected in the socio-economic profile of vendors. A fifth of the heads of vendor households were, or had been, in managerial or professional employment – a higher percentage than among council tenants as a whole at that time. It was also this group, particularly those still in work, who tended to have the higher household incomes, the higher-value properties and thus wider subsequent housing choices. Thus, we have a group of households in relatively high-status jobs with generally long, and often exclusively, adult council-housing histories finally moving on to a diversity of destinations within the general owner-occupied sector.

Concluding observations: pulling up the ladder, halting the escalator

The overt theme of this chapter is not that there was some golden age of council housing which we can recapture in order to address the housing problems of early twenty-first-century Britain. The world has moved on in terms of attitudes, aspirations, lifestyles, employment patterns and so on. But council housing was a key ingredient of these transformations, providing access to high-quality state rental housing for the early postwar generations, which they were subsequently enabled to purchase with deep discounts. However, a council-housing sector which had been part of an escalator of expanding opportunities in the 1950s and 1960s had become a dead end by the end of the twentieth century. The brave new world of the postwar welfare state, promising an expansion of middle-class opportunities, had been transmogrified into a harsher neoliberal world in which social mobility had stalled, if not gone into reverse. For some in the council-housing sector there is still the opportunity and prospect of subsidised access to home ownership but in the main it has become a tenure for those apparently surplus to the requirements of the so-called knowledge-based economy. The ladder of housing opportunity has been pulled up, the escalator has effectively stopped.

The shifting position of council housing within the British housing system is also illustrative of a more pervasive tension between the state and the market which can be found in policy debate and housing provision across a number of societies. State or non-profit housing which is too successful in terms of quality and popularity sows the seeds of its own destruction if it threatens the pre-eminence of the market, and a weakly targeted state housing sector raises question of social justice and resource efficiency. Strong targeting, however, produces the kinds of outcomes we are confronting today in which council housing has become unambiguously associated with the poor in a situation in which social mobility in other spheres is increasingly restricted.

Since the 1970s the dominant narrative in relation to council housing has been that of a failed and unpopular social experiment – a passing moment of collectivist zeal which produced mass housing estates managed by insensitive bureaucrats. Moreover, as the social, economic and policy landscape changed, council housing became guilty by association. Privatisation and lack of investment contributed to creating a housing sector ill-equipped to handle the social changes of the latter part of the twentieth century in which a new and diverse poor became increasingly concentrated in a residual tenure. As this chapter, however, has tried to show there is another story where council housing, for all its imperfections, made a significant and lasting contribution to social and spatial mobility for a section of the urban working class and offered security and dramatically improved housing conditions for the rural poor.

In drawing to a close, let us return to where we came in and, in particular, to the relationship between council housing and the market. Given the current turmoil in the owner-occupied sector, it is worth reminding ourselves that the relationship has always been supportive rather than oppositional. For example, it is often overlooked that council housing was built by private developers and represented a steady and reliable source of profit, particularly when times were hard. Also, the current level of home ownership in Britain would have been very difficult to achieve without the prior existence of a large state sector. A reliance on more market-oriented means of achieving a significant growth in owner occupation would have produced a sector of dwellings with less space and of lower build quality – and requiring many more households to enter into the kinds of unsustainable financial arrangements which are at the centre of the current difficulties.

Unlikely as it may have seemed only a few months ago, council housing may be about to experience something of a revival precisely because of an ailing market. After a long period of market triumphalism in which local councils were becoming increasingly marginal to housing provision, it seems that the current housing crisis is about to move them back nearer centre stage, with various measures being introduced to help ailing developers and struggling home owners. Some unsold homes built for home ownership may end up in the council sector. Some home-owners may end up as council tenants. There is renewed talk of some form of local-authority mortgage finance. It may be that these measures to alleviate market failure will provide the elements of a new housing escalator for poor households and a version of council housing with a more positive image and a role more in tune with the current times. Non-market housing could prove to be an attractive label.

References

Berry, F. (1974) *Housing: The Great British Failure*, London: Charles Knight.

BMRB (1986) *Housing and Savings*, London: Building Societies Association.

Bootle, R. (1997) *The Death of Inflation: surviving and thriving in the zero era*, London: Nicholas Brealey.

Cloke, P. and Thrift, N. (1990) 'Class and change in rural Britain' in Marsden, T., Lowe, P. and Whatmore, S. (eds) *Rural Restructuring*, London: David Fulton.

Cloke, P. and Milbourne, P. (1992) 'Deprivation and lifestyles in rural Wales: Rurality and the cultural dimension', *Journal of Rural Studies*, 8: 359–71.

Cole, I. and Furbey, R. (1994) *The Eclipse of Council Housing*, London: Routledge.

Department of the Environment (1977) *Housing Policy: Technical Volume Part 1*, London: HMSO.

Donnison, D. (1964) *Essays on Housing*, London: G. Bell and Sons Ltd.

Dunn, M., Rawson, M. and Rogers, A. (1981) *Rural Housing: competition and choice*, London: Allen and Unwin.

Fabian Society (2008) 'Flint: We must break link between council housing and worklessness' http://fabians.org.uk/events/speeches/flint-we-must-break-link-between-council-housing-and-worklessness.

Feinstein, L. (2008) *The Public Value of Social Housing: a longitudinal analysis of the relationship between housing and life chances*, London: The Smith Institute.

Forrest, R. and Murie, A. (1990) 'A Dissatisfied State? Consumer Preferences and Council Housing in Britain', *Urban Studies*, 27(5), 617–35.

Forrest, R. and Murie, A. (1992) 'Change on a rural council estate: an analysis of dwelling histories', *Journal of Rural Studies*, 8(1), 53–65.

Forrest, R., Murie, A. and Gordon, D. (1995) *The Resale of Former Council Homes*, London: HMSO.

Forrest, R., Leather, P. and Kennett, P. (1999) *Home Ownership in Crisis? The experience of negative equity in Britain*, Aldershot: Avebury.

Harloe, M. (1995) *The People's Home?* Oxford: Basil Blackwell.

Harloe, M., Issacharoff, R. and Minns, R. (1974) *The Organisation of Housing*, London: Heinemann.

Heraud, B.J. (1968) 'Social class and the New Towns', *Urban Studies*, 5(1): 33–58.

Jowell, R., Witherspoon, S. and Brook, L. (1986) *British Social Attitudes: the 1986 Report*, Aldershot: Gower.

Kennett, P. and Forrest, R. (2003) 'From Planned Communities to Deregulated spaces: socio-tenurial change on high-quality council estates', *Housing Studies*, 18(1), 47–63.

Malpass, P. (1990) *Reshaping Housing Policy: Subsidies, Rents and Residualisation*, London: Routledge.

Newby, H. (1980) 'Urbanisation and the Rural Class Structure: reflections on a case study', in Butte, F. and Newby, H. (eds) *The Rural Sociology of the Advanced Societies*, London: Croom Helm.

Parker, T. (1983) *The People of Providence: a housing estate and some of its inhabitants*, London: Hutchinson.

Power, A. (1997) *Estates on the Edge: the social consequences of mass housing in Northern Europe*, London: Macmillan.

Power, A. and Tunstall, R. (1995) *Swimming Against The Tide: polarisation or progress on 20 unpopular council estates*, 1980–1995, York: Joseph Rowntree Foundation.

Ravetz, A. (2001) *Council Housing and Culture: the history of a social experiment*, London: Routledge.

Redclift, N. and Whatmore, S. (1990) 'Household, Consumption and Livelihood Ideologies and Issues in Rural Research' in Marsden, T., Lowe, P. and Whatmore, S. (eds) *Rural Restructuring*, London: David Fulton.

Saunders, P. (1990) *A Nation of Home Owners*, London: Unwin Hyman.

Saunders, P. and Harris, C. (1987) 'Biting the nipple? Consumers, preferences and state welfare.' Paper presented at Sixth Urban Change and Conflict Conference, University of Kent, 20–23 September.

Shucksmith, M. (1981) *No Homes for Locals*, Farnborough: Gower.

Simon, E.D. (1929) *How to Abolish the Slums*, London: Longmans, Green and Co.

4 The right to buy

Colin Jones

The right to buy (RTB) began as a headline, arguably hard-line, policy of Mrs Thatcher's Conservative government in 1979, but it became the most significant single housing policy of the last 30 years. Giving council tenants the right to buy their homes at discounted prices raised passions on both sides of the political divide, but it became a very popular policy with the public, even with those who appeared to suffer as a consequence. Over time the RTB has also come to be seen as almost a human right and as such has become politically sacrosanct, embraced by the main political parties. Even so, from a policy perspective it has always been contentious.

This chapter assesses the impact of the RTB on the changes to the housing system since 1980. The analysis will encompass the ramifications of the RTB across tenures and neighbourhoods, its significance in the cascading of wealth, and its consequences in terms of complexity and fragmentation for housing policy, affordability problems and housing markets. The chapter will also set the RTB within the wider perspective of other fundamental influences on the housing system and regional variations. Finally, future prospects for policy will be considered. The chapter updates and extends the analysis presented in Jones and Murie (2006) where a more detailed review of the underpinning evidence is to be found.

Historic housing and policy context

Almost 30 years after the introduction of the right to buy the housing system looks very different. To fully understand the RTB it is useful to return to the 1970s. The RTB was introduced at a time of some complacency in British housing policy. The long-term postwar council-house building programme was coming to an end, although at the time this was not clearly apparent. Council housing was seen as a central element of the housing system and it had been a very effective driver for improving housing standards and meeting shortages. By the end of the decade almost a third of households in England and Wales, and half in Scotland, were council tenants. Most council houses were well built, traditional houses, with satisfied tenants, but much of the later housing of the 1970s took the form of medium- and high-rise blocks using systems-based building. There were some concerns about the quality of this new housing and fears about the difficulty of letting of some of these estates.

In parallel to the growth of council housing was the even greater rise of owner occupation (except in Scotland). The Labour government's 1977 Green Paper argued that owning one's home was a basic and natural desire, and in 1980 58 per cent of the housing stock was owner-occupied in England and Wales, while in Scotland the figure was just a third. Home ownership had become the dominant and normal tenure (except in Scotland) and the 1970s saw growing aspirations among young people to own their own home, with almost seven out of ten people wanting to buy (Jones, 1982).

The promise that council tenants would be given the right to buy was a major part of the Conservatives' appeal to working-class voters in the late 1970s and was a key issue in the general election of May 1979. The election of a Conservative government not only saw the arrival of the RTB but also a different approach to council housing. The attractiveness of council housing was diminished as rents were systematically raised in real terms (and subsidies reduced) over the next two decades, especially in the 1980s. Meanwhile subsidies to home ownership continued until tax relief on mortgage interest was phased out in the 1990s. Council-house building was also quickly curtailed and houses sold under the RTB were effectively not replaced.

The evolution of the right to buy

The RTB is very simple in terms of the individual rights and the opportunity it offers, and its overall goal of expanding home ownership. Judged in these terms it is a very successful policy, with more than 2.3 million council houses sold since its introduction in 1980. But the policy of selling council houses was not entirely new. Up to this point there had been some 200,000 sales to sitting tenants in areas where local authorities had chosen to exercise their discretionary power to sell (Murie, 1975). The RTB removed local authority discretion, provided a higher discount to value for purchasers and gave tenants the right to a local-authority mortgage. Discounts were based on period of residence, with tenants entitled to a 33 per cent discount after 3 years, rising by 1 per cent a year up to 50 per cent. There were some amendments in the mid-1980s to make the scheme more attractive: providing higher discounts (especially for flats); reducing to two years the qualification period needed before tenants could purchase; and reducing to three years the subsequent period of residence required, within which the discount would have to be repaid if the property was resold.

Following the election of a Labour government in 1997, limits to the reduced monetary discount were introduced in 1998 in England and Wales, but the essentials of the scheme remained (and continue) unchanged. Nevertheless subsequent policy changes have diluted the attractiveness of the RTB and the simplicity of the scheme has been eroded by regional variations, especially brought about by the devolution of housing policy to the Scottish government. Recent amendments have been particularly driven by considerations of value for money, but also in England by concern about abuses by companies. In England and Wales the eligibility and repayment periods were raised in 2005 to five years and owners who sell within ten years must now first offer the property back to their former landlord. In Scotland the 'modernised' RTB was introduced in 2002, increasing the eligibility period to five years and lowering the maximum discount for new tenants from that date.

Over the last decade maximum discounts have become less generous and now vary by region. The lowest in absolute terms, £15,000, applies to the modernised RTB in Scotland but long-standing tenants are not subject to such a ceiling. In all other regions there is a maximum discount that ranges from £16,000 up to £38,000. The lowest figure applies to Wales, all but two London boroughs and nine local authorities in the South-East of England with the highest housing pressures. The discount therefore represents a relatively low percentage of the average valuation for a property in London of £147,000 in 2006–7.

In Scotland the devolved government has followed a distinct approach. The concept of 'pressured areas' was introduced in 2002: within these the modernised right to buy could be suspended, initially for five years. For an area to be designated pressured, the local authority has to demonstrate an affordable-housing shortage; so far nine out of 32 authorities have successfully applied for parts of their area to be designated. These areas are generally villages, but pressured-area status has been granted in a suburb of Glasgow and parts of Aberdeen. More recently the Scottish government has announced plans to stop all sales of new council houses. This measure is more symbolic than substantial as very few council houses are being built. Similarly, pressured-area status – limited as it is to suspending sales to tenants who have moved in since 2002 – is less effective than initially appears.

The RTB therefore was originally a very generous national scheme that replaced a discretionary scheme with little or no subsidy. Initially the RTB was made even more generous but over the last decade the subsidy has been reduced and the terms have become less attractive to potential purchasers. There is also now a regional – even local – discretionary dimension to the policy, and so to a degree it is beginning to turn back to the pre-1980 position. Local differences have been heightened by the increasing number of council-housing stock transfers (see Chapter 5) that have meant that many new tenants in the sector are not eligible for the RTB.

RTB sales over time

The introduction of the RTB was followed by the anticipated dramatic take-up by tenants who had wanted the opportunity to buy their home. But the subsequent pattern of sales – shown in Figure 4.1 for England and broadly similar in other parts of the UK – was far less predictable. This latent demand was certainly the initial thrust for sales but, rather than fading away then, sales surged again with the house-price boom of the latter half of the 1980s and the growing reality of the financial benefits of buying rather than renting. During the first half of the 1990s the owner-occupied housing market was in the doldrums and so were RTB sales, and they began to grow again only as house prices rose at the end of the decade. The 1990s also saw the gradual establishment of resale markets as the original purchasers moved on (contrary to the government's expectations) or died, and this reinforced and encouraged the surge in sales by increasing the marketability of these houses as financial assets.

Sales have fallen away dramatically since 2003, dropping by more than two-thirds in England to the lowest point since the introduction of the RTB. This decline is consistent across every region of England and Wales. Sales have fallen least in Scotland but even here sales are down by almost a half. Part of the explanation lies in the reduction in the maximum discounts, making the RTB less financially attractive.

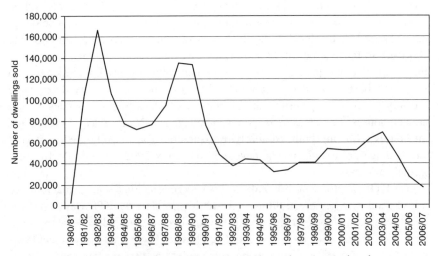

4.1 Sales by local authorities through the right to buy in England.
Source: Department of Communities and Local Government.

Impact on owner occupation

Today the aspirations for home ownership articulated in the 1970s have been largely achieved, as 70 per cent of housing is now owner-occupied in England. The growth of the tenure in Scotland has been more spectacular, with the owner-occupied proportion of the stock doubling to reach 65 per cent. The RTB played a significant part in this transformation, contributing about a third to the growth of home ownership over this period. Put another way, new build for sale has outnumbered RTB sales by about two to one. However, in Scotland in particular, and also in the North-East of England and London, the RTB has been more important than new building in promoting the level of home ownership. It has been of least significance in the southern regions of England, especially the South-East and the South-West. However, these figures belie the symbolic signal represented by the RTB, together with the initial surge in sales, in promoting the belief that aspirations to own could be achieved.

In strict statistical terms the RTB has played a partial role in a movement toward buying one's own home, derived in large part from rising real incomes. Dissection of the impact of the RTB on home ownership over time reveals that the major impact on the growth of owner-occupied stock relative to new house-building was in the 1980s. Since 1990 sales have been greater than new building in only a limited number of years and a small minority of the regions – the North-East in 2002 and 2003, London in 1999 and 2000 and Scotland in 1991–4. The RTB's most significant influence on the owner-occupied *stock* is therefore relatively historical, but the largest impact on the growth of owner-occupied *markets* followed later, with the expansion of resales in the 1990s.

The pool of RTB purchasers has not proved to be finite, as initially anticipated, because a continual flow of new tenants and the dynamics of demographic change have meant that there has been a persistent stream of potential buyers. The stereotypical purchasers of the 1980s were an older couple, over 45 years of age, with grown-up children and at least one member in full-time employment. Today there is a younger generation of purchasers, who are still most likely to be two-parent families but whose children are more usually of school age. RTB purchasers have become a more diverse group, encompassing single parents and the retired, receiving financial assistance from relatives. Household incomes are generally low (but not the lowest) and most purchasers are drawn from a social background of the lower middle class and the skilled working class. In many places the incomes of these households would have been sufficient to enable them to buy on the market – probably a less spacious house. Many have variable incomes, with county-court judgements against them, and it is important to note that much of the demand during this decade has been financed by sub-prime mortgages.

Resale markets have matured and resales have been integrated into the local housing market in all areas, typically accounting for at least 10 per cent of the market. The prices of these houses are generally lower than equivalent housing not built by the public sector. This negative differential varies across areas with resales in some areas as much as 25 per cent cheaper than equivalent mainstream housing nearby. In contrast, where there are severe market pressures the differential can almost disappear for popular house types and popular areas. Resales have found a niche in the housing market as starter homes or as affordable housing for low-income families. But some of the best housing in the highest-demand areas is not affordable and former council flats in parts of London are readily marketable at prices in excess of £200,000 (Jones and Murie, 2006).

Consequences for council housing

The stock of council housing has fallen by the order of a half in England, although only about a third of this can be attributed to the right to buy, with the remainder accounted for by demolitions and transfers of stock to housing associations. Stock transfer to registered social landlords outnumbered sales under the right to buy by the order of almost five to one in 2006–7. The regional breakdown of the remaining stock is given in Table 4.1 and shows that the largest concentration of council housing is in London, but over three-quarters of this comprises flats. Nevertheless, some initial fears that the right to buy would ultimately leave only flats in the

Table **4.1** Regional council-housing stock and current annual depletion rates

Region	2007 stock (thousands)	Percentage flats	RTB sales 2006–77	Depletion rate 2006–7
North-East England	154	27	2,080	1.28
Yorkshire and Humberside	248	34	2,445	0.92
East Midlands	205	32	1,628	0.77
Eastern England	186	40	1,113	0.61
Greater London	452	77	2,221	0.49
South-East England	189	48	1,139	0.56
South-West England	120	43	627	0.49
West Midlands	214	39	2,315	1.04
North-West England	204	39	3,329	1.38
Wales	154	^	1,248	0.82
Scotland	362	^	7,288	2.01

^ Not available

Sources: Crown Copyright, DCLG live table 670 (last updated August, 2008; Scottish Government, Housing Statistics for Scotland, 2008; Welsh Assembly Government, Statistical Release 211/2008 (December 2008)

sector have proved unfounded, with the council stock in most regions still predominantly consisting of houses. Current annual depletion rates are now less than 1 per cent, except in the North-East and North-West of England and in Scotland.

At the beginning the RTB was presented by the government as a policy to promote home ownership that would not have any adverse impact on other tenants, because purchasers would have stayed as tenants anyway, and there is evidence that this was initially true (Forrest and Murie, 1984a, 1984b; Foulis, 1985). The immediate impact of the RTB on lost lettings was very limited as a consequence, and it was not until the early 1990s that there was any noticeable impact. Even so, the cumulative effect of the RTB (with virtually no replacement) has led to a loss of 80,000 annual social-housing tenancies in England since the early 1980s (Jones and Murie, 2006).

RTB sales have been predominantly concentrated in the larger and better stock, not only reducing access to council housing but also having a disproportionate impact on the availability of the attractive stock to existing and new council tenants. The implications can be seen in terms of a mismatch between demand and supply, causing overcrowding to increase, whether of council tenants or of the statutory homeless living in temporary accommodation. Vacancies are also increasingly focused in the less desirable estates.

A number of consequences have followed, which have in turn had a knock-on effect on RTB sales. Families with expanding housing requirements living in two-bedroom council housing, finding their opportunities to move to a three-bedroom home limited, have opted to buy their home with a view to selling and then trading up and buying a three-bedroom house (Jones and Murie, 1999). Indeed Jones (2003) found that many people had planned such a strategy of moving on before they bought their council house.

The silent cumulative effect of the RTB is a slow asphyxiation of the tenure as it was in the 1970s. Council housing is sometimes described as the tenure of last resort but in many parts of the UK there are social-housing shortages and the homeless have to stay lengthy periods in 'temporary' private rented accommodation. At the same time council housing has become a transient staging-post for many younger tenants on the way to buying on the open market. Council housing has increasingly taken the mantle of providing housing for people at particular stages of their lives: for the young, for the elderly and for others during periods in which they have limited resources.

The promotion of the private rented sector

One unexpected development of the RTB has been the promotion of the private rented sector. The sector experienced significant long-term decline from the early twentieth century. Following the reforms of the 1988 Housing Act, which reintro-duced market rents and reduced security of tenure, new investment began to develop in the late 1990s. The RTB has influenced this in three ways. First, the cumulative impact of the RTB on re-lets is an important factor in reducing the supply of social housing and contributing to a shortage of housing to rent, and also to increasing rent levels in the private sector. Second, local authorities faced with record numbers of homeless have had to turn to private-sector leasing to resolve their housing deficit. Third, RTB resales have contributed by offering the opportunity of a source of new supply to the sector.

RTB resales are attractive to private landlords because they are relatively cheap, often selling at a discount relative to comparable properties. In some cases former RTB properties are unattractive or difficult to sell for owner occupation because of weak resale markets in areas where such markets have not been established or sustained. There is, for example, no resale market for flats in multi-storey blocks, or for isolated purchases on large estates. This is partly brought about by the lend-ing criteria of major mortgage-providers, who will not fund, for example, the purchase of flats higher than five storeys above ground-level. As a consequence, many of these dwellings are sold at knock-down prices at auctions.

There is only limited formal evidence on the scale of this effect. Jones (2003) found that a quarter of properties bought under the RTB in areas of inner London in 2002 were being rented out three years after their initial purchase. The equiva-lent figures for provincial cities in the study were much lower – 7 per cent in Birmingham and 3 per cent in Leeds. A wider study of Birmingham by Murie and Rowlands (2008), based on a comparison of the 1981 and 2001 Censuses, finds substantial growth in large council-built estates in the city. The most extreme example is the large 1960s council-built estate of Ladywood, where RTB sales had accounted for 27 per cent of the original stock and the private rented sector now represented 43 per cent of this private stock. The statistics for other estates are less dramatic, but the private rented sector appears to account for at least a fifth of all original RTB sales in equivalent estates. Murie and Rowlands (2008) hence argue that there is an emerging picture not of mixed social-rented/home-ownership estates but of mixed social-rented/private rented or social-rented/private rented/home-ownership estates. In particular there is the potential for the least popular and attractive estates to revert to being rented estates while the best estates will remain mixed-tenure, with private renting as well as social renting.

Wider perspectives and consequences

The wider agenda of the RTB policy has embraced wealth generation and the pro-motion of socially mixed neighbourhoods (discussed in other chapters). With more than two million purchases under the scheme it can be argued that the RTB has achieved a massive transfer of wealth from the state to low-income households.

This has been achieved not only through the discounts but more importantly also as a consequence of the rise in capital values as resale markets developed. The major criticism lies in the lottery of the process that is very much dependent on the location and type of council house occupied. The major beneficiaries have been those who purchased at the outset of the RTB. The households excluded from the wealth redistribution are generally low-income council tenants living in the unpopular council-housing stock because they do not have the financial ability to find any alternative. For these households, not only have the opportunities of the RTB passed them by but so too their chance to be allocated a good-quality council house is much more limited.

Notwithstanding the inherent inequity of the RTB between tenants, it can be argued that a similar scheme offering broadly the same opportunities would have been necessary to meet the pressure of growing aspirations for home ownership as real incomes increased. From this perspective a marketisation of the stock was inevitable. It can be further argued that through resale markets these homes are bought by local people who traditionally would have been housed locally by the council and so there is no or little effect on communities. The problem with this argument is twofold: local housing markets are open and this inevitably creates the potential for 'locals' to be outbid – for example, through the buying of former council houses as retirement or second homes in rural communities. Second, the 'market' solution has not been entirely successful, with changes to the structure of households, the increasing number of households and the failure of the private house-building industry to satisfy the growing demand for house purchase, especially at the bottom of the market. The cumulative effect of the RTB through historically low social-housing lettings combined with these phenomena, and despite the rise of the private rented sector, has created widespread affordability problems recognised by the government (ODPM, 2005). This has led to calls for a new social-housing programme and the replacement of housing sold under the RTB (Shelter, 2005), and this argument has to a degree been accepted by the government (CLG, 2007; Scottish Government, 2007).

The cumulative impact of the RTB has also wrought changes to the management of council-built estates, especially of those that consist predominantly of flats. The emergence of mixed-tenure estates of freeholders, leaseholders and private and council tenants who may also be in freehold or leasehold properties represents a series of challenges for estate management, including the apportionment of responsibility and financial liability for management, repairs and maintenance. Owners attracted to these properties are often first-time purchasers on low incomes who struggle to pay substantial annual expenditures. The maintenance and upgrading of mixed-tenure estates therefore unleashes a range of tensions between tenants who want a high level of service and owners or leaseholders who often seek to minimise services and extend maintenance periods to reduce costs. From the point of view of owners modernisation may not make financial sense where the properties remain of low value. The outcome of these frictions can be substantial administrative headaches and delays, higher unit management costs and barriers to major comprehensive redevelopment programmes.

The future of the right to buy

There was a collapse in the take-up of the RTB even before the 2007 credit crunch, which affected the whole housing market through lending criteria becoming more restrictive. The impact of the post-credit-crunch housing finance climate is particularly unfavourable to the right to buy. As noted earlier, much recent house purchase under the RTB has been supported by sub-prime lending. Indeed, although it has not been widely recognised, much of the sub-prime lending in the UK has been focused on RTB sales, as have the high level of repossessions. In the post-credit-crunch financial environment this source of lending will be substantially diminished for some years to come.

The reduced maximum discounts, as noted earlier, have had a major impact on RTB sales by reducing the financial incentive to buy, and sales have nose-dived, as Figure 4.1 indicates – for the first time in a housing boom. Historically RTB purchasers have been able to receive 100 per cent mortgages on the actual price because their discount in effect represented their deposit. The capping of the discount in nominal terms – certainly in parts of the South-East – to less than 10 per cent of the average valuation has reduced the potential to achieve such an arrangement. This position is more aggravated in a new era of conservative lending criteria that will now require larger deposits and are therefore likely to substantially reduce RTB opportunities, at least in certain regions.

These curtailments of demand must also be seen in the context of the current predominance of the young, the elderly and the unemployed among council tenants. These groups are unlikely again to find credit so easy, and many of the best and largest properties have been sold – although Table 4.1 shows that there is still a high proportion of houses left (except in London). Many of the houses where resale markets have been sustained have also been sold, and in other areas where resales have been problematic, mortgages will be difficult to find in the new financial environment.

The conclusion must be that the heyday of the RTB is over: sales are at their lowest since its inception, both in absolute terms and in relative terms as measured by depletion rates. Furthermore, the scope for revival appears very limited. In policy terms this means that, unless there is some substantial initiative to make the RTB more financially attractive, it will wither on the vine. In fact policy discussions in the devolved administrations have pointed in the reverse direction. The Welsh government is committed to seeking powers to suspend the RTB in areas with acute shortages, as part of its 'One World' agreement between the Labour and Nationalist coalition partners. In December 2007 the Welsh government applied for the extra powers to do this by the laying of a Legislative Competency Order. It is envisaged that there will be area suspensions of the RTB scheme on application from local councils (Assembly of Wales Government, 2007).

The Scottish National Party, prior to its installation in government, had a manifesto commitment to review the RTB. To date it has only announced its intention to withdraw the RTB for new council housing but an indication of its thinking is given in a recent green paper (Scottish Government, 2007). It poses the question whether there is any potential for varying the discount by type of property or locality as a means of creating greater local flexibility. The Housing Executive (2007) in Northern Ireland reports that the house-sales scheme is to be reviewed for the devolved government 'to make it more sensitive to local need'.

These ideas are still embryonic but potentially suggest that the RTB can be transformed into a local policy tool. However, it is unclear that these policies will be little more than sophisticated ways of restricting sales on a local basis rather than developing greater incentives in areas of low owner occupation. It is possible to postulate a scenario where certain house types, or houses in areas that are in surplus, could be offered at higher discounts to generate cash flow to build new housing to meet specific needs. However, there are a number of difficulties in this proposition. High discounts reduce the potential revenue generated, so a number of houses will have to be sold to fully account for the new build costs (even if there is truly no replacement required for the houses sold). At the same time, while take-up in the past has been seen to be responsive to discounts, in the current context the likely credit constraints on most council-tenant households are likely to dampen demand.

Extensions of the right to buy

After 2005 the government's strategy in England continued to seek a rise in owner occupation to 75 per cent (CLG, 2007), and policy documents heralded the achievement of over one million more people owning their own homes than in 1997. With the slowdown in the take-up of the RTB, while there was a continuing promotion of home ownership, the government sought new approaches. These included the remodelling of existing schemes to aim at social tenants more widely, including council tenants who did not want to buy their existing home.

Since 1980 there have been parallel but voluntary schemes for participating housing association tenants to become owner occupiers. These schemes have developed over time but broadly offer qualifying tenants either the opportunity to buy a property on the open market at a reduced cost or on a shared-ownership basis. These schemes did not apply to sitting-tenant purchase but instead to the purchase of another property. The amount of cash incentive payable was dependent on geographical location. In 1996 further schemes were introduced that, while not offering a statutory right, enabled participating housing-association tenants to purchase the homes they lived in at a flat-rate discount equivalent to those of the other, parallel schemes. In all cases the participation of the housing association was dependent on funding from the Housing Corporation.

The Right to Acquire was introduced in 1996, giving a mandatory right for some social tenants to acquire their home with a statutory-purchase flat-rate grant. It applies to all new build and to rehabilitation-for-rent schemes that received Social Housing Grant, and to all tenanted property transferred to a registered social landlord from a public sector or council landlord on or after 1 April 1997.

At the general election of 2005 the Labour Party promised a comprehensive plan for increasing home ownership that encompassed a new 'HomeBuy' scheme, offering up to 300,000 council and housing-association tenants the opportunity to buy part of their home, increasing their equity over time if they wished. The government has now rebranded its long-standing shared-ownership scheme under the HomeBuy title and has introduced a range of shared-equity opportunities in April 2006, targeting social tenants. Two of these schemes are now considered.

One of these is MyChoiceHomeBuy, which offers a shared-equity product in partnership with the private sector. This scheme is aimed mainly at helping tenants who earn between £20,000 and £60,000 per annum to buy their own home on the open market. The key component is a shared-equity loan to cover between 25 per cent and 50 per cent of the property value. A low interest rate is charged on this loan and it is redeemed in full when the property is sold. The scheme is cash-limited and priority was originally given to social tenants and public-sector key workers but the income criterion will exclude many council tenants. It is also available to households who have previously owned properties but are now unable to buy without assistance – for example, in the case of relationship breakdowns, or of families who are overcrowded in their existing homes.

The Social HomeBuy scheme potentially provides opportunities for existing housing-association or local-authority tenants to buy a share in their rented home. Tenants can purchase a minimum initial share of 25 per cent of the home. The remaining unowned equity is retained by the social landlord, which charges the household rent on this share. Buyers receive a discount on the initial share purchase pro rata with the Right to Acquire (RTA) discount (currently between £9,000 and £16,000 – depending upon the local-authority area in which the property is located).

The emphasis is therefore on a continuing stimulation of home ownership through inclusion of households the RTB has been unable to reach. In 2005 the government announced that it planned to assist over 100,000 people into home ownership through these HomeBuy schemes by 2010 (CLG, 2007). The schemes combine elements of the existing shared-ownership scheme to enable social tenants to buy a share in their own home, with a discount applicable that is similar to the existing RTA. Social HomeBuy appears to be aimed at council tenants who cannot afford the cost of the RTB, but its application is restricted as only eight local authorities were participating by April 2007 (as well as 78 housing associations) (Cooper, 2007). The two-year pilot was completed in March 2008 and it is now a voluntary scheme for local authorities and housing associations.

The statistical trends for the RTB do not suggest a positive prognosis for Social HomeBuy and take-up by council tenants. This is to a degree confirmed by Rowlands and Murie (2008), who report only 207 sales under the pilot scheme by the end of March 2008, and these were mainly by housing-association tenants. The scheme was only a pilot, with very limited numbers of local authorities participating, but the conclusion must be that the full scheme will not have any substantive impact on the council-housing sector. It seems unlikely that the 100,000 target above (equivalent to 25,000 per year, just above the current annual level of RTB sales) will be achieved and that Social HomeBuy's contribution from council tenants will be extremely limited.

These schemes lack the simplicity of the RTB. There are doubts about the ease of take-up by households and the budget constraints applicable significantly constrain their availability, unlike the RTB which has never been subject to such budget limits. The limited discount of £9,000–16,000 also raises the issues of fairness in relation to the RTB, and of the attractiveness of the schemes to potential target groups. There is also a fundamental problem in that their success is predicated on the owner-occupied housing stock being available, and over the last decade new house-building has not kept pace with the rate of new household formation (ODPM, 2005). Overall these schemes are unlikely to create a new wave of council tenants moving into owner occupation.

The changing policy debate

The right to buy, an essential part of 'Thatcherism', continued unquestioned in government through 17 years of Conservative power. Under New Labour from 1997 the policy persisted, although after 2005 the government rejected the Conservative Party's arguments for extending the RTB in England to housing-association tenants. In many ways the surprise is that there has not been more debate – for example, about the discounts on flats. Devolution in Scotland brought some new thinking and the Welsh Assembly is now seeking new powers to control the RTB. Since 1997 the changes have emerged slowly and there are common threads in the reasons for these developments. This is particularly reflected in the reductions of discount, and in concern to address value for money, abuse of the policy and the adverse consequences of the RTB. The Scottish 'modernised' RTB reduced the incentives to purchase but only applied for new tenants and while the pressured-area designation process was slow and cumbersome, it is significant in ending the universality of the scheme. At the same time Scotland is the only region where the Conservatives' maximum discount of £50,000 is still in force for long-standing tenants. In comparison, the stiffer cash limitations introduced on discounts for all tenants in England in 1999 and the further reforms in 2003 seem bolder and have severely reduced sales.

In the last decade arguments to restrict or remove the RTB have been voiced more stridently than in the late 1980s and 1990s – but it continues, probably because its negative consequences for the council stock are now very limited. Governments have so far amended the RTB but have not repealed it – indeed there is a view that it is very difficult to contemplate such repeal without a challenge under Human Rights legislation. Policy changes over this latter period can at best be described only as preserving the status quo (and even this is unlikely), and do not redress the past impact of the RTB on access to housing. All of the changes may be argued by the critics to be too little and certainly too late for the council-housing sector.

There is also a current argument that the abolition of the right to buy could restrict the funds available to address the social-housing shortage (Wilcox, 2007). In fact, in many ways this issue has always been at the crux of the debate about the RTB and is therefore a long-standing issue. The Conservative government explicitly decided against reinvestment at the outset. The long-term lost opportunity associated with the right to buy is the failure to use the receipts generated through sales creatively to improve housing opportunities and to spread the benefits to households other than those able to buy their house – to homeless people and the badly housed and to tenants on the worst estates and in obsolete properties. In the present context continuing the right to buy without reinvestment would mean continuing to miss this opportunity but it is also true that revenues from sales will now be insufficient to revive the council or social rented housing tenure. There is the further argument that the RTB itself is a barrier to investment, as local authorities do not see the logic of building new council houses, even if funds were available, only for them to be sold off. This view underpins the Scottish Government's abolition of the RTB for new housing.

The Labour government now accepts that there are social-housing shortages but has a continuing enthusiasm for promoting home ownership, and in recent years there has been a policy focus on the unaffordability of owner occupation, especially for key workers in the South-East, but also for council tenants. There is an implicit understanding that the RTB will not address these problems, and the HomeBuy scheme (partly an extension of the RTB) has been designed specifically to generate an alternative avenue into home ownership. RTB sales may have dropped to a trickle, having topped two million altogether, but there is still a substantial unfulfilled demand for home ownership – a demand coming from 75 per cent of social tenants, according to the 2001 English Housing Survey (Munro et al., 2005). There is therefore a latent demand for home ownership by social tenants as in the 1970s, but the difference is that the council-housing sector is now depleted. The scope of the RTB is now much diminished, as the segment of the housing market that the RTB applies to is smaller – both because of the previous impacts of the policy and because of other privatisations and stock transfers – and the stock in general is less attractive to purchase. The type of tenant in the sector has similarly changed, and the aspirations of these tenants seem more unrealistic than those of the tenants in the 1970s, even if discount limits were raised again. The HomeBuy schemes are restricted by being cash-limited and for the reasons discussed above are not likely to tap into this 'demand' from council tenants.

Conclusions

The sale of council houses has been the biggest and most sustained privatisation programme in the UK and has had a profound effect on the housing system. It has generated around £40 billion in cash receipts and is not yet exhausted. The policy has been generous and has made a real and positive difference for households that have bought their houses under the scheme. It has had a 'second-round' effect on the housing market through the subsequent resales, an impact that continues but varies with the local housing market. The latent demand for home ownership identified in the 1970s proved to be only the beginning as succeeding households took up the opportunities afforded by the scheme. There were no explicit goals when it was introduced but it is safe to say it has exceeded its original ambitions.

Many of the negative predictions made at the time of its introduction have proved true, if not quite as quickly as its critics suggested. By the beginning of the 1990s the availability of re-lets began to be affected and the development of resale markets encouraged more sales; ultimately the cumulative impact has left the council-housing sector (and the social rented sector more generally) less attractive and housing a narrower section of the population. The funds generated have not been used to improve the housing opportunities of homeless or badly housed households.

There have been some unexpected consequences, especially with regard to the promotion of the private rented sector. The growth of private renting was unanticipated in 1980, never mind a role for the RTB in such a revival. The expansion of owner occupation through the RTB has not been totally sustainable and the mixed-tenure estates of owner occupiers, private and social tenants have in turn created management difficulties, with long-term question marks over the maintenance of housing.

Much of the RTB's success was based on its simplicity and generosity to purchasers, but in the last decade the discounts have become subject to lower cash ceilings and the rules have been subject to greater complexity. Numbers of sales have dropped substantially because of these changes. These developments have more recently been compounded by the aftermath of the sub-prime credit crunch. With many RTB purchasers in recent years dependent on sub-prime finance, it seems highly likely that this source of finance will be less available for the foreseeable future, reinforcing existing trends.

The operation of the RTB highlights the intricate and changing outcomes over time of what appears to be a simple policy. These outcomes are interwoven with the changing structure of society, rising real incomes and the increased desire for home ownership, a general move toward a more market-oriented economy and changing housing policy. In particular, the wider policy context within which it has operated has substantially shifted, with the New Labour government even more fully committed to the idea of a property-owning welfare state than the governments of Margaret Thatcher.

It has not been possible here to deal with every facet and implication of the policy. The outcome of the RTB is a transformed social-housing sector, but without any attempt to define an explicit role formally. Arguably, if the RTB had not been established then some alternative form of privatisation would have occurred.

From this perspective a major issue is the extent to which the RTB has been a lottery, providing much bigger rewards for households that were in the right place at the right time than for those in less attractive properties or those waiting to become tenants. And beneath the complexities of the policy there is a fundamental issue of the balance between meeting aspirations and meeting need.

Thirty years after the introduction of the RTB it remains an emotional and important element of housing policy and the message from the constituent governments of the UK is that it will continue, albeit with more constraints. Council tenants unable to afford to buy their home are now offered the opportunity to purchase just a share in their home. Nevertheless, the heyday of the RTB is over and even if more generous discounts are reintroduced it seems that the privatisation of the social-housing stock using this vehicle has more or less run its course. Its legacy is that today's housing system is very different from the late 1970s and that, for better or worse, it was the most significant driver of this transformation.

References

Assembly of Wales Government (2007) 'Assembly Government applies for affordable housing powers' http://new.wales.gov.uk/news/presreleasearchive/1835893/?lang=en.

CLG, Department of Communities and Local Government (2007) *Homes for the Future: more affordable, more sustainable*, London: CLG.

Cooper, Y. (2007) Parliamentary Answer, 20 April Hansard, House of Commons, London. http://www.parliament.the-stationery-office.com/pa/cm200607/cmhansrd/cm070420/text/70420w0002.htm.

Forrest, R. and Murie, A. (1984a) *Right to Buy: Issues of Need, Equity and Polarisation in the Sale of Council Houses*, School for Advanced Studies, University of Bristol.

Forrest, R. and Murie, A. (1984b) *Monitoring the Right to Buy*, School for Advanced Studies, University of Bristol.

Foulis, M. (1985) *Council House Sales in Scotland*, Central Research Unit, Edinburgh: Scottish Office.

Housing Executive (2007) *Housing Review*, Belfast: Housing Executive.

Jones, C. (1982) 'The Demand for Home Ownership', in J. English (ed.) *The Future of Council Housing*, London: Croom Helm.

Jones, C. (2003) *Exploitation of the Right to Buy Scheme by Companies*, London: Office of the Deputy Prime Minister.

Jones, C. and Murie, A. (1999) *Reviewing the Right to Buy*, Birmingham: University of Birmingham.

Jones, C. and Murie, A. (2006) *The Right to Buy*, Oxford: Blackwell.

Munro M., Pawson, H. and Monk, S. (2005) *Evaluation of English Housing Policy 1975–2000 Theme 4: Widening Choice*, London: ODPM.

Murie, A. (1975) *The Sale of Council Housing*, University of Birmingham.

Murie, A. and Rowlands, R. (2008) *The Changing Council Estate: Privatisation, Tenure and Social Mix*, Mimeo: University of Birmingham.

ODPM (Office of the Deputy Prime Minister) (2005) *Sustainable Communities: Homes for All*, Cm 6424, London: HMSO.

Rowlands, R. and Murie, A. (2008) *Evaluation of Social HomeBuy Pilot Scheme for Affordable Housing: Final Report*, London: CLG.

Scottish Government (2007) *Firm Foundations: the Future of Housing in Scotland*, Edinburgh: Scottish Government.

Shelter (2005) *Generation Squalor: Shelter's National Investigation into the Housing Crisis*, London: Shelter.

Wilcox, S. (2007) 'A Financial Evaluation of the Right to Buy', *UK Housing Review 2006–7*, London: Chartered Institute of Housing.

5 The evolution of stock transfer

Privatisation or towards renationalisation?

David Mullins and Hal Pawson

The two outstanding trends directly affecting British social housing since 1979 have been a reduction in the stock of social rented homes and a gradual redistribution of the remaining stock from local authorities to non-profit-sector landlords. In the 25 years to 2006 the number of homes rented from local authorities fell from its peak of 6.1 million to only 2.6 million. Over the same period housing associations have grown from less than 10 per cent of all social housing to over 45 per cent and look likely to exceed 50 per cent by 2010 (see Table 5.1).

Throughout the UK the two most important processes contributing to the change in the size and composition of the social rented sector have been individual sales to tenants under the right to buy (see Chapter 4) and council-housing disposals to non-profit landlords through stock transfer. Another key driver was the virtual ending of local authority new build after 1980 and the substitution of housing association development, but generally at a much lower rate than previous municipal construction.

This chapter explores the experience of stock transfer from local authorities to housing associations over the past 20 years, drawing on a series of studies undertaken by the authors[1]. After summarising the national context and evolution of the stock transfer programme, we identify a recurring theme of critics of the policy that equates stock transfer with privatisation. We address this theme by considering the extent to which the transactions involved in stock transfers could be described as 'privatisation', then by unpacking the concept of privatisation and by comparing stock transfer with the right to buy as exemplars of the different processes that are referred to in the privatisation literature. In a final discussion we review the impact of 20 years of stock transfer on relationships between

Table 5.1 Council-housing decline and housing association growth, Great Britain, 1981–2006 (dwellings, thousands)

	1981	1986	1991	1996	2001	2006
England						
Housing association	410	475	608	942	1,424	1,850
Local authority	4,798	4,439	3,899	3,470	2,812	2,086
Wales						
Housing association	24	25	28	45	55	66
Local authority	290	254	222	207	188	156
Scotland						
Housing association	36	50	–	91	137	252
Local authority	1,027	962	–	691	558	363
Great Britain						
Housing association	470	550	–	1,078	1,616	2,168
Local authority	6,115	5,655	–	4,368	3,558	2,605

Source: Wilcox (2007)

privatisation and democracy, and consider whether attempts at central steering could be regarded as steps towards 'renationalisation'.

National context and programme evolution

The origins of stock transfer in 'voluntary' local initiatives and its subsequent evolution into a central element of housing policy in the UK have been outlined by Malpass and Mullins (2002). Building on this account, Mullins and Murie (2006) have developed a typology suggesting four main stages in the evolution and maturation of stock transfer. Table 5.2 updates the story of this process as it has applied in England (the experience has been somewhat different in Wales and Scotland) and highlights the key features of each phase.

In the most recent period, since 2001, there have been growing tensions between the desire of government to steer the process and its outcomes on the one hand and the desire of stock transfer landlords to maximise their independence on the other. These tensions were reflected in the wider conflict between housing associations and government over the drafting of the Housing and Regeneration Bill, 2008. Housing associations emphasised the importance of independence for their classification as non-public bodies and consequent exclusion from the Public Sector Borrowing Requirement (PSBR)[2]. Meanwhile, government proposals for wider regulation of community investment activities by housing associations could be seen as a continuation of the steering of stock transfer landlords in this regard since the early 2000s.

Table 5.2 Evolution of stock transfer, 1988–2008

Dates	Character of policy	Key features	Completed transfers		Ballots lost	Homes transferred (000s)
			Whole	Partial		
1988–92	Voluntary origins	Individual authority initiatives (various motivations). DoE approval, subject to positive ballot and compliance. Learning by all players (many non-players). Mainly rural/suburban LAs with good-condition stock, new HAs set up in most cases.	18	0	15	94
1993–6	National programme	Transfer replaces tenants' choice and HATs as main Government demunicipalisation programme. Annual bids, limits to approvals, levy on receipt, transfer landlord size limits (to avoid monopolies). Housing benefit impacts outweighed by PSBR benefits. Slight broadening of take-up.	34	5	11	137
1997–2000	Widening take-up	Spread to urban areas and Labour-controlled LAs. New models: include Local Housing Companies and estate ('partial') transfers to existing HAs. Regeneration focus emerges. Incentives: governance models, funding for negative value and overhanging debt transfers (ERCF, LA debt write-off), levy holiday, coercion: all LAs to consider transfer option, a key factor in performance assessments.	38	36	14	260

| 2001–8 | Policy delivery – towards re-nationalisation? | Decent Homes Standard (Public Service Agreement-led), new public money in return for private leverage/delivering decent homes. Transfer as 'delivery mechanism' for Treasury – one of four options (+ PFI, ALMO, major repairs allowance). All LAs to undertake option appraisals by 2005 (with tenant involvement). Coercion and incentives strengthened ('soft and hard levers'), tighter monitoring. Regeneration focus strengthened. Relaxation of transfer package size rules. Re-emergence of 'gap funding' for negative value transfers. Increasing concern at inability of government to steer assets of mature stock transfer associations to areas of greatest housing needs. Conflicts over the independence and non-public identity of housing associations in the Housing and Regeneration Bill 2008 continue the tensions associated with increased central steering. | 89 | 74 | 37+ | 656 |

Adapted from Mullins and Murie (2006)

Voluntary origins

Taylor (1999) drew attention to the persistent use of the word 'voluntary' in government policy documents about transfer. This language can be traced to the origins of the policy in the individual initiatives of three authorities (Chiltern, Sevenoaks and Newbury) in the late 1980s, using powers contained in earlier legislation (Housing Act 1985 and Housing and Planning Act 1986), to transfer their housing to newly established bodies. They did this for several reasons; to reduce right-to-buy stock losses (since new housing association tenants would not enjoy this right), to access finance outside PSBR restrictions and to 'protect against predatory takeovers' under the Tenants' Choice scheme (Mullins *et al.*, 1992). The latter motivation was very real at the time, as the Conservative government was actively promoting demunicipalisation through Housing Action Trusts and Tenants' Choice. In contrast to these schemes, which were thought likely to fragment local municipal housing stocks and, in the case of Tenants' Choice, possibly to transfer estates to private landlords (Mullins, 1990; Tulloch, 2000), early transfers were usually presented as voluntary initiatives to preserve and improve local stocks of social rented housing.

Between 1988 and 1992, there was a considerable sense of experiment and learning, not least for the two-thirds of the 49 local authorities proposing transfer who either dropped their proposals or had them defeated at ballot (Mullins *et al.*, 1993: 173). Central government was learning, too; the Department of the Environment (DoE) incrementally expanded its guidelines for responding to each application and developed standard methodologies for ballots and valuations and guidelines for stock-condition surveys and consultation. Consultants helped shape the process through advice to local authorities, transfer landlords and (later) tenants on feasible organisational and financial models.

National programme

This 'voluntary' phase began to close in 1993 when the Government introduced an annual (cash-limited) transfer programme and a levy to be paid from the local authority's capital receipt. The rationale for the new regime was largely associated with public-expenditure control, with programme limits and with the transfer levy predicated on the cost to the Treasury of increased Housing Benefit subsidy (as a result of housing moving out of Housing Revenue Accounts in surplus, which picked up the tab for council tenants' Housing Benefit).

The first serious financial appraisal of the costs and benefits of transfer was carried out by DoE and the Treasury in 1993. This modelled the hypothetical impact of a programme of 100 transfers of 500,000 homes over the following five years. This concluded that such a programme would reduce the PSBR by £240 million, as compared with local authority stock retention with existing capital expenditure on maintenance (NAO, 2003).

As well as introducing the annual programme, the 1993 regime brought further new centrally determined dimensions reflecting government thinking about competition, choice and voice. For example, it limited to 5,000 the stock that could be transferred to a single landlord 'to avoid the risk that future transfers will perpetuate a local monopoly by creating a single new predominant landlord in an area' (DoE, 1992: 7). There were also new requirements to ensure tenant access to independent advice to inform their ballot choices, partly in response to research evidence of the level of resources allocated to promoting 'yes' votes (Mullins *et al.*, 1992).

Widening take-up

The third phase of stock transfer was signalled in 1996 by two forms of assistance to the process: new constitutional options and financial incentives to stimulate transfers in areas with stock in poor condition, with low or negative stock valuations and/or where the valuation was insufficient to redeem the local authority's housing debt (the 'overhanging debt' scenario). The distinction between these two forms of assistance is more fully discussed elsewhere (see Mullins and Pawson, 2009 forthcoming). Such mechanisms were intended to extend transfer into urban areas where the backlog of disrepair was greatest, but which had hardly been involved at all in the first seven years of transfer. Constitutional innovations included a 'Local Housing Company model' (Zitron, 1995) intended to attract Labour-controlled authorities (none of which had transferred before 1995) by increasing the proportion of board members that could be nominated by the local authority from 20 per cent to 49 per cent. This 'tripartite' model established a norm of a third, local authority, a third resident and a third independent membership for most stock transfer boards from 1996. In Scotland some ex-Scottish Homes stock was transferred to non-housing association landlords, including WESLO and Waverley (though these later sought and achieved registration with Communities Scotland).

The main new financial incentives were provided by the Estates Renewal Challenge Fund and the introduction of Treasury funding to redeem 'overhanging debt'. Set up specifically to facilitate transfers of negative-value run-down estates, ERCF underwrote 41 schemes involving nearly 50,000 dwellings and absorbing £500 million of ERCF funding (Wilcox, 2008–9). Geographically, ERCF was significant in widening the remit of the transfer policy to encompass urban neighbourhoods, including a number in Inner London, an area previously untouched by transfer. While a number spawned new landlords, many of the smaller ERCF transactions involved handovers to existing housing associations, which incorporated the received stock into existing structures (Pawson *et al.*, 2005).

In England, Treasury funding for overhanging debt totalling £133 million was secured to facilitate the Coventry and Burnley transfers in 2000. Subsequently, such assistance has been provided to more than 70 transfers at a gross cost of some £3 billion[3]. A second stream of treasury funding to facilitate transfers, known as 'gap funding' – whereby CLG made grant payments to housing associations taking on stock transfers to cover business-plan gaps – was closed with applications made within the 2006 transfer programme[4]. Treasury-funded debt write-off as an element of the transfer deal has also been adopted as standard practice in Scotland, where the cost for the 2003 Glasgow/GHA transfer alone amounted to over £900 million (Social Housing, 2003; Mullins and Pawson, 2009 forthcoming).

This phase of transfer policy also involved greater coercion of local authorities to consider the transfer option, making the label 'voluntary' increasingly inappropriate. In 1995–6 all stock-holding authorities in England were required to demonstrate in their local-housing strategy submissions to central government that transfer had been considered. Government offices began to base part of their assessments of local authority housing performance on whether the transfer option had been appraised. While many authorities had anticipated that a change of government in 1997 would reduce pressure to transfer, it soon became clear that there was little fundamental change in policy. The coercive elements of the third-phase approaches were further developed under subsequent Labour governments, when the requirement for option appraisal was strengthened and the Housing Inspectorate incorporated assessments of the transfer and other disposal options Arm's Length Management Organisations (ALMOs) and the Private Finance Initiative (PFI) into performance judgements about delivery of the strategic enabling role.

Policy delivery: towards renationalisation?

The most recent phase of transfer policy was signalled by the Treasury's Comprehensive Spending Review in 2000, by the Housing Green Paper (DETR and DSS, 2000a) and by the Government response to comments on the Green Paper (DETR and DSS, 2000b) published in the same year. While still officially promoted, transfer was now seen as one 'delivery option' to enable local authorities secure sufficient funding to meet the newly established Decent Homes Standard. The other options were to delegate management to an Arms Length Management Organisation (ALMO), to set up a Private Finance Initiative (PFI) scheme or to make use of Major Repairs Allowance within the context of retained ownership and management. In any event, authorities were required to undertake an inclusive appraisal process to determine the most appropriate of these options. This new requirement for options appraisals was implemented from 2001 with support for local authorities available through the newly created Community Housing Task Force (CHTF). Additionally, stronger links were made between transfer, regeneration and neighbourhood renewal to achieve 'sustainable communities' (Mullins et al., 2004).

This phase consolidated central-government control of transfer policy, integrating it into the Treasury-led approach of establishing Public Service Agreements (PSAs) with spending departments. Release of funding to departments was conditional on very specific benefits being demonstrated. In the case of social housing investment the PSA was based on the 'Decent Homes Standard'[5] introduced by Government in 2001:

> as part of its desire to link increased spending to better outcomes, . . . (by) ensur(ing) that all social housing meets set standards of decency by 2010, by reducing the number of households living in social housing that does not meet these standards by a third between 2001 and 2004, with most of the improvement taking place in the most deprived local authority areas. (ODPM, 2004)

In tune with the second-term Blair administration's focus on policy delivery and evidently informed by 'principal–agent' concepts from economics (Mullins and Murie, 2006), stock transfer was now seen as a 'delivery mechanism' to meet the Decent Homes Target. The so-called 'PSA Plus review' of delivery of the Decent Homes Target (ODPM, 2003) referred to the 'many agents Government relies upon to deliver decent homes', about 'incentives to help drive delivery forward' and about 'a staircase of support, persuasion, soft levers, hard levers and intervention that can be used to minimise and respond to delivery risks' (ODPM, 2003a: 10). Inevitably this was seen as requiring more comprehensive monitoring than hitherto – 'the only way to keep track of whether the target is being delivered' (ibid.: 62) – and a monitoring and evaluation framework was commissioned for transfer landlords, adding to the regulatory burden for new transfers completed after 2001.

Again influenced by economic theories of public choice, as well as responding to criticisms of lack of options in the past, the new policy framework identified a menu of options for securing Decent Homes investment, and from which local authorities and tenants could choose. This approach was seen as a significant departure by the Public Accounts Committee in its Fortieth Report (UK Parliament, 2003) which considered that:

> Until recently, the 'off the public sector balance sheet' finance represented by transfer was generally local authorities' only option to carry out repairs and renovation needed on their housing stock. A range of options is, however, available now, such as better funded retention and renovation by local authorities, direct access to the Private Finance Initiative, and the establishment of Arm's Length Management Organisations. The Government's recent review of social housing (The PSA Plus review) recommended the removal of the barriers to these different options. (UK Parliament, 2003: Summary)

From 2001 to 2004 the CHTF supported local authority stock-options appraisals with 'tenants at the heart' and more inclusive approaches to 'hard-to-reach groups' (Mullins *et al.*, 2004). The increasing focus of stock transfer on wider regeneration was partly a consequence of the move of the programme into more deprived communities, particularly under ERCF, and partly a result of increased Government attention to neighbourhood renewal, as evidenced by increasing reference to these topics within stock transfer guidance and associated good-practice advice (HACAS Chapman Hendy Associates, 2002). This emphasis was further strengthened by the PSA Plus review, which identified decent homes as a 'key component of sustainable communities' (ibid.: 7) and stated that 'where wider regeneration is an issue the delivery of decent homes should form part of a wider strategy for neighbourhood renewal' (ibid.: 8).

A related issue was a growing conviction of Government that successful regeneration has to be resident-led. The stock-options appraisal process and the subsequent establishment of new landlord bodies (transfer housing associations and ALMOs) provided opportunities for small numbers of residents to enjoy very high levels of involvement through membership of steering groups, shadow boards and boards. Issues of capacity building and empowerment of residents to take on these roles were given increased emphasis within official stock transfer guidance (ODPM, 2005). From 1996 it had been possible for up to 49 per cent of transfer housing association boards to comprise tenants. Later a 'community gateway model' was developed to enable existing Tenant Management Organisations to take fuller control of their homes and to develop mutual tenant-controlled governance structures for stock transfer landlords (Confederation of Co-operative Housing, 2001). Tenant-majority boards had been the norm for Scottish transfer associations since the 1980s. However, in both England and Scotland since 2003 most new landlords have adopted the 'tripartite' model (one-third tenants, one-third local authority and one-third 'independents').

Another important policy shift introduced in this phase was the removal of the upper limit on the size of transfer housing associations[6]. This enabled new transfers in Wakefield and Liverpool to progress as single entities, and removed constraints on Housing Corporation approvals for reunification of group structures – for example, in Bradford, Coventry and Sunderland. Evidently the potential for scale economies was now given precedence over the putative advantages of smaller landlords in avoiding monopoly and promoting choice.

Over and above the very substantial public funding made available to facilitate transfers in this era via local authority debt write-off (see above), a 'gap funding' mechanism was re-established from 2004–5 to assist transfer associations whose projected rental and other income over 30 years would otherwise be insufficient to meet estimated stock-upgrade costs, salaries and other liabilities (ODPM, 2005). In the three years to 2008, some 31 transfers (a majority being partial transfers) have been facilitated in this way, at a cost totalling almost £700 million.

However, since gap-funding demand has been far in excess of this amount, such assistance has been heavily rationed.

We can see in this phase an increasing taste for centralisation and policy prescription that could be better described as 'renationalisation' rather than 'privatisation' of housing post-transfer. The increasingly close alignment of transfer-landlord aims and central-government objectives raises fundamental questions. Tighter regulation was criticised by housing associations as stifling innovation and reducing the value of transferring stock to the 'independent sector'. A key question is whether governments had supported the independent sector because of any intrinsic merits or simply because it is non-local-authority and off the PSBR balance sheet. Even if the policy choice was not based on any intrinsic advantages of non-profit organisations, there was still a danger that tighter control would reduce some of the innovation and performance advantages they had offered to date (Mullins and Murie, 2006).

These arguments were replayed by the housing association sector in response to proposals in the Housing and Regeneration Bill, 2008, for what was seen as more onerous and extensive regulation proposed for community investment activities, and greater potential for political steering of regulatory judgements. The argument that such increases in public control might jeopardise the status of housing association investment outside the PSBR was deployed cautiously in these debates.

Stock transfer as privatisation

In this section we want to explore the idea, found throughout the history of stock transfer policy, that it is a form of privatisation. This idea is found particularly in political and media debates and in some academically informed critiques of the policy, as the following discussion indicates. Stock transfer has frequently been depicted by some critics as full-blooded privatisation (and, hence, at odds with traditionally accepted fundamentals of social housing). This was the focus of a number of successful campaigns by Defend Council Housing (www. defendcouncilhousing.org.uk) to defeat transfers at ballot stage, and prior to 1997 such views were a critical obstacle to transfer being adopted by Labour-controlled urban authorities where the backlog of stock-investment needs was greatest. Indeed, as Malpass and Mullins note, the idea of transfer:

> had to overcome resistance from tenants fearing loss of hard-won social rights, from staff fearing the loss of reasonable terms and conditions and from local councillors whose power base is threatened. (Malpass and Mullins, 2002: 678)

It has been relatively unusual for such accounts to be linked to the academic literature on privatisation and its key components, nor has there been much comparison of different aspects of housing policy in respect of the extent to which they meet components of the privatisation construct. We attempt such an analysis below, comparing stock transfer with the right to buy in relation to seven components of privatisation found in academic literature on the topic[7].

The privatisation tag

The tag 'privatisation' has often proved a potent ingredient in local campaigns against transfers. However, contributions going much beyond a simple assertion of the link are few and far between. For example, the Centre for Public Services (2004: 23) simply states that 'LSVT is privatisation of local-authority housing, as the council retains no control of the stock'. Similarly, Walter (2007) categorises transfer as one of 'the government's three privatisation options', although, like Robbins (2002) he also alludes to the 'asset-stripping' character of the process (especially bearing in mind that many transfers include land as well as buildings).

Others have emphasized the perceived hegemonic role of the financial institutions from which transfer (and other) housing associations source their funds. Glynn (2007: 128), for example, emphasises a view that (all) housing associations are 'in hock to private finance' and, hence, must place the interests of financiers ahead of those of tenants. While acknowledging that associations are not, themselves, profit-making bodies, Glynn contends that: 'The banks, building societies and other lenders all expect a competitive rate of return on their investments in the form of interest, so housing associations are providing profits second-hand' (ibid.: 127). Mooney and Poole (2005) acknowledge that historically even local authorities have had to borrow 'private money' to fund council-housing investment; 'What is [however] new is that [banks] will have [a key role] in policy-making and in shaping the future management of transferred housing' (ibid.: 35). In the context of the Glasgow/GHA stock transfer, Mooney and Poole cite the view that GHA, being a private (albeit non-profit-making) company, 'would be required to operate like a profit-making company to ensure that lenders saw a healthy return on their investment and on their loans' (ibid.: 35). This, it would seem, connects with another contention, that 'the welfare role of social housing will be severely curtailed if not completely eroded as a result of stock transfer' (ibid.: 34).

The mechanisms through which financial institutions exercise the kinds of dominant influence over housing-management policy and practice attributed to them is rarely explored in these critiques. As noted earlier, however, it is clear that loan covenants and financial ratios have increased the centrality of business planning for housing organisations, and in view of their level of debt to assets stock transfer associations have limited scope for decision-making (Mullins *et al.*, 1995). Moreover, the unwillingness of funders to extend or amend loan agreements without substantial increases in margins during the 2008 credit crisis, and the impact on financial ratios and covenants of the slump in the value of land and unsold housing for sale and shared ownership, triggering the need to amend loan agreements, has highlighted the degree of external control of housing association business plans. Nevertheless, the critics cite little convincing evidence of their implicit assertion that stock transfer landlords (and/or all housing associations) tend to be 'hard-nosed' operators, fundamentally more akin to the classic rapacious private landlord than to the archetypal caring local authority. Earlier analysis demonstrating that transfer housing associations record significantly lower eviction rates than local authorities (Pawson, 2004) would seem to suggest the opposite. Moreover the model of debt finance adopted for transfers in the UK can be contrasted to more direct investment by profit-takers in the structures of housing companies elsewhere in Europe – for example, in the system of category A and B shares used by some housing companies in Finland [8].

In a more closely argued critique Ginsberg (2005) sees 'true privatisation' as one of three possible interpretations of stock transfer. For Ginsberg the term, in this context, denotes a scenario where 'transfer marks a decisive shift towards monopolistic private landlordism, with public control and accountability fading away over time' (ibid.: 132), and where change in the character of 'social housing' will be 'driven by the increasingly commercial interests of the landlords, albeit regulated by inspectorates and partnerships with local authorities' (ibid.: 133). While acknowledging that 'the evidence in support of this interpretation is limited, so far' (ibid.: 132), Ginsberg's analysis is that a staged process leading to the ultimate destination of full privatisation is the most likely long-term impact of stock transfers. Some aspects of this argument are developed further by Malpass's consideration of future scenarios for housing associations in Chapter 6 of this book.

Components of privatisation

The wider academic literature on privatisation of public services and assets suggests that it may involve several distinct processes. For example, Heald (1984) identifies four forms of privatisation:

- *Commercialisation*, which involves shifting the way in which services are paid for from the taxpayer to the service-user
- *Contracting out* the management of public services to the private sector
- *Sell-offs* of public assets to the private sector
- *Deregulation*, enabling private companies to compete in public-service provision and reducing the burden of regulation to make market entry easier.

Murie's (1993) analysis of housing restructuring in the UK added further processes to Heald's list. For example, demunicipalisation, or the removal of assets and services from local authority control, was a clear ideologically driven change at that time. Meanwhile other changes, such as policies to move council rents closer to private rents and to introduce HRA business planning and resource accounting for housing, could be interpreted as 'preparing services for privatisation'.

Some changes of direction were apparent under New Labour's post-1997 'modernisation' policies (see Mullins and Murie, 2006). Best Value provided a broader framework for choices about contracting out services. Useful lessons were learned by housing associations from Best Value pilots on the skills required to be a good contractor – knowledge of products, costs and the contractor market, and of good contract-management skills (Mullins, 2002). The focus on 'contracting-out' which had shaped the Conservatives' 1995 Consultation Paper *More Choice in the Social Rented Sector* was still evident in Labour's 2000 Green Paper *Quality and Choice: The new way forward for housing* and was elaborated in the PSA Plus review (ODPM, 2003b), which sought a level playing-field for a number of contracting-out models.

The main driver for housing 'privatisation' has been to secure investment 'off balance sheet', so that first new homes (built by housing association with private finance) and then the backlog of repair in existing stock could be tackled without increasing borrowing as defined by PSBR (Hawksworth and Wilcox, 1995). This is perhaps a technical view of privatisation, but it has been a key policy driver.

Finally, there is the popular image of privatisation, reflected in some anti-transfer campaigns, that views the process as asset-stripping in which historic state-subsidised public goods are exploited for commercial gain. This raises questions about the valuation of assets at transfer and the controls needed to prevent unacceptable profit-taking.

Stock transfer transactions: privatisation or what?

We now proceed to a fuller analysis of the application of these concepts to stock transfer and to compare this experience with the sale of former social rented dwellings to sitting tenants under the right to buy. Both processes have clearly led to demunicipalisation, or 'reduced municipal ownership and development activity' Murie (1993). But what other aspects of stock transfer could be considered privatisation?

- Does it move decision-making from administrative to market modes?
- Does it enable consumers to make choices?
- Does it turn social housing into a source of private profit?

In this section we focus on the transactions involved in stock transfer, preparing the ground for a structured comparison with the right to buy in the next section. The basic transaction involved in stock transfer is the sale of a body of tenanted properties (often an entire local authority stock), with associated land and amenities, to a registered housing association at a price determined by a

Government valuation model; this is based on tenanted market value, which reflects continued use as social rented housing, and takes into account the condition of the stock, required improvements and projected rental and other income over a 30-year period. Classically, the purchase is financed by private borrowing by the new landlord, although an increasing proportion of more recent sales have involved an element of explicit public funding (Pawson and Smith, 2008).

As it has evolved in England, this is essentially an administrative transaction involving application for a place on a Government programme, formal consultation with tenants, registration with the regulator, agreement between the two parties, approval by the Secretary of State and the securing of private finance. A distinctive feature of this process is the very significant 'voice' given to existing tenants, whose vote in a ballot has significantly shaped most transfer proposals and seen around a quarter of such proposals defeated (Munro *et al.*, 2005). Subsequent transactions involving transferred assets (for example, sales of vacant properties, or mergers with other social landlords) remain administrative rather than market-based, requiring the approval of the regulator, and usually of private funders, and consultation with tenants (although not a further ballot).

In Glasgow a two-stage transaction, with council stock being passed initially to a city-wide housing association in readiness for later break-up and hand-over to smaller, locally based associations, was envisaged for the 2003 transfer. Subsequently, however, it became apparent that the model's inherent complexity and cost were likely to result in the completion of only a few of the 62 second-stage transfers (SSTs) that had originally been planned.

Even RTB sales by transfer landlords have tended to be initially covered by agreements with the local authority (on income-sharing) as well as remaining bound by national rules on the entitlements of qualifying tenants. Over time, the debts of transfer landlords decrease and their stock is improved, giving greater potential for new borrowing to finance other activities which may be more market-orientated (for example, non-grant-funded rented housing).

The brief description above has established that most aspects of initial transfer transactions are administratively determined, following rules specified by legislation or regulation. A transfer landlord's ability to enter into subsequent transactions (involving the former council stock) is severely constrained and there are few early opportunities to exploit the transferred asset in a purely commercial fashion. While sales of tenanted properties require Housing Corporation consent, scope sometimes exists for disposal or commercial development of land around housing sites. Over time, as initial debt is repaid and asset values have appreciated, the 'headroom' to engage in more commercial activities increases. It is often said that one of the main changes introduced by stock transfer is the discipline of private borrowing and the associated need to keep within the 30-year business plan. Usually this results in a more commercial approach than operated under the local authority. We return to this question later in the chapter.

Comparison with the right to buy

Table 5.3 assesses stock transfer against some of the component elements of privatisation referred to in the discussion of Heald (1984) and Murie (1993) above. To place the resulting observations about transfer in a broader context, our analysis compares stock transfer with the right to buy, a policy that might be seen as a more clear-cut example of privatisation. A striking feature of this analysis is how few aspects of privatisation are fully exemplified by either policy and how many 'ifs and buts' qualify any simplistic reading-off of privatisation characteristics from the implementation details of these programmes. The only unqualified 'good fit' between our account of these processes and the main components of privatisation shown in Table 5.3 is with demunicipalisation. To some extent this leads on to our conclusion that both policies have transferred risk from government, since these housing assets are no longer the responsibility of local authorities to manage, let and maintain and new investment no longer increases the PSBR. However, this is not quite the full story, since local authorities retain some responsibilities after selling leasehold flats, and government regulation to some extent mitigates the risks taken by lenders in the case of transfers. Loan agreements provide for lenders first call on the assets in the event of the landlord's business failing.

There is qualified support for the view that both processes involve commercialisation, in which the burden of costs for services is shifted from the taxpayer to the user. However, in the case of the right to buy these costs have been highly subsidised through discounts for initial purchasers, and historically there were additional subsidies for subsequent purchasers in the form of mortgage-interest tax relief. As to stock transfer, some of the strongest early criticisms related to the higher rents charged to new tenants and expectations that existing tenants' rents would rise to meet these once the guarantee period expired. However, it was recognised that for many tenants these cost increases would be cushioned by the state as 'Housing Benefit would take the strain'. Subsequent national policy changes held housing association rent increases close to inflation through a price-capping formula, and later a rent-restructuring programme made it clear that state policies rather than commercial drivers would be the main determinants of user charges by transfer landlords. This latter example also illustrates our conclusion that, far from stock transfer being associated with deregulation, it has in practice been accompanied by a growth in regulation – particularly after 2000, when transfer landlords were cast in the role of delivery agents for the Government's Decent Homes policy and subjected to 'hard and soft levers and intervention' to secure compliance with Government aims.

The biggest contrast in our assessment of impacts of the two processes is in relation to consumer choice and private profit. Perhaps it is no coincidence that these two archetypal characteristics of markets are found to coincide in the case of the right to buy but to be largely absent from stock transfer. This contrast is most

Table 5.3 Stock transfer and right to buy as forms of 'privatisation'

Form of privatisation (and definition)	Right to buy	Stock transfer
Demunicipalisation: Reducing municipal ownership and development.	YES – reduced LA stock by around 3 million properties between 1980 and 2003.	YES – reduced LA stock by 1.3 million dwellings between 1988 and 2008.
Transfer of risk: Risk of maintaining the assets and protecting future income no longer borne by the state ('off balance sheet').	YES – responsibility for maintenance transferred to individual owners. BUT some responsibilities to provide services to leaseholders remain.	Technically YES – HA borrowing is outside PSBR and responsibility for assets is with HAs. BUT borrowing is effectively underwritten by HC regulation and lenders have first call on assets in event of landlord bankruptcies.
Commercialisation: Increasing user charges and reducing subsidy and tax finance of state activity.	Partly YES – after resale, user charges reflect market processes (house prices, mortgage rates and repair and maintenance). BUT the initial transaction is administrative rather than market-based and initial sales are heavily subsidised. Also, until 2000 mortgage interest tax relief an important subsidy to purchasers.	Partly YES – transfer landlords must ensure rental and other income enables loans to be repaid; higher rents for new tenants one outcome of this. BUT HA rents increasingly regulated from mid-1990s and state policies on rent restructuring have underpinned post-2000 transfer HA business plans.
Contracting out: Outsourcing the management of services where responsibilities and assets remain state-owned.	NO – ownership of assets is transferred to individual owners. BUT owners of flatted properties are required to secure leasehold management services from a third party (who may be either the local authority or a private contractor).	Technically NO – ownership of assets transfers to HAs. BUT after 2000 Government has viewed transfer landlords as one delivery agent to achieve Decent Homes Standard. Other agents (ALMOS, PFI) closer to contracting-out model (no asset transfer).

(Continued)

Table 5.3 Stock transfer and right to buy as forms of 'privatisation' *Cont'd*

Form of privatisation (and definition)	*Right to buy*	*Stock transfer*
Deregulation: Reducing or removing state regulation of private activity.	Partly YES – housing moves from a tight and specific regulatory regime to one where financial regulation is important but other safeguards are in the general application of law.	NO – stock transfer a highly regulated process and all (other than very small) HAs routinely subject to heavy regulation. Funding policies have attempted to harness HA assets to subsidise new social housing. BUT difficult to see how any regulatory intervention to influence use of surpluses accrued by transfer landlords could be implemented without threatening landlords' 'independent' status.
Promotion of consumer choice: Enabling consumers to choose between alternative providers and options to meet their needs.	Partly YES – BUT qualifying tenants are restricted to a choice of tenure limited to the property they were allocated administratively. Future applicants for social housing have less choice as best properties are sold. After resale, properties integrated within broader market and subject to usual search and choice process (constrained by income and information).	Largely NO – despite rhetoric of tenant choice, choices have largely been made by LAs. Even when these were enforced, size limits had little impact on tenants' ability to choose between landlords. BUT considerable evidence of increased 'voice': greater tenant involvement after transfer and post-2000 option appraisals emphasise early involvement of tenants.
State investment exploited for private profit: Assets undersold, historic state investment fuels current private profits.	YES – existing tenants are the intended beneficiaries of 'underselling of assets' through discounts. This was presented as a way of enabling a new group to enter owner occupation (although exploitation by relatives and abuse by others apparent). Subsequent market transactions are unlikely to involve similar groups (most resales are to people who already own properties). Profit is generated in resale markets, especially in high-cost areas.	Largely NO – low asset valuations reflect requirement to continue as social tenancies. Valuation process intended to be cost-neutral. Status of transfer landlords as non-profit-distributing protects tax-payer. BUT undervaluation through cautious assumptions and changes in economy led to strong surpluses in some cases. Concerns about 'fat cat remuneration' of senior staff and, post-2003, board member payments. High consultancy costs constitute a 'leakage' of public funds to private sector.

Source: Framework adapted from Murie (1993); stock transfer evidence drawn from case studies in this chapter, right-to-buy evidence based on discussion with Alan Murie

clear-cut in relation to the scope for private profit. RTB policy was designed to confer a benefit on groups of tenants who were thought to have been unlikely to enjoy home ownership otherwise. It was anticipated that they would benefit from any increases in value of their property and from the discounted purchase price on resale. The extent of profit enjoyed by subsequent purchasers is determined by housing-market dynamics (but still influenced by former landlord management effectiveness in the case of flatted blocks).

It is arguable that in buoyant markets any benefits to subsequent purchasers of ex-RTB properties have been at the expense of both the local authority that lost the opportunity to retain an appreciating asset and future social-housing applicants who have been deprived of access to these homes. In contrast, the stock transfer valuation process is designed to be cost-neutral between the local authority and the new landlords, who are also non-profit-distributing. One might think that these two factors would provide a watertight defence against critics who equate transfer with private profit. However, some loopholes in this defence have been identified in studies of the valuation process which suggest that assets have been consistently under-valued (after allowing for their use being confined to social-housing tenants) (Gardiner *et al.*, 1991) and that the state has only weak leverage on the use of accumulated resulting surpluses. Assertions of private profiteering also draw on 'fat cat' critiques of executive pay after privatisation, a charge liable to be compounded by the recent trend towards adoption of board-member payment by many larger housing associations. Housing Corporation data for 2006 shows that while newly created transfer landlords universally eschewed such payments (sometimes as a result of specific commitments in transfer-offer ballot documents not to pay boards), the incidence of payment regimes was similar across longer-established transfer housing associations and larger traditional housing associations – at around a quarter (Pawson *et al.*, 2009). Also, taking into account the considerable sums that have leaked from transfer receipts to meet consultancy costs, it is clear how a case for charges of private profit-making could be mounted.

Although it is natural to think of policy beneficiaries in terms of the tenants, it is also important to widen the consideration of the scope for private profit. A range of private-sector organisations are involved in repairs and maintenance, and in property lettings and sales, which benefit from the increasing size of the private sector. The right to buy has increased the share of the market which they manage, and in which they are the key exchange professionals, and the areas of public-sector employment and management are equally diminished. This raises a wider set of issues about the impact of different forms of accountability and exchange processes. While the right to buy may be seen as providing particular consumers with very much increased power, it does nothing to address the lack of entitlements or power of other tenants or future tenants. Stock transfer, on the other hand, provides existing tenants with at least a one-off opportunity to make a direct democratic choice based on the terms of the offer document. It may be argued that the transfer landlord then has a written contract with tenants and residents which they are obliged to fulfil, although, as the research has indicated, they may not deliver on every aspect of it. After this moment of enhanced control, stock transfer could diminish control if the new landlord does not provide opportunities for tenants to have a 'voice'; however, regulation to date has placed a strong emphasis on providing for the tenant voice to be heard.

Key stakeholders for transfer landlords are their regulator, funders and boards. The role of these stakeholders may be compared with that of local authority elected members under the pre-transfer regime. How do new forms of accountability to residents through board membership affect these relationships? Assessed against agendas about consumer control, both the right to buy and stock transfers can be seen as flawed. While some element of enhancement may be identified in each case, it is equally evident that there are real losses. Some of these issues also become empirical questions: did the household exercising the right to buy already have choices available to them? Did their income and household circumstances give them the possibility of open-market purchase? If so, then the choice that is expanded is not a choice to buy, it is simply a very particular opportunity to buy (on preferential terms) the specific house occupied at that time. The discussion of choice must also relate to the next cohort of tenants, and it has repeatedly been argued that the increased choice of one cohort may be the reduced choice of another. In a similar way, the choice exercised by one cohort of tenants to support stock transfer will not be available to the next cohort; early transfers followed a model in which new tenants were at a disadvantage compared to existing tenants and paid higher rents as well as enjoying lesser tenancy rights.

Stock transfer and democracy – what's choice got to do with it?

A key theme within the privatisation debate is the charge that stock transfer has been a profoundly undemocratic process designed to achieve demunicipalisation (moving housing away from local democratic control) through undemocratic means. Despite the rhetoric of consumer and citizen choice associated with aspects of the process (ballots and tenant's-friend advisers), we tend to agree with this aspect of the critique of stock transfer.

While transfer has been promoted with considerable reference to the concept of consumer choice, how much choice is there in practice, who gets to make these choices and under what constraints?

In the transfer process most of the initial strategic choices have tended to be made by governments, by councillors or by senior staff advised by consultants. Tenants have since the early 1990s been provided with independent advice but have usually been faced in a ballot with the option either of transferring to a specified new landlord or of remaining with the council and then having to abide by the majority view.

This process is more akin to voice than choice. And although they have signified greater tenant involvement, the stock-option appraisal guidelines promoted by central government in England in the context of its Decent Homes programme (ODPM, 2003c) have not altered this in any fundamental way. (See Mullins and Murie (2006) for more detailed discussion of tenant involvement in option appraisal.) Much of the criticism of option appraisal has focused on the absence of a fourth, status-quo option for tenants of 'underfunded' local authorities: to enjoy stock improvements while remaining under municipal control (Centre for Public Services, 2004).

In contrast the Scottish Homes transfer process of the 1990s incorporated greater emphasis on competition and contestability, with ballots in some cases providing tenants with an opportunity to choose between several potential successor landlords. The extent to which tenants benefited from this is, nevertheless, questionable. However, the largest housing transfer in the UK, to Glasgow Housing Association (GHA), has been at the centre of the greatest debates about democracy and choice in stock transfers, with attention focusing on delivery of the proposed second-stage transfers to local community-based landlords. As seen by many tenant activists, GHA's ballot promises included a clear commitment to break up its holdings by handing on packages of stock to community-based landlords in the tradition of small-scale transfers familiar in Glasgow. Such undertakings were made in speeches by leading politicians (both local and national) involved in the process at the time. However, Glasgow City Council, aware that the costs of an SST process would be substantial and that the requisite funding was not built into the GHA business plan, worded its ballot prospectus carefully, committing the transfer housing association to undertake SSTs only if these could be shown to be 'financially neutral' to the landlord, therefore protecting remaining tenants from any adverse consequences. While the terms of the prospectus are a matter of record, controversy has continued to rage around the twin claims (a) that SST was an unconditional 'transfer promise' and (b) that GHA has not only failed to deliver but has actively obstructed the process. The regulatory inspection judgement that '. . . GHA has tried to make SST happen within its financial limits and the conditions set at the time of the transfer' (Communities Scotland, 2007: 6) received little or no media coverage. Nor, more importantly, did the Communities Scotland judgement that GHA was well on track with its massive investment programme displace criticisms of failure to deliver smaller, locally accountable landlords (Pawson et al., 2009).

In England, policies on size limits and the independence of local landlords within group structures – all advocated on the grounds of reducing monopoly and promoting choice – have not played out in real choices for users (see Audit Commission, 2001 for discussion of stock transfer groups). However, there has been considerable policy emphasis on involving residents in option appraisals and ballots, particularly through the stimulus provided by CHTF between 2001 and 2004. Moreover, transfer landlords are generally acknowledged to have been successful in increasing the voice of tenants through improved tenant involvement and feedback (Mullins *et al.*, 1995; Pawson and Fancy, 2003; Pawson *et al.*, 2009).

Conclusion

In concluding this chapter it is worthwhile reflecting upon one final dimension of both the stock transfer and right-to-buy policies. If we think back to the 1970s, local authority managers were the key gatekeepers in cities and towns: they were almost always the largest single landlord and their investment and development activities were fundamental in changing the shape and pattern of opportunities in housing. The way that they allocated housing and maintained and repaired properties had a crucial impact on spatial and social patterns within cities, on segregation and on the opportunities of individual citizens. Thirty years on, the management of the city and its housing stock is much more fragmented, and is arguably less coherent. In some cases the local authority (or stock transfer) role as a landlord is still dominant, but discretion over rents is more limited and new-build and acquisition programmes are generally very small.

Stock transfer has taken on different meanings in different phases of its evolution. Initially a 'voluntary' response to a hostile policy environment for local authorities, transfer soon became the major driver for growth of the 'independent' social-housing sector. While beneficial to governments' wish to secure improvements to the social-housing stock without recourse to public expenditure, this process heightened concerns about decreasing ability to steer the sector, particularly in relation to the growing mismatch between assets and investment needs. This led to growing regulation of the transfer process itself and of the new landlords consequently established, to such an extent that we might detect a trend towards 'renationalisation' rather than privatisation of the housing association sector. Debates around the 2008 Housing and Regeneration Bill reflect the tension between governmental steering and sector independence that have played out through the history of the stock transfer policy.

Stock transfer has involved a transfer of assets from local government to the independent sector in a process which can certainly be described as demunicipalisation and which some have described as privatisation. The debt exposure of the new landlords and their covenants with lenders have clearly set constraints on the ways in which these businesses have developed in the early years after transfer, and these constraints have been emphasised in a period of credit crisis in 2008. Over time a degree of strategic choice has been possible, and consequent concerns have been raised about the inability of governments to steer resources controlled by these independent organisations to meet needs. However, the extent of risk transfer to the new organisations has been mitigated by the 'comfort blanket' provided by regulation and the first call on assets enjoyed by lenders.

Some stock transfer landlords have begun to operate in more commercial ways, but there is little evidence that this has been at the expense of tenant security or of traditional social purposes. Indeed, it can be argued that stock transfer has provided a way of injecting private finance into housing regeneration that has avoided the worst excesses of privatisation, such as asset-stripping or gentrification accompanied by displacement of existing residents. While some stock transfer landlords have begun to adopt a portfolio approach to asset management, harnessing assets on high-value sites for more market-orientated activities, the main beneficiaries of regeneration programmes have been existing social-housing tenants. This is a far cry from a profit-maximising approach of privatisation that might have seen the clearance of social tenants from high-value sites.

Stock transfer is not a management contracting-out model, since long-term asset transfer is involved, but it has increasingly been described as such in principal–agent views espoused by governments. Deregulation has not been a feature of stock transfer: indeed, conflicts over the absence of a level playing-field with the private sector and drives to increase regulation beyond core social-housing activities mark current relations between sector and government.

Finally, there has been very little real consumer choice in the process of transfer and in its outcomes, although there have certainly been important efforts to increase user voice. Exploitation for private profit has not been a feature of the stock transfer sector, although there is some vulnerability in relation to executive and non-executive remuneration and isolated proposals for flotation of housing associations to replicate models found in other countries. Nevertheless, Ginsburg's vision of a staged process to full privatisation seems a long way from the recent contests over the Housing and Regeneration Bill and dangers of 'renationalisation' and the recasting of housing associations as 'public bodies'.

Notes

1. We would like to acknowledge the support of the former Department of Environment, which commissioned the first two of these evaluations (Mullins *et al.*, 1992, 1995) and the Joseph Rowntree Foundation, which funded the most recent two (Pawson and Fancy, 2003) and (Pawson *et al.*, 2009). We would also like to acknowledge earlier work with Peter Malpass (Malpass and Mullins, 2002) and Alan Murie (with whom an earlier version of some of the arguments in this chapter was developed).
2. We use the term PSBR throughout to refer to the conventions used over the entire period discussed to include or exclude borrowing from the public accounts. In the recent period a new term, Public Sector Net Cash Requirement (PSNCR), has taken over for technical definitions of public and private borrowing but is still less widely used than PSBR.

3. This funding to enable Exchequer payments to the Public Works Loan Board to write off overhanging debt was still available at the time of writing in late 2008.
4. Thanks to Decent Homes and Housing Finance Team, Communities and Local Government for clarifying this point in November 2008.
5. A Decent Home was defined as meeting the statutory minimum fitness standard under the Housing Act 1985, in a reasonable state of repair, with reasonably modern facilities and services and a reasonable level of warmth (DTLR, 2002). Using this definition 1.7 million social sector dwellings were 'nondecent' in April 2001.
6. The limit had already been breached by, for example, the transfer of 12,000 homes by Bromley to Broomleigh Housing Association in 1993 by special dispensation of the Secretary of State, and later by allowing group structures in which municipal stocks were split between two or more subsidiaries controlled by a parent association.
7. We are grateful to Alan Murie for his contribution to the development of this approach firstly in the framework used in his 1993 article in the *Scandinavian Journal of Housing and Planning Research*, Murie (1993), and later in discussions with David Mullins whilst working on *Housing Policy in the UK* (Mullins and Murie, 2006).
8. Category B shares are held by pension funds and other investors with the expectation of a profit, while category A shares are held by municipalities in lieu of a transfer receipt.

References

Centre for Public Services (2004) *The Case for the Fourth Option for Council Housing and a Critique of Arms Length Management Organisations*, http://www.european-services-strategy.org.uk/publications/essu-reports-briefings/4thoptionreport/4th-option-council-housing.pdf

Confederation of Co-operative Housing (2001) *Stock Transfer: Creating Community Controlled Housing*, Confederation of Co-operative Housing.

DETR and DSS (2000a) *Quality and Choice: A Decent Home for All. The Housing Green Paper*, London: DETR, DSS.

DETR and DSS (2000b) *Quality and Choice: A Decent Home for All. The Housing White Paper*, London: DETR, DSS.

DoE (1992) *Local authority housing in England: Voluntary transfers – Consultation paper*, London: DoE.

Gardiner, K., Hills, J. and Kleinman, M. (1991) *Putting a Price on Council Housing: Valuing Voluntary Transfers*, STICERD Welfare State Programme Paper No. 62, London: London School of Economics.

Ginsberg, N. (2005) 'The privatisation of council housing', *Critical Social Policy* 25(1), 115–35.

Glynn, S. (2007) 'But we already have community ownership: Making council housing work', in Cumbers, A. and Whittam, G. (eds), *Reclaiming the Economy: Alternatives to Market Fundamentalism in Scotland*, Glasgow: Scottish Left Review Press.

HACAS Chapman Hendy (2002) *Beyond Bricks and Mortar: Bringing Regeneration into Stock Transfer*, Coventry: Chartered Institute of Housing.

Hawksworth, J. and Wilcox, S. (1995) 'The PSBR Handicap', in Wilcox, S. (ed.), *Housing Finance Review 1995/96*, York: Joseph Rowntree Foundation.

Heald, D. (1984) 'Privatisation and Public Money' in Steel, D. and Heald, D. (eds), *Privatising Public Enterprises*, London: Royal Institute of Public Administration.

Malpass, P. and Mullins, D. (2002) 'Local authority stock transfer in the UK: from local initiative to national policy', *Housing Studies* 17(4), 673–86.

Mooney, G. and Poole, L. (2005) 'Marginalised voices: resisting the privatisation of council housing in Glasgow', *Local Economy* 20(1), 27–39.

Mullins, D. (1990) *Tenants' Choice: The Role of the Housing Corporation*, Report by CURS for DOE. University of Birmingham.

Mullins, D. (2002) 'Redefining "Competition" as "Competitiveness" – The Best Value Activities of Registered Social Landlords', *Public Money and Management*, 22: 25–30.

Mullins, D. and Murie, A. (2006) *Housing Policy in the UK*, Basingstoke: Palgrave.

Mullins, D. and Pawson, H. (2009 forthcoming) *After Stock Transfer: Britain's New Social Landlords*, Basingstoke: Palgrave.

Mullins, D., Niner, P. and Riseborough, M. (1992) *Evaluating Large Scale Voluntary Transfers of Local Authority Housing: Interim Report*, London: HMSO.

Mullins, D., Niner, P. and Riseborough, M. (1993) 'Large Scale Voluntary Transfers', in Malpass, P. and Means, R. (eds). *Implementing Housing Policy*, Buckingham: Open University Press.

Mullins, D., Niner, P. and Riseborough, M. (1995) *Evaluating Large Scale Voluntary Transfers of Local Authority Housing*, London: HMSO.

Mullins, D., Beider, H. and Rowlands, R. (2004) *Empowering Communities, Improving Housing: Involving Black and Minority Ethnic Tenants and Communities*, London: ODPM.

Munro, M., Pawson, H. and Monk, S. (2004) Summary Theme Report: Choice Review of English Housing Policy.

Munro, M., Pawson, H. and Monk, S. (2005) *Evaluation of English Housing Policy 1975-2000 – Summary Theme Report: Choice*, London: ODPM.

Murie, A. (1993) 'Privatisation and restructuring public involvement in housing provision in Britain', *Scandinavian Housing and Planning Research* (10), 145–57.

National Audit Office (2003) *Improving Social Housing through Transfer*, Report by the Comptroller and Auditor General, HC 399 Session 2002–3.

ODPM (Office of the Deputy Prime Minster) (2003a) *Sustainable Communities: Building for the Future*, London: ODPM.

—— (2003b) *Review of the Delivery of the Decent Homes Target for Social Housing (PSA Plus Review)*, London: ODPM.

—— (2003c) *Delivering Decent Homes – Option Appraisal*, London: ODPM.

—— (2004) *A Decent Home – the definition and guidance for implementation*, London: ODPM.

—— (2005) *Housing Stock Transfer Manual: 2005 Programme*, London: ODPM, http://www.communities.gov.uk/documents/housing/pdf/138475

Pawson, H. (2004) 'Reviewing Stock Transfer', in Wilcox, S. (ed.) *Housing Finance Review 2004/05*, Coventry and London: Chartered Institute of Housing and Council of Mortgage Lenders.

Pawson, H. and Fancy, C. (2003) *Maturing Assets: The Evolution of Stock Transfer Housing Associations*, Bristol: Policy Press.

Pawson, H. and Smith, R. (2008) *Second Generation Stock Transfers in Britain: Ministerial Mission accomplished?* Paper presented at European Network for Housing Research Conference, Dublin, 6–9 July.

Pawson, H., Fancy, C., Morgan J. and Munro, M. (2005) *Learning Lessons from the Estates Renewal Challenge Fund*, London: ODPM.

Pawson, H., Davidson, E., Morgan, J., Smith, R. and Edwards, R. (2009) *Second Generation: The Impacts of Stock Transfers in Urban Britain*, http://www.jrf.org.uk/publications/impacts-housing-stock-transfers-urban-britain

Robbins, G. (2002) 'Taking stock: regeneration programmes and social housing', *Local Economy* 17(4), 266–72.

Social Housing (2003) Glasgow unlocks public-private funding for £2.25 billion works, *Social Housing*, April 2003.

Taylor, M. (2000) *Stock Transfer Past and Present: A Summary of Research Evidence*, Research Review no. 6, Edinburgh: Scottish Homes.

Tulloch, D. (2000) *Tenants' Choice: Ten Years On*, Report No. 4, Stirling: University of Stirling, Housing Policy & Practice Unit.

UK Parliament (2003) Press Notice issued alongside Committee of Public Accounts Fortieth Report, *Improving Social Housing Through Transfer*, http://www.parliament.uk/parliamentary_committees/committee_of_public_accounts/pac240703_pn40.cfm

Walter, A. (2007) 'Give us real choice', *The Guardian* 29 March 2007, http://www.guardian.co.uk/commentisfree/2007/mar/29/comment.society

Wilcox, S. (ed.) *UK Housing Review 2008/09*; Coventry and London: Chartered Institute of Housing and Building Societies Association (Table 68d).

Zitron, J. (1995) *Local Housing Companies*, Coventry: CIH.

6 The rise (and rise?) of housing associations

Peter Malpass

The transformation of housing associations[1] in England since 1974 is little short of spectacular and demands explanation, especially in the context of a housing system that had seemed to be most unlikely to change in this way. As Figure 6.1 (p. 104) illustrates, the rate of change in the other parts of the United Kingdom has been less dramatic; different traditions and circumstances require separate explanations. Not only were housing associations numerically insignificant throughout the UK in the early 1970s but there was no sign that their prospects were about to improve. They were completely overshadowed by the local authorities, which owned nearly six million dwellings and appeared to occupy an impregnable position as the dominant suppliers of affordable rented housing. Moreover, the Housing Finance Act, 1972, had introduced a subsidy system for housing associations that was widely regarded within the sector as completely unworkable, and in 1973 the Housing Corporation's new chairman had found an organisation 'conscious of its own futility', beset by a mood of 'deep, bleak gloom' (Housing Corporation, 1977: 1). The Corporation had been set up in 1964 specifically to support experiments in cost-renting, which had been wound up in 1972, and co-ownership, which saw very little new investment after 1973. At that time the Corporation had no remit in relation to the housing-association sector as a whole and therefore had an uncertain future.

This chapter addresses the questions of how and why housing associations in England emerged from the undergrowth to achieve a position of such strategic significance in the present period. It goes on to consider the future facing housing associations in light of the changes following the Cave (2007) review of regulation in England. It is important to avoid a narrow perspective focused on housing associations themselves. A main theme of the chapter is that the growth of housing associations needs to be understood in terms of forces, factors and perceptions affecting other parts of the housing system. They have benefited from, on the one hand, the inability of the private market to provide sufficient quantities of afford-able housing, of acceptable quality, for people on low and modest incomes, and on the other hand the political judgement that local authorities were no longer to be seen as the main providers of social rented housing. A second, related, theme is that the housing-association sector as it exists today is largely the product of policy action by successive governments since the mid-1970s, although this is not to deny that housing associations have been able to influence the course of events and to shape the policy and regulatory environment within which they operate (Mullins, 1997; Mullins and Murie, 2006). A third theme is that the transforma-tion of the position of housing associations should be seen as a product of changes that were mostly incremental and opportunistic. There is no suggestion that anyone in 1974 foresaw and planned the displacement of local authorities by housing associations in the ways or to the extent that have emerged in recent times.

The question of how housing associations have achieved their current ascend-ant position can be approached by looking at the ways in which they have been boosted and transformed by policy action. It is, of course, impossible to say where they would have found themselves if things had been different, but it seems highly unlikely that, in the absence of the financial assistance and other forms of support since 1974, they would have made much progress. The housing-association sector has been through two main phases since 1974, and in England it is about to enter a third. An overview of the housing-association sector needs to recognise that, although 1974 was a crucial year, nothing comes from nowhere. The Housing Act, 1974, marked a new beginning in a number of ways, but it was nevertheless also building incrementally on a series of changes that had taken place over the previ-ous decade or more. In the early 1960s the government introduced an experimen-tal initiative to explore the potential for unsubsidised cost-rent and co-ownership housing, which did not produce many dwellings but did give rise to some vibrant new organisations, some of which went on to become large and successful hous-ing associations. Also during the 1960s a number of other new associations were set up, many to take advantage of funding opportunities offered by the Greater London Council and/or the financial support provided by Shelter, the campaign for homeless people, which was set up in 1966. At the same time some of the longer-established associations were actively modernising themselves, and so, overall and despite the short-term problems of the early 1970s, it can be said that the sector was better equipped than it had ever been to take up the challenges presented by the new Act.

The 1974 Act inaugurated a peculiarly helpful and benign financial and regula-tory framework which allowed housing associations to grow and mature in a virtually risk-free environment for almost 15 years. Research has shown that housing associations, represented by their National Federation, were able to influ-ence a number of key factors in this pioneering approach to regulation in Britain

(Cowan and McDermont, 2006; Emsley, 1986; Malpass, 2000). In particular the Federation was able to secure agreement to register virtually all associations, rather than use the register as a device to reduce the size of the sector. This victory has had long-term implications. The Housing Corporation provided not only development loans but also capital grants that typically covered 80 per cent or more of scheme costs. The fair-rent system meant that associations did not have to fix their own rents, and inflation tended to improve their financial situation by eroding the burden of debt incurred on new projects. Even when associations did manage to get into difficulties, the Corporation always found a bigger and stronger association to take them over.

The next phase of housing-association development started in 1989, when a number of far-reaching reforms were introduced. First, the Housing Corporation lost its responsibility for housing associations in Scotland and Wales, where new bodies, Scottish Homes and Tai Cymru, were established (both were absorbed into the devolved governments after 1998). Second, the government moved ahead with developing the use of private finance (then referred to as mixed funding), initially to cover an average of 25 per cent of scheme costs. The introduction of private finance alongside grant aid required legislative amendments to take new housing-association lettings out of the fair-rent system; in order to give comfort to private lenders unfamiliar with the sector, regulated tenancies and fair rents were phased out and replaced by assured tenancies, which required associations to set their own rents, and gave them the power to vary them if necessary. This was part of a strategy of redistributing risk from the state to associations and their lenders. Also in 1989, the housing-association sector began to grow, not only through its own investment but through the transfer of local-authority housing. The first large-scale voluntary transfer was in fact completed in December 1988, and others soon followed.

Further major changes to the funding and regulatory framework in England were introduced as a result of the Housing and Regeneration Act, 2008. The Act provides for the creation of a new organisation, the Homes and Communities Agency (HCA), incorporating English Partnerships, the investment functions of the Housing Corporation and some parts of the Department of Communities and Local Government. The HCA is responsible for investment and for the management of the national affordable-housing programme. The Act also provides for the regulatory role performed by the Corporation since 1974 to pass to a new independent regulator, the Tenant Services Authority (TSA). According to one insider's view '. . . the very fabric that has held the system of affordable housing in place is being unpicked' (Marsh, 2008: 20).

Dimensions of change and transformation

Precise figures for the number of dwellings in the sector are not readily available from official statistics for the years before the mid-1970s, but the Cohen Committee

(1971: 121) estimated that in 1969 there were 237,000. Nearly half of these were accounted for by the Coal Board Housing Association and were soon to be sold off, in most cases for owner occupation (Beynon *et al.*, 1999). What might be called the housing-association sector proper was therefore tiny, representing less than 1 per cent of the total stock in Great Britain. Today associations have over 2 million homes, 8.2 per cent of all dwellings, and although their share is less than the profit-seeking private rented sector, they seem certain very soon to overtake the shrinking local authorities to become the second-largest sector in the housing system. Figure 6.1 shows this strong growth in the total stock of housing-association dwellings, especially in England, most of which has been due to transfers from local authorities. The relatively small additions derived from new building in recent years are shown in Figure 6.2.

Accounts of the rise of housing associations refer to growing complexity and increasing concentration of strength and power among a small number of large organisations (Mullins and Murie, 2006: 207). Although there remain large numbers of small associations they account for a very small proportion of the housing stock. In 2007 a third of the total housing-association stock in England was owned by associations of more than 10,000 dwellings, up from a quarter in 1998 (Dataspring, 2007; Malpass, 2000). The majority of larger associations are now typically organised into often elaborate group structures, which are responsible

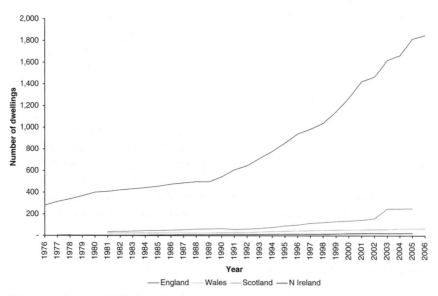

6.1 Housing association stock.
Source: Wilcox, 2007.

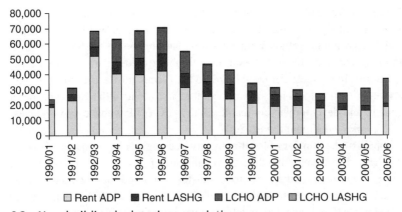

6.2 New building by housing associations.
NB: the data in this chart do not include the unknown number of dwellings produced by Section 106 agreements where there is no grant element.
Source: Wilcox, 2007.
Key: *ADP:* Approved Development Programme; *LASHG:* Local Authority Social Housing Grant; *LCHO:* Low Cost Home Ownership.

for more than two-thirds of the stock. These groups provide a number of potential advantages, including economies of scale and the opportunity to exploit the operational and tax benefits of linked charitable and non-charitable subsidiaries. The abolition of corporation tax relief provided the main stimulus to accelerating group formation in the late 1990s (Audit Commission and Housing Corporation, 2002). Groups also allow open-market operations to be kept separate from social housing. One spur for the rush into collaboration was the decision by the Housing Corporation in 2004 to introduce 'investment partnering', a process involving the distribution of 80 per cent of investment resources to just 80 associations or consortia. This reflects a long-established view within the Housing Corporation that there are too many associations, and it has always tended to channel grant to a relatively small number, thereby over time helping to reshape the sector. References to the emergence of a 'super-league' of large, developing associations have been made over a number of years (Malpass, 2000: 237), and have resurfaced in 2008 (Marsh, 2008: 22).

Diversity has always been a feature of the sector; indeed, historically the idea of a coherent 'sector' or 'voluntary housing movement' is almost certainly inaccurate and misleading. Some organisations were charities, others were limited-profit companies run on philanthropic lines, while others again were working-class self-help organisations of a quite different political outlook. It is likely that people involved in the varied sorts of housing organisations operating in the early twentieth century would have been more aware of the differences than the similarities

(Malpass, 2000: 69). The way the language has changed is revealing: 40 years ago the phrase 'voluntary housing' was widely used, but no one would do so today (although the voluntary ethos remains strong among board members, and in Scotland in particular). Instead, they now talk about themselves as social businesses that are 'in business for neighbourhoods'. Places for People, for example, now describes itself not as a housing association but as 'one of the largest property management and development companies in the UK' (PFP website, www.places-forpeople.co.uk, and annual report, 2007).

The impact of the transfer of local-authority housing stocks to housing associations has helped to change the character of the sector in a number of ways: at a macro level, dwellings acquired by stock transfer accounted for 45 per cent of the housing-association sector in England in 2007 (Dataspring, 2007); stock transfer has created more than 80 new associations with more than 4,000 dwellings at the point of transfer (in some cases many more). These associations have a different stock profile, reflecting the pattern of investment by local authorities over the years (that is, very little new building since 1980), and a strong geographical focus within one local-authority set of boundaries. They also have different governance arrangements, typically having boards consisting of one-third local councillors (or nominees), one-third tenants and one-third independents. Stock transfer has increased the proportion of the housing-association stock owned by large organisations (see Chapter 5).

Housing associations have been transformed by their ever closer relationship with government policy. Since the early 1970s they have moved from the margins, where they subsisted on very limited amounts of state support, but where they enjoyed considerable freedom from regulation and freedom to innovate. As they have moved towards the centre of the policy stage, housing associations have had more resources to deploy and as a consequence they have been able to make a greater impact than their predecessors. 'Larger associations have effectively been incorporated into the machinery of government, and as a consequence enjoy considerable influence over the way in which programmes are delivered' (Mullins and Murie, 2006: 210). But the price to be paid has been acceptance of much more intrusive forms of regulation and control. Associations find themselves subject to pressures coming from different directions: central government, through the national regulator, seeks to pursue its investment and other goals, while some local authorities look for partner associations that have some sort of local presence; meanwhile, the opening of the grant market to private developers represented a new challenge.

Why housing associations?

Housing associations have their origins in nineteenth-century initiatives by individuals or groups of concerned people coming together to respond to the perceived failings of the private-market mechanism. At times during the twentieth century new associations were formed by people who were equally critical of local authorities. In this sense, then, housing associations have always been defined by what they are not, and their reason for existing was, and remains, that they fill gaps and/ or do certain things better than the market and state sectors. Different rationales for supporting housing associations have applied at different times. The diversity within the housing-association sector has undoubtedly helped it to respond to government initiatives identifying problems in private renting in the 1960s; later housing associations were favoured because they offered an alternative to local authorities, and now they have the additional role of supporting the owner-occupier market through various low-cost home-ownership schemes.

In the past a common stance taken by both local councillors and their senior staff was that housing associations didn't do anything that they couldn't do better themselves. And for much of the twentieth century local government in Britain had sufficient power and autonomy to ensure that central government generally went along with its view. Other countries did things differently, and it has often been observed that Britain was unusual in Europe in developing a form of social housing that was directly owned and managed by local authorities. In a sense, therefore, the shift towards a non-municipal pattern of provision can be seen as adoption of the European model, but this is far from an explanation. By 1974 housing associations and their forerunners had been around for many years but had failed to convince governments that they were capable of achieving very much (Malpass, 2000). They were chronically unable to raise sufficient capital to make a significant numerical impact, and they had struggled to establish a positive image within central and local government. For example, in 1933 an official report had suggested an expanded role, but the local authorities were actively opposed and in the view of the permanent secretary in the Ministry of Health housing associations 'were bodies neither efficient nor easy to deal with, as their members were not normally men of affairs. He considered, therefore, that they had only a very small contribution to offer at the price of much inconvenience' (quoted in Malpass, 2000: 99). In the period after 1945 housing associations were swept aside as local authorities were given the lead in the postwar housing drive. And in the early 1960s, when they were given a role in the development of what would now be called the intermediate housing market, they failed to impress (Emsley, 1986). The creation of the Housing Corporation in 1964 and its re-launch in 1974, with a wider remit to finance and regulate housing associations as a whole, can be seen as a sign of government thinking that if housing associations were to make a bigger contribution they would have to be carefully and closely managed from the centre. In the policy initiatives of both the early 1960s and the mid-1970s the reason for resorting to housing associations was not that they were especially attractive but that there was no real alternative.

The fact that the decision by the Conservative government in 1961 to promote cost-rent and co-ownership schemes prompted the creation of a number of organisations that have subsequently become some of the largest and best-known housing associations was very much an unforeseen consequence, for at the time the focus was on finding ways to reinvigorate the private rented sector. Governments had virtually given up expecting a revival of investment by the traditional small landlords and were looking for new organisational and financial models that would provide unsubsidised homes aimed at a section of the market with incomes substantially above the average among council tenants. The involvement of housing associations came only after the builders and mortgage-lenders made clear their lack of enthusiasm and long-term commitment; the government fell back on housing associations essentially because they were there (Malpass, 2000: 134-5).

During the 1960s and 1970s housing associations were often referred to as the 'third arm' of housing. As private renting continued its seemingly inexorable decline, housing associations were seen as having a role to play between owner occupation and council housing, preventing the emergence of an increasingly two-tenure housing system, especially in urban areas. This applied to the development of both new-build cost-renting and co-ownership in the 1960s and to the role accorded to housing associations in inner-city rehabilitation of existing properties in the 1970s. In Housing Action Areas designated under the Housing Act, 1974, it was expected that housing associations would be involved alongside the local authority and private owners in order to promote choice for consumers. In view of subsequent developments it is important to appreciate that throughout the 1960s and 1970s housing associations were seen as tackling problems in the private rented sector, and that they were working alongside local authorities, complementing rather than competing with them. Apart from the cost-rent and co-ownership schemes, housing associations were providing homes that were similar to those provided by local authorities, and for much the same kind of tenant; indeed local authorities had the right to nominate a majority of tenants from their own waiting-lists.

After 1979 the rationale changed, but what made housing associations attractive to government was that they were not local authorities. Initially, however, housing associations suffered from the heavy policy concentration on expanding owner occupation, more or less to the exclusion of all other considerations. Housing associations were now perceived as part of the public sector, and therefore as targets for cuts and privatisation by the Thatcherite Conservative government. The introduction in 1974 of 100 per cent public funding (grants and loans through the Housing Corporation) had altered the perception of housing associations, and it was only as a result of a campaign led by their National Federation that charitable associations were excluded from the right to buy. Not until the late 1980s did Conservative housing policy begin to accept that there was a continuing need for affordable rented housing, but by this stage antipathy towards local government had reached the point where it was inconceivable that resources would be channelled towards local authorities to meet the demand for new building. It was at this time that there was a discernible shift to an attack on council housing in principle; the housing minister in 1987, William Waldegrave, was quoted as saying,

> I can see no arguments for generalised new build by councils, now or in the future. . . . The next great push after the right to buy should be to get rid of the state as a big landlord and bring housing back to the community.
>
> (Quoted in Malpass, 1993).

In this context, housing associations had two advantages that helped to propel them towards the centre of housing policy: first, they represented a politically acceptable form of subsidised renting, although the government's attempt to bracket them with private landlords under the label of the 'independent rented sector' failed to gain much support. Housing associations could be, and were, presented as small-scale, community-based organisations, free of the remoteness and bureaucracy alleged to characterise the large urban council-housing departments. Second, and arguably much more significantly in the long term, they were capable of being defined as non-public bodies for accounting purposes, which meant that any loans raised from private institutions did not count as public expenditure (as the same loans would have done if borrowed by local authorities).

This is an illustration of the incremental and opportunistic way in which housing associations have been transformed; it was associations themselves (supported by senior executives within the Housing Corporation) that responded to the squeeze on resources in the early 1980s by exploring the feasibility of raising private loans (Malpass, 2000: 178). Once this was shown to be possible it was taken up as government policy and significant legislative changes followed in the Housing Act, 1988, to embed the use of private finance. A key factor in the success of this development was that, as a result of the form and level of state support for housing associations since the Housing Act, 1974, many more associations were large enough and financially and organisationally strong enough by the late 1980s to take on substantial private loans and the commercial risk that came with them. The 1974 Act was undoubtedly a direct response to immediate problems created by the unworkable subsidy system and the need to decide what to do with the Housing Corporation. As such it was not envisaged that over time it would help associations to build up large portfolios of unmortgaged assets which would allow them to grow further through private borrowing. It follows that it was also not foreseen that the wider regulatory role for the Corporation would subsequently provide comfort to private lenders and assist associations seeking to increase their borrowing.

In the early 1990s, as local authority house-building continued its downward trend, housing associations enjoyed record levels of investment, resulting from the combination of large amounts of government support and the injection of private finance. 1990 was the first year since before 1919 that housing associations built more new homes than local authorities, and since then the trend has continued, with local authority completions falling to tiny numbers. Also in the early '90s housing associations were beginning to receive growing numbers of homes transferred from local authorities. Again this was a piece of opportunism: a number of local authorities in England decided to sell all their council houses to newly formed housing associations in response to aspects of the Housing Act, 1988, that were seen as a threat to social housing – specifically, the so-called 'tenants' choice' and proposals for housing action trusts. Taking the homes out of local authority control was a way of retaining the integrity of the stock within localities, preventing its fragmentation and privatisation. Once this had been shown to work it was taken up as mainstream housing policy in 1992 (Malpass and Mullins, 2002; Mullins and Pawson, this volume).

Stock transfer should be understood as primarily a process of demunicipalisation rather than a positive endorsement of housing associations as such (see Chapter 5). Indeed, it is interesting that in the great majority of cases the decision was made to set up a new organisation, and it is significant that the governance arrangements widely adopted in stock-transfer associations are different from traditional associations. The housing-association sector provided a convenient home for ex-council stock, but the process was more push than pull. The objective was, and is, to get as much council housing as possible out of the clutches of democratic local government and into new ownership. In this sense the right to buy worked very well for 20 years, but stock transfer has the added benefits of both (potentially) finishing the job and preserving some much-needed social rented housing.

The rise of housing associations, especially in more recent years, can be explained in terms of the government's need for housing-policy delivery agents that are more dirigible, more controllable, than purely market-based actors and institutions. As governments of both main parties at Westminster turned away from local authorities as suppliers of housing services, so they needed to cultivate housing associations to do those things that councils previously undertook and which the market can never provide. A good example of this is the involvement of housing associations in regeneration, especially the remodelling of council-built estates. It has been accepted for more than a century that the task of dealing with rundown housing cannot be left to the market. In the past a significant proportion of the council stock was built to replace municipally redeveloped private housing, but now the humiliation of local authorities is highlighted by their reliance on others to renovate their own estates.

Another area of work that has become increasingly important to housing associations in the last 15 years is low-cost home ownership. As consumer preference for home ownership has risen, and particularly as problems of affordability have mounted since the recovery of the market from the early 1990s slump, governments have diverted investment resources away from renting into various shared-ownership schemes, for which housing associations are well suited. They provide a convenient organisation to own, and draw rent on, the proportion of the home that the occupier cannot afford to buy. In the early 1990s housing associations in England produced 3,000–4,000 dwellings through home ownership schemes each year, under 15 per cent of total output (Malpass, 2000: 226), but in 2006–7 the figure was more than 18,000, or 44 per cent of the total (Housing Corporation, 2007).

Having reviewed some housing-specific reasons for the rise of housing associations, it is important to acknowledge that there has been a wider process of change affecting a range of local-government services. Since the early 1990s successive governments have promoted changes to the established pattern of services provided by town-hall departments. Initially the Conservatives emphasised the benefits of 'market testing' and demanded compulsory competitive tendering of a number of services, including housing management. It has been claimed that the notion of new public management, with its emphasis on businesslike approaches and market-based providers, gave way to 'modern management', which is concerned with long-term effectiveness and joined-up government as well as short-term efficiency (Newman, 2000: 47). Other observers have noted that the drive for market-based methods of policy coordination were unsuccessful and prompted a response in terms of a new style of service delivery based on complex partnerships, coalitions and networks spanning the public, private and voluntary sectors (Rhodes, 1999: xviii). After 1997 Labour changed the tone, but the underlying message of 'modernisation' remained much the same, summed up in a pamphlet by Tony Blair in 1998:

> The days of the all-purpose local authority that planned and delivered everything are gone. They are finished. It is in partnership with others – public agencies, private companies, community groups and voluntary organisations – that local government's future lies.
>
> (Blair, 1998: 13)

Housing associations were ideally placed to benefit from this emphasis on local authorities working with other organisations that would actually provide services.

Looking ahead

In one sense the future of housing associations seems assured. Despite the claim that 'social housing isn't working' (Dwelly, 2006), most observers agree that it is necessary to maintain a viable social rented sector (Hills, 2007). If there were no social rented sector it would be necessary to regulate the bottom end of the private rented market, and as Murie, Pocock and Gulliver (2007: 31) have argued, 'We have no experience of making such a regulatory regime work and countries without significant social rented sectors have much more severe problems associated with segregation and inhuman housing conditions'. So a social rented sector of some sort is needed, and given the improbability of a return to large-scale investment in new building by local authorities, the future seems to lie with housing associations as the established alternative. However, it is difficult to be entirely confident about which way events will play out, partly because of contrary indicators. On the one hand, there are signs of government continuing to embrace housing associations as agents of policy implementation. As associations have become ever more closely involved with the delivery of policy objectives and targets, so governments have become more assertive and constraining (Mullins and Murie, 2006: 188). The Decent Homes standard, choice-based lettings, rent restructuring and development partnering are all examples of policies introduced since 2000 that have had a significant impact on the operation of housing associations. On the other hand, there are signs that government is moving towards a stance that is more open to market-based organisations, which implies a reduction in its capacity to steer organisations and to control what gets done (at the very least it implies the adoption of different techniques for ensuring achievement of policy goals). However, there is little evidence of government reducing its grip on associations.

In thinking about what lies ahead for housing associations there are questions about what sort of social-housing sector we will have, where it will sit in relation to the public–private distinction for accounting purposes, and what relationship it will have with government and government policy objectives. Questions about how closely associations remain tied to the pursuit of government policy objectives are linked to their role in the overall housing system. The interest of ministers in social housing was reflected in the commissioning of two reports in 2006: John Hills's report on the future roles of social housing in England was published in February 2007, and Martin Cave's review of regulation came out in June 2007.

As has been stressed above, housing associations have been evolving and changing for many years, and there is no reason to suppose that the future will be any less dynamic. They have shown that they can adapt to new demands, and deliver the sorts of outputs demanded by government. They have responded positively (often enthusiastically) to government-sponsored initiatives, including low-cost home ownership, which go beyond the traditional focus on affordable rented housing. They have also taken the initiative in some areas (such as private finance). As a third sector (like a third political party in an essentially two-party system), housing associations are pulled in different directions; sometimes the public-service ethos has been to the fore, sometimes, as in the present period, it is the business model that dominates. The picture is made more complicated by variation within the sector; at any given time some associations will be more committed to the prevailing *Zeitgeist* than others.

The housing-association sector of the future will need to be financially and organisationally robust; successful organisations will be those that can survive with less financial support from government and in a more openly competitive environment. Signs of the direction of travel have been appearing for more than a decade – since the attempt in the run-up to the Housing Act, 1996, to make direct access to social housing grant open to private for-profit developers. This was then implemented in the Housing Act, 2004, and the changes proposed in the Cave review of the regulation of social housing can be interpreted as a logical progression, providing the basis for a regulatory environment that will be more acceptable and attractive to the for-profit sector. In one sense, therefore, the Cave review is consistent with a long term trend from regulatory capture to regulated competition (Mullins and Murie, 2006: 155), but it may come to be seen as marking the start of a new, and potentially radically different, phase of development.

The appointment of Professor Cave in December 2006 came after several years of debate around the location of responsibility for investment, regulation and inspection. One of the issues that had been discussed over many years was the co-location within the Corporation of responsibility for investment and regulation. The view within both the Corporation and its sponsoring government department had remained that there were significant advantages to keeping the two functions together, and this was still the case in the mid- and late 1990s (DoE, 1995; Housing Corporation, 1998). The housing green paper of 2000 suggested an expanded role for the Housing Corporation, although as Murie (2008: 229–30) notes, at the same time questions were raised among ministers and their advisers about whether the Corporation was the right sort of organisation for the new era. It was then decided that the responsibility for inspection was to be given to the Audit Commission, and that the Corporation should continue to handle both investment and regulation. This can be seen as setting up an incoherent and unsustainable distribution of responsibilities, which later provided a reason for asking Professor Cave to conduct a thorough independent review.

Although Cave's report did not attract as many headlines as the Hills review, it may well turn out to have more far-reaching and long-lasting significance. The stated purpose of the review was to establish a regulatory system for social housing which would be clearer and more effective than the existing set of arrangements. The terms of reference were 'to establish objectives . . . for social housing regulation and to propose . . . the system which the review recommends, and the institutional arrangements which will be most capable of achieving those objectives' (Cave, 2007: 29). Cave argued that the objectives of regulation should be: to ensure continued provision of high-quality social housing; to empower and protect tenants; and to expand the availability of choice of provider at all levels in the provision of social housing. The pursuit of these objectives was to be based on two main principles: a minimum degree of intervention consistent with the achievement of the objectives, and uniformity of approach across all providers of social housing. The first principle was presented as 'the accepted standard of better regulation' (Cave, 2007: 11), and the second was justified in terms of the shift towards an approach to regulation from the point of view of the service offered to tenants. This idea of regulating a service rather than a particular set of providers can be referred to as a move from sector regulation to domain regulation (Cave, 2007: paragraph 4.6).

The title of the report of the Cave review was *Every Tenant Matters* and the focus on tenants is presented as a major change in the approach to regulation:

> The review's primary initial conclusion is that the regulatory arrangements need to be much more focused on the needs of tenants. For the last thirty years or so, the focus of social housing regulation has been on regulating providers. The review concludes that now is the time to set a new and long term strategic direction for the regulation of social housing. The focus for the future should be on regulating social housing for the benefit of consumers. This conclusion is grounded in the view that increasing consumer power and choice is what tenants want and that it will, over time, improve the perfor-mance of providers and reduce the need for more intrusive regulation.
>
> (Cave, 2007: paragraph 2.76)

The increased focus on tenants is the first of three important changes proposed in the review. The others are that regulation and investment should be separated and become responsibilities of different organisations, and that regulation of social housing as a whole should be brought together under a new independent regulator with a remit covering all providers, in what the review refers to as a 'mixed econ-omy for the provision and management of social housing' (Cave, 2007: paragraph 2.63). The mixed economy envisaged by Cave includes the possibility that devel-opment, ownership and management might be unbundled and provided by differ-ent organisations (Cave, 2007: paragraph 5.122). This is echoed in a Scottish Government housing-policy discussion paper (http://www.scotland.gov.uk/ Resource/Doc/201716/0053780.pdf). Cave makes no detailed case for recom-mending the end of co-location, probably because it was a prior assumption already accepted by government. It is suggested that one of the problems of the existing regime is that it encourages 'policy passporting', which means the ten-dency to implement policy through regulation.

In the future envisaged by Cave, the distribution of funds for the supply of new homes will be managed by the Homes and Communities Agency, in a process that 'requires little conventional regulation' (Cave, 2007: 18). However, in order to qualify for grant aid developers would need to meet the standards and specifications set for social rented housing. If they wish to have a longer-term involvement in the management of rented homes they would also need to be 'registered providers of social housing' (the replacement term for registered social landlords in England), and the regulator will have responsibility for the 'housing standard' set by the Secretary of State. In relation to low-cost home-ownership schemes, however, developers can receive grants to build and they can retain ownership without having to register.

The review considered various options for the institutional arrangements for regulation, including the possibility that the Audit Commission might take on the role. The decision to recommend a new independent regulator seems to have been influenced by lobbying from the lending industry, the power of which is acknowledged by Cave: he quotes evidence from the Council of Mortgage Lenders to the effect that regulation provides comfort to lenders said to be worth £200–400 million in interest charges each year (Cave, 2007: paragraph 2.38). In the context of a report which highlights the aim of empowering tenants, it is useful to remember the power and influence wielded by other stakeholders, not least the lenders and private developers. Cave interpreted his brief in a liberal fashion, going beyond regulation to include policy proposals about how the regulator should encourage new types of provider and promote different forms of ownership. Choice for tenants is associated with a wider range of providers, offering different services, terms and conditions. It is at least possible that the more that private, for-profit providers are brought into social housing the more the danger that corporate interests and concern about shareholder value will trump tenant power.

The Cave review went with the grain of government policy, emphasising tenant empowerment and the increased involvement of profit-distributing organisations. For example, the phrase 'mixed economy of affordable-housing providers' was already in use and the Housing Corporation was talking about the 'market for grant' (Housing Corporation, 2007). The review can be seen as a potentially highly important step in the development of social housing, moving towards a more fully privatised sector. In order to bring in more private companies to build and manage social housing, two conditions had to be met: the demise of the Housing Corporation and a new regulatory environment acceptable to private companies.

The review received a favourable response from government (CLG, 2007: 38–40), but the subsequent Bill differed from Cave's vision in a number of important respects. In particular, it failed to establish a system of domain regulation, embracing all providers. Local authority housing (including homes provided by arm's-length management organisations) remained outside the scope of the Tenant Services Authority, a situation described by the Chartered Institute of Housing as a fundamental shortcoming of the Bill (CIH, 2007). The proposed arrangements for the regulation of private, for-profit organisations differ from those for housing associations, so Cave's objective of domain regulation remains a long way off. The National Housing Federation was even angrier, describing the Bill as the 'greatest threat ever to the independence of housing associations' (NHF, 2008). The basis of this criticism is that the Bill gave increased explicit statutory powers to the regulator as compared with the pre-existing regime – including, for example, the power to force registered providers to enter into merger agreements, even against their will. The NHF claimed that the Bill provided for the regulator to fine registered providers for failing to implement government directives. As the Bill passed through Parliament it was amended in ways that allayed most of the Federation's concerns (Murie, 2008: 278).

The implication of visibly increased powers, expressed in statute, is serious, in that it could lead to housing associations being reclassified as public bodies, which would have the effect of transferring the private borrowing of housing associations (in excess of £35 billion) onto the government's balance sheet. This is arguably the greatest dilemma for the government in its thinking about the future of the sector: it clearly wishes to increase its control over an important part of the housing system (in order to improve its chances of securing the housing outcomes that it wishes to see), but the more it goes in that direction the more it undermines a key advantage of housing associations, namely the claim that they are private bodies for accounting purposes. It has been claimed that the success of housing associations in harnessing private finance for a social purpose constitutes the best example of not-for-profit public–private partnership in the modern era (Marsh, 2008: 21, Mullins and Murie, 2006: 179). But the sustainability of this approach is jeopardised by the threat of public-sector designation on the one hand and by a backlash against encroachment by private, for-profit companies on the other. The more that government encourages competition in the social housing domain the more strongly housing associations will insist on a level playing-field, which is likely to include demands from some associations to be allowed to convert to PLC status. The chief executive of Places for People has already gone on record as saying that 'there is now a clear need to access equity finance' (Cowans, 2008: 41), which seems to reveal a yearning to be able to issue dividend-bearing shares as a way of raising development finance. Ministers in 2008 may have been adamant that PLC status is not an option, but ministers of housing come and go, and governments – and circumstances – change.

Conclusion

This chapter has argued that the rise of housing associations in the past should be seen as incremental and opportunistic. It follows that it is inappropriate to think in terms of grand strategy when looking ahead. Any overall, long-term coherence in the way the housing system develops almost certainly owes more to path-dependency than strategic thinking. If we stand back far enough to take a long-term view of what is today called social housing, it is arguable that there is a consistent direction of travel, away from the overwhelming municipalist and collectivist dominance of the period from 1919 to 1979. From 1974, as local authority housing came under increasing attack, housing associations were growing and gathering strength, which enabled them to cope with the post-1989 reintroduction of private finance. The Cave review can be seen as setting up the next phase, with greater emphasis and reliance on private finance and profit-seeking companies. History, of course, does not repeat itself, but there is a sort of symmetry about the prospect of a twenty-first-century form of social housing that is overwhelmingly non-municipal and provided by a mix of charities, not-for-profit organisations and for-profit companies. It may be that council housing will be seen as a peculiarly twentieth-century phenomenon, and social housing will in future be provided by organisations that have more in common with their nineteenth-century predecessors: they will be essentially private-sector organisations, relying mainly on private finance, which they will obtain by a mix of loans and share capital, just as housing associations did before 1974. In retrospect, commitment to local democratic accountability and squeamishness about profit distribution may appear rather quaint notions (as, perhaps, they do already to the senior managers in some of the more thrusting and progressive 'housing development and management companies'). Thus the Cave review can be seen as making the regulatory environment acceptable to the for-profit sector, and as such its importance is potentially profound.

Insofar as there is a strategic approach within government it seems to be to rely as far as possible on the market for the provision of housing to the majority of the population. In a fundamental sense this represents a continuation of the stance that has underpinned housing policy in the UK for a hundred years. What is different now is the structure and character of the housing market, with owner occupation having replaced private renting as the mass tenure. This restructuring of the housing market has been depicted as a significant influence on the development of social housing, and earlier accounts (Harloe, 1981, 1995; Malpass and Murie, 1999) have tended to refer to municipal housing settling down to a long-term residual role. It is now possible to revise this conclusion in light of more recent evidence, which suggests that municipal housing has a very limited future and that the residual role is only part of what social housing will be required to do in future. In the coming period it looks as if it might be better to think in terms of the social provision of housing rather than a social-housing 'sector'; this may be a more accurate way of referring to the mixed economy of providers. An entrepreneurial social business model (or models) may predominate, but the sector will remain small, and may shrink further. There remains considerable scope for further privatisation within the social-housing domain, and an apparent willingness to explore its potential.

In terms of the role of social housing, it has been argued that 'The strategic focus of social housing is changing from letting social rented housing to promoting mixed-tenure housing and more diverse neighbourhoods and community activities' (Mullins and Sacranie, 2008). The need to provide decent, affordable and well-managed housing for the least well-off and most vulnerable people in society will continue, but it is clear from the historical evidence that neither housing associations nor local authorities were ever entirely confined to this residual role. They always embraced higher-income groups as well, and models of housing that anticipated a future in which the market would provide for all but the least well-off need to be revised. The evidence, both historical and contemporary, suggests that markets fail to provide decent, affordable, value-for-money housing for a wider proportion of the population, embracing what has come to be called the intermediate market: people who are not the residualised poor but who are nonetheless unable to afford open-market prices. The size of the intermediate market will vary over time and the prescribed solutions will also vary, but it seems that it will be organisations located within the mixed economy of social-housing providers that will be used as the agents of policy implementation.

Of course, there is much about the future that remains unknowable, but housing systems tend to change only slowly, and as established organisations with increasing financial and organisational strength, housing associations are in a good position to defend their interests and shape their development, although the tensions inherent within the third sector provide a complicating factor. Housing policies can change more quickly and unpredictably, and here there are many sets of tensions to consider. Three of the most relevant are: the wider relationship between housing and the economy; the relationship between housing and the welfare state (particularly the significance of housing wealth as a way of paying for non-housing services); and the way that government resolves the temptation to try to control the third-sector and for-profit organisations (with their own business objectives) on which it relies for the achievement of public policy objectives.

The Cave review and the Housing and Regeneration Act mark the start of a new and potentially very different phase of development for housing associations. It is possible to develop a rather apocalyptic view of the meaning and implications of Cave. The demise of the Housing Corporation certainly suggests that the scale of change now envisaged by policy-makers is more than fine tuning. This could be the end of social housing and housing associations as we have known them. Parallels with those other paragons of nineteenth-century mutuality, the building societies, spring to mind: in 1900 there were 2,000 building societies, but they then went through a prolonged phase of mergers and takeovers, reducing their number to about 100. These then mostly converted themselves into profit-distributing banks. Who is to say that housing associations, which also used to number about 2,000, are not already going through the same sort of sequence?

Despite the assurances given by Labour ministers about issues such as PLC status, it is not hard to imagine a future Conservative government pressing forward with the privatisation of social housing. Development is the most easily privatised function, and it could well be that in future new supply will increasingly come from for-profit companies, and that housing associations will have to buy what they can afford on the open market and concentrate much more on the ownership and management functions.

On the other hand, it could be that (as has often been the case in the past) reform is more threatening as it approaches than it turns out to be in practice. We may find that the commitment to the values of not-for-profit social housing will prove to be highly resilient and/or that for-profit companies show little interest in expanding their activities in this direction.

There is perhaps a third scenario, in which fragmentation of the 'sector' becomes apparent. While many, including the majority of small organisations, will carry on as not-for-profit landlords, doing little or no development work, some of the bigger and more dynamic associations will transfer to PLC status, while others develop their hybrid character, retaining not-for-profit arms and growing for-profit activities within complex group structures. One factor working in favour of housing associations is the government's continuing need for a set of organisations that are dirigible, unlike for-profit companies where shareholder value is always likely to override the pursuit of public policy objectives. In the famous phrase used by Aneurin Bevan, who was no friend of housing associations, 'If we are to plan we have to plan with plannable instruments and the speculative builder, by his very nature is not a plannable instrument'. That is as true now as when he said it in 1946.

Notes

1. Strictly speaking, since 1996 housing associations have been just one category of registered social landlord, but for current purposes the term housing association is preferred because it has greater historical utility, having become in 1935 the generic label for independent limited-profit and charitable organisations primarily concerned with the provision of rented accommodation that is affordable by people on low incomes.

References

Audit Commission and Housing Corporation (2002) Group Dynamics. *Group Structures in the RSL Sector.* London: Audit Commission.

Beynon, H., Hollywood, E. and Hudson, R. (1999) *Regenerating Housing*, Coalfields Research Programme, Discussion Paper no. 6 http://www.cf.ac.uk/socsi/resources/regenerating%20housing%20-%206.pdf.

Blair, T. (1998) *Leading The Way: a new vision for local government*, London: Institute for Public Policy Research.

Cave, M. (2007) *Every Tenant Matters: A review of social housing regulation*, London: DCLG.

CIH (2007) *Housing and Regeneration Bill Briefing for Members*, http://www.cih.org/policy/hous-regen-breif-nov07.pdf.

CLG (Communities and Local Government) (2007) *Delivering Housing and Regeneration*, London: CLG.

Cohen Committee (1971) *Housing Associations*, London: HMSO.

Cowan, D. and McDermont, M. (2006) *Regulating Social Housing*, London: Glasshouse.

Cowans, D. (2008) 'From meeting housing needs to matching housing aspirations', in Chevin, D. (ed.) *Moving Up a Gear: New Challenges for housing associations*, London: Smith Institute.

Dataspring (2007) *Housing Associations in 2007*, http://www.dataspring.org.uk/

DoE (Department of the Environment) (1995) *Housing Corporation: Prior options study*, London: DoE.

Dwelly, T. (2006) 'Social housing isn't working', in Dwelly, T. and Cowans, J. (eds) *Rethinking Social Housing*, London: Smith Institute, 8–15.

Emsley, I. (1986) *The Development of Housing Associations*, London: Garland.

Harloe, M. (1981) 'The recommodification of housing', in Harloe, M. and Lebas, E. (eds) *City, Class and Capital*, London: Edward Arnold.

—— (1995) *The People's Home? Social Rented Housing in Europe and America*, Oxford: Blackwell.

Hills, J. (2007) *Ends and Means: The future roles of social housing in England*, London: LSE.

Housing Corporation (1977) *Annual Report 1976–7*, London: Housing Corporation.

—— (1998) *Building a Better Future: Revitalising neighbourhoods*, London: Housing Corporation.

—— (2007) *The National Affordable Housing Programme: pre-prospectus*, London: Housing Corporation.

Malpass, P. (1993) 'Housing Policy and the Housing System Since 1979', in Malpass, P. and Means, R. (eds) *Implementing Housing Policy*, Buckingham: Open University Press, 4–22.

—— (2000) *Housing Associations and Housing Policy*, Basingstoke: Macmillan.

Malpass, P. and Murie, A. (1999) *Housing Policy and Practice*, Basingstoke: Macmillan, 5th edition.

Malpass, P. and Mullins, D. (2002) 'Local Authority Housing Stock Transfer in the UK: from local initiative to national policy', *Housing Studies*, (17)4, 673–86.

Marsh, P. (2008) 'New landscapes in affordable housing', in Chevin, D. (ed.) *Moving Up a Gear: New Challenges for housing associations*, London: Smith Institute.

Mullins, D. (1997) 'From Regulatory Capture to Regulated Competition: an interest group analysis of the regulation of housing associations in England', *Housing Studies*, (12)3, 301–20.

Mullins, D. and Murie, A. (2006) *Housing Policy in the UK*, Basingstoke: Palgrave.

Mullins, D. and Sacranie, H. (2008) 'Competing Drivers of Change in the Regulation of Housing Associations in England: a multi-layered merging perspective', paper presented to the Housing Studies Association conference, University of York, 2–4 April.

Murie, A. (2008) *Changing Housing Direction: the Housing Corporation 1964–2008*, London: Politico's.

Murie, A., Pocock, R. and Gulliver, K. (2007) *Hills, Cave and After: renewing social housing*, Birmingham: Human City Institute.

Newman, J. (2000) 'Beyond the New Public Management,' in Clarke, J., Gewirtz, S. and McLaughlin, E. (eds) *New Managerialism, New Welfare?*, London: Sage.

NHF (National Housing Federation) (2008) *Housing Bill Bulletin*, 9 January http://www.housing.org.uk/Uploads/File/Campaigns/Independence/4ppA4HousingBill_Bulletin.pdf.

Rhodes, R. (1999) Foreword to Skoker, G. (ed.) *The New Management of British Local Governance*, Basingstoke: Macmillan.

Wilcox, S. (2007) *UK Housing Review 2007/2008*, Coventry: Chartered Institute of Housing and London: Council of Mortgage Lenders.

7 The transformation of private renting

Peter A. Kemp

The privately rented housing market in Britain has been significantly transformed since the 1970s. Indeed, over that period it has developed in ways that would not have been expected by most, if not all, commentators back then. Although private renting has been a tenure in transition since the early years of the twentieth century, the nature of that transition changed from the late 1980s and early 1990s as the sector entered a period of modest revival following seven decades of decline and decay. It is now clear that private renting has entered a new and different trajectory from that which characterised it for much of the twentieth century.

At one level, it is hardly surprising that private renting (as well as owner-occupation and what we now call social housing) has changed. For housing tenures are not fixed or immutable sets of social relations around the ownership, occupation and pricing of accommodation. They represent institutional arrangements that to some extent are historically and socially specific, which vary (albeit within limits) over time and space (Kemp, 1987). As the wider economy and society change, so too do the social relations embodied in housing tenures. Thus, for example, what is means to be a private tenant in the early years of the twenty-first century is not the same as it was in the 1970s, still less in the nineteenth century (Kemp, 2004). Moreover, housing tenures are also relational in the sense that how one is perceived will be influenced by how the others are seen (Gray, 1982).

The structure of this chapter is as follows. The next section briefly locates private renting within its historical context. This scene-setting is important because, as a tenure in decline for much of the twentieth century, the nature and role of private renting in the 1970s was heavily influenced by that history. After that, the chapter presents an overview of private renting in the 1970s and thereby provides a baseline against which to compare the sector today. Thereafter the chapter examines the dimensions of change over the past quarter-century, before looking in more detail at the factors that have prompted those developments. It then considers the future prospects for private renting and, finally, presents conclusions.

Historical context

For much of the twentieth century, private renting was in decline, shrinking in size both absolutely and as a proportion of the housing stock. Few new dwellings for private letting were constructed after the Second World War and many existing ones were sold into owner-occupation or demolished in slum clearance schemes (DoE, 1977; Holmans, 1987). Rent controls, which until 1965 were highly inflexible in design, prevented landlords from charging an economic rent; and, along with an unhelpful tax regime, made it uneconomic for them to undertake major repairs or improvements on the ageing stock of dwellings that remained in the sector (Nevitt, 1966). Their incentive to do so was further weakened by the excess demand that existed for rented housing, which meant that landlords could relatively easily find tenants for their properties even if they were in a poor state of repair (DoE, 1977).

Although property conditions were often poor, the privately rented sector provided a supply of low-rent accommodation, particularly at the bottom end of the market (Cullingworth, 1963). Outside of slum-clearance schemes, the poorest households were often not a priority for rehousing by local councils and instead had little choice but to rent from private landlords. Most low-income tenants could not afford to pay an economic or a market rent, even if landlords had been allowed to charge them. Moreover, the Milner Holland report (1965) showed that, under the housing tax and subsidy arrangements then in place, a newly built house would cost less to buy with a mortgage or to rent from a local authority than it would to rent an identical one from a private landlord.

Along with rent control, the fact that it was cheaper to buy a dwelling than to rent it privately in the context of housing shortage, helped to create a gap between the price at which a vacant house could be sold to an owner-occupier and that at which it could be sold to another landlord if it was tenanted (Hamnett and Randolph, 1988). This 'value gap' gave landlords an incentive not to re-let their properties when they became vacant but instead to sell them into owner-occupation; it also created an incentive for less scrupulous landlords to harass their tenants in order to persuade them to leave. The incentive for landlords to winkle out their tenants was increased by the Conservative Government's 1957 Rent Act, under which properties that became vacant ceased to be subject to rent controls and could therefore be re-let at a market rent (Kemp, 2004).

The future of private renting had become very politicised by the 1950s, with the Conservatives promoting rent decontrol and Labour advocating municipalisation (Kemp, 2004). The 1957 Rent Act was politically controversial, and made still more so by the publicity surrounding the nefarious activities of the landlord

Peter Rachman in central London in the late 1950s and early 1960s. Labour made considerable capital out of the Rachman scandal (Banting, 1979) and generalised the problems it highlighted to the private rental sector as a whole. It was presented as further proof that the private landlord had failed as an institution (Kemp, 2004). The Milner Holland Committee (1965), which was set up in the wake of the Rachman scandal, concluded that there was an acute shortage of rental housing in London and that, although most tenants were satisfied with the way their landlord treated them, abuse was too common to be regarded as an isolated problem.

Labour's 1965 Rent Act strengthened security of tenure for private tenants and introduced 'regulated tenancies' with 'fair rents' to be set by rent officers employed by local councils (Doling and Davies, 1984). The new system of regulated tenancies was intended to be more flexible than previous forms of rent control and to provide landlords with regular rent increases while ensuring that they were not able to take advantage of local shortages of accommodation (Donnison, 1967). The Minister for Housing, Richard Crossman, hoped that rent regulation would 'take rents out of politics' (Banting, 1979). Although it was not entirely successful in that respect, it did remain in place for a third of a century, with only relatively minor modifications, until the 1988 Housing Act.

Private renting in the 1970s

Crossman believed that it was too late to save the privately rented sector and that the future of housing provision lay with owner-occupation and local authorities (Banting, 1979). Certainly, since 1945, house-building had been largely confined to local authorities and the market for owner-occupation, with scarcely any for private rental. Following the introduction of a new financial regime under the Housing Act 1974, housing associations became a heavily subsidised alternative to council housing and a substitute for the private landlord (Malpass, 2000). Private renting continued to decline rapidly in the 1970s, shrinking in size by about 80,000 dwellings per annum (see Figure 7.1). Many commentators believed that private renting was in irretrievable decline (Eversley, 1975) and, indeed, some feared and others hoped that it would disappear altogether.

Meanwhile, the image of private renting seemed to worsen, especially in comparison with owner-occupation and council housing. Private renting was associated with greedy or unscrupulous landlords letting poor-quality or even slum housing at exorbitant rents on insecure tenancies to vulnerable households. The reality, of course, was far more complex than this kind of stereotype might allow, but there was enough corroborative evidence in the case files of housing-advice centres to give it credence (Kemp, 2004). For new households, the sector was in effect seen as a 'waiting-room' until entry was gained into owner-occupation or, failing that, council housing; for many of those who remained it was a tenure of last resort (Whitehead and Kleinman, 1986).

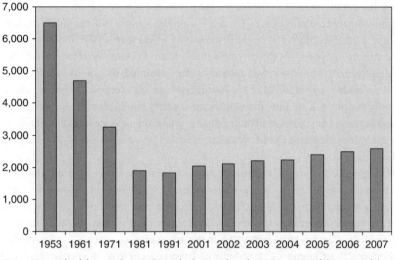

7.1 Households renting privately in England, 1953–2007 (thousands).
Source: Crown Copyright, DCLG live table 801; last updated Oct 2008.

By the 1970s, private renting had also become much less central to policy debates (Kemp, 2004). In 1975, for example, the Labour Government set up a review of housing finance, which subsequently evolved into a review of housing policy more generally and became known as the Housing Policy Review (DoE, 1977). It focused very largely on the two main tenures of owner occupation and council housing and gave little consideration to private renting, which was instead relegated to a Review of the Rent Acts. The latter was concerned mainly with tidying up and rationalising the existing system of controls rather than with a fundamental appraisal of the role of the sector in the modern housing market (Cullingworth, 1979). The 1977 Rent Act did little more than consolidate the legislation that was already in place and introduced no major innovations (Stafford and Doling, 1981).

Although a number of measures were passed in the 1970s that affected private landlords and tenants, the changes they introduced were relatively marginal and failed to address key problems facing the sector (Kemp, 2004). Following the recommendations of the Francis Committee (1971), the 1974 Rent Act brought furnished accommodation within the regulated-rent system. An important reason for this development was that some landlords were seeking to avoid rent regulation by letting their accommodation with a minimal amount of furniture. At the same time, the 1974 Act excluded lettings made by resident landlords from the regulated-tenancy framework.

More important, at least in the longer term, was the Housing Finance Act 1972, which introduced rent allowances for private and housing-association tenants and a national rebate scheme for council tenants (Cullingworth, 1979). This was a significant turning point for the private-rental sector. Previously, rent control and, subsequently, rent regulation were seen as the principal means by which rents were to be made more affordable for low-income private tenants. Whereas previously only people getting out-of-work social security benefits or the means-tested pension received assistance with their housing costs, the new system of rent allowances extended income-related assistance with the rent to other low-income tenants.

While rent control was a blanket mechanism, rent allowances were tailored to the individual needs and financial circumstances of the tenant. Moreover, they provided a mechanism for facilitating the regular rent increases in the private market envisaged under rent regulation. As Holmans (1987) has pointed out, they helped to protect low-income tenants from the rent increases that could be expected to result from the transfer of their lettings from old controlled to new regulated tenancies under the 1972 Housing Finance Act. This 'cushioning' role became even more important after rents were deregulated on new lettings under the 1988 Housing Act (see below).

Not only had the private sector declined considerably over the years, its role within the housing market had also changed. The decline had been concentrated in unfurnished lettings, so that a growing proportion of the sector comprised furnished accommodation. Increasingly, the sector was providing less long-term unfurnished housing and more short-term, immediate-access furnished accommodation (Kemp, 1988). By this time, unfurnished lettings were dominated by older tenants, many of whom had low incomes. They mostly rented houses or flats and had lived at their present address for many years, often dating back to when private renting was the majority tenure. Meanwhile, furnished lettings were largely occupied by young, single and childless households; they tended to rent rooms or flats and had generally lived at their present address for only a year or two (Whitehead and Kleinman, 1986; Kemp, 1988).

A survey of private tenants in England in 1978 found that just over two-thirds had a regulated tenancy under the Rent Act 1965, of whom one-third (or about one-fifth of all tenants) had a fair rent registered with the Rent Officer service. Seven per cent of private tenants had a controlled rent extant from the pre-1965 Rent Acts. Meanwhile, about one in twenty private tenants was renting from a resident landlord and one in six were either living in rent-free accommodation or otherwise renting tied accommodation (Todd et al., 1982).

The 1978 survey also found that the ownership of privately rented housing was diverse and relatively small in scale. Over three-fifths of private lettings in 1978 were owned by individuals, and only a tenth by property companies. About a fifth were owned by employer landlords (Todd et al., 1982). Meanwhile, a survey of landlords in 'densely rented' areas of England and Wales in 1976 found that the median size of holding of non-resident individual landlords was only five to nine lettings, while for companies it was 50–99 lettings (Paley, 1978). Thus, private letting in the late 1970s was a fragmented, small-scale and largely unmodernised sector of the market economy (Kemp, 1988).

The end of decline

By the time that Labour left office in 1979 the private rented sector had declined to 2.3 million dwellings or 11 per cent of the housing stock in Britain. All the evidence seemed to suggest that the sector would continue to shrink in size for the foreseeable future. It was no surprise, therefore, that the decline of private renting continued into the 1980s, notwithstanding the election of a radical Conservative Government determined to roll back the state and release market forces.

Nevertheless, the turn of the next decade witnessed a significant, and largely unexpected (Down et al., 1994), change in trajectory for the private-rental housing market. Not only did the long-run decline of private renting come to an end, but the sector actually began to expand in both absolute and percentage terms. In fact, between 1988 and 2007 the number of households in England renting from private landlords rose from 1.7 million to 2.6 million, an increase of 52 per cent in two decades (Figure 7.1, above). Meanwhile, the sector's share of all households expanded from nine to twelve per cent, and its share of the rental market as a whole from a quarter to two-fifths.

Over the past 20 years, the private rented sector has not only grown in size; it has also changed in other important ways. Perhaps the most fundamental change has been in the terms upon which tenants rent their home from private landlords. In 1988, about nine out of ten lettings in England were either regulated under the Rent Acts or not part of the open market. However, a new tenancy regime *for new lettings* involving rent deregulation and reduced security of tenure for tenants was introduced in January 1989 (see below). Because of the high turnover of private tenants and an influx of new landlords and properties, this new tenancy regime rapidly came to dominate the sector. By 2006–7, regulated tenancies and those not part of the open market accounted for only one in eight lettings. Meanwhile, three-quarters of private lettings in 2006–7 were deregulated tenancies on which landlords could charge market rents. Most of them (85 per cent) were assured shortholds, which give tenants relatively little security of tenure. Similar trends occurred in Wales and Scotland (Bailey, 1999).

Thus, over the past two decades, the sector has rapidly changed from one mainly comprising lettings regulated or controlled by the Rent Acts to one dominated by deregulated tenancies let at market rents. This transformation in tenancies has meant that private renting is now much more explicitly affected by market forces than it had been in the 1970s and 1980s. Moreover, a greater proportion of the privately rented stock is now let by landlords who regard their properties as an investment. Private individual landlords who have non-commercial motives accounted for over a third of privately rented addresses in England in 1993, but by 2001 this had fallen to one in six (Crook and Kemp, 1996a; Rugg and Rhodes, 2008). A substantial influx of 'buy-to-let' landlords, investing with the help of mortgage finance, has brought the sector into much closer contact with the financial markets. Thus, the private rental housing market is now much less of a 'stagnant backwater of the market economy' than it was in the 1970s (Kemp, 2004).

The composition of the private tenant population has also changed since the 1970s. There has been a sharp decline in the proportion of tenants aged 60 or more, as older people who had always rented privately died or moved in with their children or into a residential home. Meanwhile, single-adult households and childless couples have both become more important. As a whole, private tenants are now much younger than they were in the 1970s. Far fewer private tenants are retired and, at least compared with the 1980s, far more are either in paid work or higher education (see Kemp, 2004).

The image of private renting has also changed in some respects when the 1970s are compared with the present day. To a significant extent, the image of 'Rachmanism' – of unscrupulous landlords letting slum property at exploitative rents – has faded and no longer dominates debates about private letting. Investment in rental housing has become a dinner-table topic and is seen in a more respectable light than it was in the 1970s. The daily newspapers and other forms of mass media frequently give coverage to what is now referred to as 'buy-to-let' as well as to the relative merits of buying or renting one's home (Kemp, 2004). Renting from a private landlord is no longer something to feel embarrassed about, but instead is widely regarded as an appropriate and suitable housing option for some people. The latter change has been in part facilitated by the influx into the sector of new-build and higher-quality properties than was previously the case. A much larger proportion of the privately rented stock comprises modern properties and the sector is no longer so heavily concentrated in inner city areas but is more spatially dispersed.

Thus, in a variety of ways the privately rented housing sector has been transformed compared with the 1970s. The next three sections – on housing policy, supply and demand – seek to examine what has driven this turn-around in the sector's fortunes. What they show is that, although housing policy has been important, social and economic developments have also been crucial in creating the transformation of private renting over the past two decades.

The role of housing policy

During the Conservatives' first two terms of office, reviving the privately rented sector was not a central focus of their housing policy; instead, the emphasis was firmly fixed on expanding home ownership and curtailing the role of local authorities. The Conservatives' vision for private renting was limited to managing decline in the long-stay accommodation market and encouraging the provision of short-stay accommodation for mobile households and people saving up for a deposit prior to buying their own home (see Crook, 1986; Whitehead and Kleinman, 1986).

The Housing Act, 1980, included a package of modest measures aimed at stimulating the privately rented sector (Crook, 1986). First, easier rules for regaining possession were introduced for resident-landlord lettings. Second, the remaining controlled tenancies, extant from the pre-1965 years, were converted into regulated tenancies. Third, the phasing in of increases in fair rents and the interval between fair-rent increases, were both reduced from three years to two. Fourth, a new form of tenancy known as 'shorthold' ('short tenancies' in Scotland) was introduced. These were regulated tenancies of from one to five years, which gave the landlords the power to regain possession after the fixed term. Initially, all shortholds had to have a fair rent registered, but this requirement was subsequently dropped. Finally, in England and Wales (but not in Scotland) a new form of tenancy known as 'assured tenancies' was introduced. These were lettings by approved landlords of newly built property at market rents. The landlord-approval scheme can be seen as an attempt to shed the negative image that had dogged private landlordism for many years (Kemp, 2004).

By the mid-1980s it was becoming clear that the measures introduced in the Housing Act, 1980, were having only a limited impact on the sector and had failed to halt decline (Crook, 1986). Following their election for a third term of office, however, the Conservatives made a more concerted attempt to revitalise private renting. The 1988 Housing Act deregulated new private lettings and made it easier for landlords to regain possession of their properties (Whitehead and Kleinman, 1989). Under this legislation, all new private lettings were to be new-style, assured tenancies unless the landlord issued the prospective tenant with a specific notification that they were to be 'assured shorthold tenancies' ('short assured tenancies' in Scotland). The minimum term for an assured shorthold was reduced from one year to six months.[1]

The Conservatives argued that rent control and security-of-tenure legislation – in addition to the attractions of home-ownership – had been the main reason for the decline of private renting (DoE, 1987). However, as a temporary measure to kick-start investment in the private rented sector, the 1988 Budget extended the Business Expansion Scheme (BES) to include companies letting on assured tenancies, for a limited period, until the end of 1993. The BES was originally introduced in 1983 with the objective of encouraging small businesses as part of the 'enterprise culture' that the Conservatives were hoping to encourage. It provided tax relief to investors on the purchase of shares in BES firms and exemption from capital-gains tax if the shares were held for at least five years (Crook et al., 1995).

Approximately £3.4 billion was raised by around 900 public and private residential property companies within the BES, a substantial sum in a period of little more than five years. BES companies purchased an estimated 81,000 properties, but about three-quarters of them were linked to housing associations, universities or building societies wishing to offload repossessed homes. Most directors of the other BES companies reported that they would probably sell their dwellings when property prices picked up. The net yields on BES companies were uncompetitive compared with alternative investments and, consequently, even those directors who wished to keep their company going thought it unlikely that they would be able to continue in business (Crook *et al.*, 1995).

An estimated £1.7 billion in tax relief was claimed by investors in BES rental housing companies, which at £21,000 per property acquired was equivalent to 44 per cent of the cost of the average BES property (Crook *et al.*, 1995). The BES did bring a new generation of investors into the residential lettings market (Hughes, 1995) and brought the sector to the attention of the financial institutions. It also brought (albeit often temporarily) many modern dwellings into a rental market that, for much of the post-1945 period, had been associated in the public mind with sub-standard accommodation. But otherwise, it was a very expensive way to give a temporary boost to new investment in the private rental housing market (Crook *et al.*, 1995).

The cessation of decline in private renting took place just as both the Housing Act 1988 and the BES extension came into affect. It might, therefore, be tempting to attribute this recovery to those two initiatives. Certainly, rent deregulation and the changes to security of tenure made it much more attractive to let accommodation privately. And the fact that the Labour Party made it clear that it would not reintroduce rent controls when it was returned to office helped to reduce the political risk associated with investment in the sector. Yet, despite deregulation, the yields on private lettings were still uncompetitive with alternative investments, taking into account relative liquidity and investment risk. Moreover, the 81,000 BES properties that were bought over the five-year life of the initiative accounted for only a small share of the increased rental supply (Crook and Kemp, 1996b).

Although the 1988 Housing Act was a critical precursor, and the BES an important stimulant and advertisement for investment, the recovery in the private rental sector was also encouraged by the housing slump that began at about the same time and continued into the early 1990s. During this period, in the face of rising unemployment and increased interest rates, mortgage arrears and possessions increased to record levels. Meanwhile, property transactions declined sharply, house prices fell in real as well as in nominal terms, and around a million home owners found themselves with negative equity (Dorling and Cornford, 1995; Forrest and Murie, 1994). One result of this slump was that some owner-occupiers who needed to move, but were unable to sell their property, opted to let it and rented somewhere else instead. Meanwhile, people who might have become first-time buyers delayed house purchase and rented their accommodation from a private landlord.

Hence, the housing market slump of the early 1990s in England increased both the demand for, and the supply of, privately rented accommodation. Crook *et al.* (1995) found that, in 1993/94, about one in ten of all privately rented addresses in Britain were owned by what they termed 'property slump landlords' who were unable or unwilling to sell because of the state of the owner occupied housing market. Crook and Kemp (1996b) estimated that these landlords accounted for around half of the increase in lettings since 1988.

The Conservative Government took further steps to encourage investment in the privately rented sector in 1996. By this time, the owner-occupied housing market had recovered from the slump as prices and transactions began rising once again, potentially threatening to stall the revival in private renting. The Housing Act 1996 made assured shortholds the default tenancy instead of assured tenancies. This change, in effect, signalled a view that private renting was a short-term tenure rather than a long-term housing solution (Kemp, 2004).

Meanwhile, in order to encourage the financial institutions into residential lettings, the Finance Act, 1996, introduced a new investment vehicle called 'housing investment trusts' (HITs), which had a reduced liability to pay tax. The Conservative Government hoped that attracting financial institutions into the private rental housing market would help to modernise the ownership of the sector. It was believed that financial institutions could bring a stain-free reputation to private landlordism and achieve economies of scale and more efficient management than small-scale landlords. Finally, because of the large sums for investment available to the financial institutions, it would be possible to increase the size of the privately rented sector in a way that would not be possible by relying on investment from private individuals (Crook and Kemp, 1999).

Despite the tax relief on offer, not a single HIT was ever established. Estimates of the likely returns on HITs found that they were not competitive with alternative investments, even when tax relief was taken into account (Crook *et al.*, 1998). The rules governing HITs prevented them from operating like a normal property company. And the lack of sufficiently large and otherwise suitable portfolios available for purchase in the privately rented sector meant that they could not invest the amounts required in the short timescale specified by the rules governing HITs (Crook and Kemp, 1999). Thus, the dominance of the privately rented sector by small-scale landlords was itself an obstacle to investment in the sector by financial institutions (Crook and Kemp, 2002).

The Labour Government elected in 1997 made it very clear that they had no intention of reintroducing rent controls in the privately rented market. A well functioning, market rented sector aimed at younger and mobile households in particular was a central part of Labour's housing policy, just as it had been for the Thatcher and Major Conservative Governments. This reflected the political consensus that had developed that the sector played several important, if small-scale, roles in housing provision (Best *et al.*, 1992). The emergence of this consensus helped to eliminate the political risk that had for so long helped to undermine investment in private renting.

Labour's interventions in the private rental sector mainly focused on the edges of the market and were largely aimed at improving management and maintenance standards by 'rogue landlords'. In England and Wales, local landlord-accreditation schemes were encouraged and a rent-deposit scheme and licensing of houses in multiple occupation (HMOs) were introduced. Similar initiatives were introduced in Scotland, along with compulsory registration of most privately rented properties. Meanwhile, local authorities were beginning to make use of the privately rented sector to accommodate homeless people, an initiative that had originally been encouraged by the Conservative Government of John Major.

Like the Conservatives, the Labour Government was keen to attract the financial institutions into privately rented housing. The Barker (2003) inquiry into housing supply recommended that measures be taken to encourage institutional investment in privately rented housing in order to increase the size of the sector. Labour followed that advice and introduced new tax rules to allow the setting up of REITs – property investment trusts along the lines of US real estate investment trusts. However, as yet not a single residential REIT has been established (Jones, 2007). Thus, the investment vehicles introduced by the Conservative and Labour Governments (HITs and REITs respectively) failed to entice financial institutions into the private rental sector.

Buy-to-let

The most striking development on the supply side of the privately rented sector at the turn of the century was the 'buy-to-let' (BTL) scheme, an initiative developed from the bottom up by the industry itself (Gibb and Nygaard, 2005; Kemp, 2004). Buy-to-let was originally introduced by the Association of Residential Letting Agents (ARLA) and a panel of mortgage-lenders in September 1996 (Ball, 2006). ARLA's key motive was to help ensure that their members continued to have a high level of lettings business at a time when landlords were beginning to sell, as house prices and transactions recovered from the early 1990s slump (Kemp, 2004).

BTL involved the provision of loan finance to moderate and high net-worth individuals wishing to invest in housing to let (Ball, 2006). Previously, the mortgage-lending criteria and products available to landlords were limited and expensive. Private landlords typically had to pay a premium of around 2 per cent over the mortgage rates charged to owner-occupiers. Under the BTL scheme, however, landlords were charged mortgage rates that were closer to those paid by owner-occupiers. One condition of the scheme was that the borrower had to agree to the property being managed by a member of ARLA, thereby providing the lender with the comfort that the security for the loan was being professionally managed. In due course, other mortgage-lenders that were not part of the official BTL panel of lenders began marketing loans under the 'buy-to-let' label. In the end, 'buy-to-let' turned into a noun that referred to mortgaged investment in private rental housing (Kemp, 2004).

As Table 7.1 shows, there has been a very marked expansion in BTL lending by mortgage-lenders. The number of loans outstanding grew from only 28,700 in 1998 to 1,024,300 in 2007, an increase of almost a million in just ten years. BTL accounted for less than one per cent of all residential mortgage loans outstanding in 1998, but for as much as ten per cent in 2007. Hence, by the end of this period, lending to private landlords had switched from being a very small part of the market to being a significant outlet for mortgage funds. Indeed, several specialist BTL lenders, such as Paragon, became significant players in this market, along with a number of ex-building societies such as the Bradford and Bingley.

Why did buy-to-let develop into such a significant market?[2] First, market conditions within the privately rented sector had significantly improved. The 1988 Housing Act had deregulated rents and introduced assured shorthold tenancies, which meant that landlords could be sure of regaining vacant possession, as could lenders in the event of the landlord defaulting on the mortgage (Rhodes and Bevan, 2003). The Labour Government had kept its promise to leave the letting framework introduced by the Conservatives in place, thereby minimising political risk.

Second, from the mid-1990s interest rates fell to historically low levels, making it financially viable to borrow money to invest in rental housing for the first time

Table 7.1 Buy-to-let mortgages outstanding at end of period

Year	Number	% of total
1998	28,700	0.4
1999	73,200	1.0
2000	120,300	1.6
2001	185,000	2.3
2002	275,000	3.4
2003	417,500	4.7
2004	576,700	6.2
2005	699,400	7.2
2006	835,900	8.6
2007	1,024,300	10.1

Source: Council of Mortgage Lenders data, cited in FT Weekend 4–5 October 2008, p. 28.

in decades. Borrowing money to buy rental property enabled landlords to gear up their investments and thereby purchase more properties than would otherwise have been possible (Rhodes and Bevan, 2003) and to achieve a higher rate of return. Typically, the properties purchased were new or modern flats and to a lesser extent houses, which were seen as having low maintenance costs and the maximum potential for sale (if necessary) to the owner-occupied market. However, some full-time or 'business' landlords invested in older property in need of refurbishment (Rhodes and Bevan, 2003), thereby doubling up as developers in order to maximise the opportunity for capital gain.

Third, lenders began to see the attractions of lending to private landlords, when previously they had been relatively circumspect about it and largely focused on lending to owner-occupiers. During the housing-market slump of the early 1990s, lenders gained experience of the landlord market. This occurred both when some of their borrowers let their home when they could not sell it, and when lenders took possession of properties of borrowers in arrears and let them for the duration. This revealed that arrears and possessions were often lower than on owner-occupied property and, therefore, that lending to landlords was not as risky as they had previously thought (Kemp, 2004). Meanwhile, the decline in first-time buyers meant that lenders had to find new outlets for their loans. One result of these developments was the emergence of a wider range of loan types and the emergence of mortgage products geared specifically to the needs of private landlords (Rhodes and Bevan, 2003).

Fourth, financial market deregulation, the relaxation of capital adequacy requirements by the regulatory authorities and the emergence of new sources of funding on the international capital market meant that mortgage lenders were awash with money to lend from the late 1990s. Competition among lenders encouraged them to provide new products in order to attract borrowers, including landlords. Mortgage-lenders gradually relaxed their BTL lending criteria, requiring lower deposits and reducing the minimum rental cover (the amount by which the anticipated rental income had to exceed the mortgage payments).

Fifth, low interest rates also meant that the returns available on building-society and bank deposit accounts were low, thereby increasing the relative attractiveness of property as an investment. At the turn of the century, the stock market fell for three years in a row, reducing the attractiveness of investment in shares. In a related development, the performance of pension funds deteriorated. Meanwhile, many companies were beginning to switch from final-salary pension schemes into defined-contribution schemes, which carried much more risk for their employees. These developments increased the attractions of rental property as a form of saving for retirement (Kemp, 2004). Certainly, research has found that some buy-to-let landlords view their property as their pension (Rhodes and Bevan, 2003; Scanlon and Whitehead, 2005). The rapid increase in house prices from 1997 also encouraged many new investors to enter the BTL market.[3]

Rental demand

The growth of private renting was not only due to increased supply from individual investors who were now willing to put their money into modern residential lettings; it also resulted from the rising demand for such accommodation. The past two decades has witnessed an expansion in the number of single-person households, including young people and older, divorced or separated adults. The increase in the average age at which people marry or have children has also helped to boost the number of people wishing to rent their home (Ball, 2006; Holmans, 1995). Thus, demographic and social change has been an important part of the recovery of private renting.

In addition, the increase in the proportion of school-leavers going into higher education has further fuelled the demand for privately rented accommodation. Students now account for one in ten private tenants, which is about three times their share of the market in 1988 (Kemp, 2004). As a result, student housing has become a sizable and distinct market niche in the rental-housing sector in university towns (Rugg *et al.*, 2002). Indeed, one notable feature of the student housing market has been the emergence of large-scale student housing companies such as Unite, letting high-quality student blocks akin to halls of residence in university towns such as Sheffield, Birmingham and Bristol.

Meanwhile, there has been a marked increase in the average age of first-time buyers and a corresponding increase in the proportion of adults under 35 years renting their home privately (Holmans, 1995). In addition to the social and demographic developments already mentioned, this delay in house purchase and increase in private renting reflected a number of financial factors. In the first place, the shift in higher-education student support from grants to loans has also helped to boost the demand for private renting. Most newly graduated students now have substantial loans to repay, thereby reducing their ability to save up for house purchase and potentially delaying their entry into owner-occupation (Andrew, 2006).

Secondly, rental demand was also fuelled by the sharp, decade-long rise in house prices from the mid-1990s, which outstripped earnings growth and made owner-occupation less affordable to low- to medium-income households (Andrew, 2006). Third, the phasing out of mortgage-interest relief for home-owners may also have made house purchase more expensive relative to renting, especially for younger households. In many locations it became cheaper to rent than to buy a house or flat (Wilcox, 2007).

At the lower end of the market, shortages of social rental housing, especially in areas of high demand, boosted the demand for private renting from people who were not a priority for rehousing but could not afford to buy their home. This is a significant segment of the market. Indeed, according to the Survey of English Housing, in 2006–7 two out of five private tenants said that they did not expect to be able to become homeowners in the future. Meanwhile, there is evidence that dissatisfaction with social housing has led to a small, but not insubstantial, exodus of tenants from that sector into private renting in search of a better home or neighbourhood (Kemp, 2004).

The influx of economic migrants, especially since the expansion of the European Union to include countries in Eastern Europe, has further increased demand for private rental accommodation, including houses in multiple occupation (Whitehead, 2008). Many of these migrants do not have the resources to purchase their home and some intend staying only temporarily; in either case, most are unlikely to gain access to social housing. Hence the private rental market, as Thomas (2006, p. 6) has pointed out, is 'the obvious default tenure on arrival' for most migrants arriving in Britain.

Looking ahead

As the partial recovery over the past several decades has made clear, there is a substantial demand for privately rented homes in Britain, especially from new and mobile households. Over the medium to long term, the likely continued growth of single-person and childless households, as well as continued immigration, will ensure that a significant minority of people will wish or need to rent privately. The long-term demand for private renting will also be underpinned by economic factors. If, as seems very likely, new housing construction remains below the level of household formation (though the two are not unrelated), long-term upward pressure on real house prices will continue to make it difficult for first-time buyers to enter the market. Likewise, even when the 'credit crunch' is over, it seems likely that banks and building societies will take a more prudent approach to lending than they did in the years leading up to it. Meanwhile, constraints on the expansion of new social housing are likely to further underpin continued demand for private renting from low-income households. The reliance of many such tenants on the local housing allowance, however, may limit their ease of access into the private rental market unless significant improvements can be made in the speed and efficiency of administration of this benefit by local authorities (Kemp, 2006).

On the supply side, the willingness of investors to enter or remain in the sector is likely to continue. There appears to be little risk of a return to rent control to frighten off investors. The reaction of the Labour Government to the independent review of the future of private renting that it commissioned (Rugg and Rhodes, 2008) suggests that it is keen to further encourage investment in the sector. The possible return of a Conservative Government in the next general election is unlikely to disturb the political consensus about private renting.[4]

Nevertheless, if the very existence of private renting is now secure, the immediate future is somewhat uncertain as a result of the credit crunch and its impacts on the housing market, mortgage-lending and the wider economy. It is widely accepted that the current financial crisis is the most serious since the Great Depression of the interwar years. But the likely depth and duration of the housing-market slump, and the economic recession more generally, are not yet apparent.

It seems likely, however, that rent arrears among private tenants and possession actions by mortgage-lenders against marginal buy-to-let landlords are both likely to increase among those who become unemployed or otherwise get into financial difficulties. Mortgage arrears and possession actions against BTL landlords are especially likely among those who bought properties between 2005 and 2007. This is for two reasons. First, because mortgage lenders relaxed their lending terms in this period, these landlords are more likely than earlier BTL borrowers to have a high loan-to-value ratio and low rental cover.[5] Second, because these land-lords invested shortly before the peak in house prices, they will more affected by the subsequent fall in values and hence more likely to experience negative equity.

Increased possessions against landlords and owner-occupiers who are in mort-gage arrears will result in the banks and building societies becoming landlords by default until they can sell them when prices and transactions eventually recover, as happened in the early 1990s housing market slump (Crook and Kemp, 1996b). The current downturn is also likely to increase once again both the supply of and demand for privately rented homes among new property slump landlords. It is also likely to create demand for private renting from households who might otherwise have bought their home, but are waiting for prices to stop falling. Rising unem-ployment will also reduce the number of renters that are able to move into the owner-occupied housing market.

While the fall in house values will reverse the capital gains that many landlords have seen over the past decade, it should also increase rental yields, thereby making buy-to-let attractive for investors who can obtain mortgage finance to buy new properties. The possibility of an increase in yields, however, may be reduced by a decline in rents if the increase in rental demand from tenants is outweighed by the rise in supply from property slump landlords.

When the fall in house prices begins to bottom-out, buy-to-let may prove to be attractive to investors looking for long-term capital gains, for the best time for landlords to buy is near the trough rather than the peak of the house price cycle. Thus, although some landlords may suffer in the credit crunch, the housing market slump may create opportunities for long-term investors to enter the market or to expand their existing portfolios. Moreover, the uncertainties in the stock market may make the tangible investment that rental housing represents seem more secure than stocks and shares. The end result could well be a further modest increase in the size of the sector while the credit crunch, housing slump and economic recession last.

Conclusions

The future of private rental housing now seems secure to an extent that was not the case in the 1970s. The era of apparently inexorable decline has come to an end and there is also now a political consensus about the need for a vibrant private rental housing market. The sector remains a relatively small part of the housing market, but the shift from long-term decline to modest revival marked a significant turning point in its history (Kemp, 2004). Although housing policy, and in particular the 1988 Housing Act, was an important factor in this revival, other developments were also critical. The implementation of that legislation coincided with the onset of a deep housing market slump that increased both the demand for and the supply of privately rented homes. Although largely a temporary impetus, it was followed by important developments in housing finance (such as the emergence and growth of BTL mortgages) and increasing real house prices that, along with the other demand and supply trends discussed in this chapter, served to expand private renting.

As well as this new trajectory, private renting in Britain has undergone other changes over the past twenty years that collectively amount to a significant transformation. The sector has a much-improved image compared with the 1970s. It has witnessed a huge surge of investment and an influx of new landlords, most of them letting modern, often high quality properties to a new generation of private tenants at market rents.[6] Buy-to-let has become a ubiquitous investment into which moderate and high income individuals may decide to invest along with other assets such as shares and bank deposits. Likewise, while most people aspire to buy their home, for younger households renting privately in the meantime is widely seen as a more acceptable housing solution than it was in the 1970s. Moreover, the Survey of English Housing shows that a higher proportion of private tenants are now satisfied with their landlord than is true of social housing tenants.

Yet this transformation has been only partial, for significant problems remain within the private rental housing market (Groves, 2004; Rugg and Rhodes, 2008). A substantial share of rental properties do not meet the Government's 'decent homes' standard; over-crowding remains a problem, particularly in London; management and maintenance standards are often quite poor, especially in relation to older properties and houses in multiple occupation; and while the Rachman image may have faded, a small minority of 'rogue landlords' still appear to operate within the sector. Moreover, these problems at the lower end of the rental market are accompanied by a legal framework that, in practice, provides tenants with relatively little security of tenure. As a result, the sector remains a problematic tenure for low-income tenants who need long-term rental housing. Nevertheless, despite these deficiencies, the private rental market is now in much better shape than it was in the 1970s.

Notes

1. The 1988 Housing Act also abolished the approved landlord scheme, strengthened landlords' grounds for possession and introduced a new harassment offence.
2. This discussion is based on Kemp (2004).
3. Since rents are more 'sticky' than house prices, the increase in house prices meant that the capital gains were offset by declining rental yields. An analysis by the National Housing and Planning Advice Unit concluded that demand from BTL investors itself had an inflationary impact on house prices, increasing them by an estimated maximum of 7 per cent in 2007.
4. However, if the Conservatives were to privatise social housing that might polarize attitudes and mobilise opposition to private landlords, which in turn could threaten the political consensus on the private rented sector.
5. By 2005 the maximum loan to value (LTV) ratio had increased to 85 per cent and the minimum rental cover had fallen to 125 per cent. In 2007 the minimum rental cover was only 120 per cent. This compares with a maximum LTV of 80 per cent and minimum rental cover of 130 per cent in 2004 (Council of Mortgage Lenders data).
6. On the debit side, it is important to note that the BTL revolution (Ball, 2006) has included not just long-term and professional landlords but also amateur and naive individuals, some of whom became over-leveraged or had only short-term investment horizons. Moreover, residential lettings have so far remained an unattractive investment to financial institutions, notwithstanding government initiatives to attract them into the sector.

References

Andrew, M. (2006) 'Housing tenure choices by the young', *Housing Finance*, 7, June, 1–13.

Bailey, N. (1999) 'Deregulated private renting: a decade of change in Scotland', *Netherlands Journal of Housing and the Build Environment*, 14, 363–84.

Ball, M. (2006) *Buy to Let: The Revolution – 10 Years On*, London: Association of Residential Letting Agents.

Banting, K.G. (1979) *Poverty, Politics and Policy*, London: Macmillan.

Barker, K. (2003) *Review of Housing Supply. Interim Report – Analysis*, London: The Stationery Office.

Best, R., Kemp, P.A., Coleman, D., Merrett, S. and Crook, T. (1992) *The Future of Private Renting*, York: Joseph Rowntree Foundation.

Crook, A.D.H. (1986) 'Privatisation of housing and the impact of the Conservative Government's initiatives on low-cost home ownership and private renting between 1979 and 1984 in England and Wales: 4. Private renting', *Environment and Planning A,* 18, 1029–37.

Crook, A.D.H. and Kemp, P.A. (1996a) *Private Landlords in England,* London: HMSO.

Crook, A.D.H. and Kemp, P.A. (1996b) 'The revival of private rented housing in Britain', *Housing Studies,* 11(1), 51–68.

Crook, A.D.H. and Kemp, P.A. (1999) *Financial Institutions and Private Rented Housing,* York: Joseph Rowntree Foundation & York Publishing Services.

Crook, A.D.H. and Kemp, P.A. (2002) 'Housing investment trusts: A new structure of rental housing provision?', *Housing Studies,* 17(5), 741–53.

Crook, A.D.H., Hughes, J. and Kemp, P.A. (1995) *The Supply of Privately Rented Homes: Today and Tomorrow,* York: Joseph Rowntree Foundation.

Crook, A.D.H., Hughes, J. and Kemp, P.A. (1998) 'Housing investment trusts and the returns from residential lettings', *Journal of Property Research,* 15(3), 229–48.

Cullingworth, J.B. (1963) *Housing in Transition,* London: Heineman.

Cullingworth, J.B. (1979) *Essays on Housing Policy,* George Allen & Unwin.

DoE (Department of the Environment) (1977*) Housing Policy Review,* London: HMSO.

DoE (Department of the Environment) (1987) *Housing: The Government's Proposals,* London: HMSO.

Doling, J. and Davies, M. (1984) *The Public Control of Privately Rented Housing,* Aldershot: Gower.

Donnison, D.V. (1967) *The Government of Housing,* Harmondsworth: Penguin.

Dorling, D. and Cornford, J. (1995) 'Who has negative equity? How house price falls in Britain have hit different groups of home buyers', *Housing Studies,* 10, 151–78.

Down, D., Holmans, A.E. and Small, H. (1994) 'Trends in the size of the private rented sector in England', *Housing Finance,* 22, 7–11.

Eversley, D. (1975) 'Landlords' slow goodbye', *New Society,* 31, 119–21.

Forrest, R. and Murie, A. (1994) 'Home ownership in recession', *Housing Studies,* 9, 55–74.

Francis Committee (1971) *Report of the Committee on the Rent Acts,* London: HMSO.

Gibb, K. and Nygaard, C. (2005) 'The impact of buy to let residential investment on local housing markets: evidence from Glasgow', *European Journal of Housing Policy,* 5(3), 301–26.

Gray, F. (1982) 'Owner occupation and social relations', in S. Merrett (with F. Gray) (eds) *Owner Occupation in Britain,* London: Routledge and Kegan Paul.

Groves, R. (2004) *Understanding the Private Rented Sector,* Birmingham: Centre for Urban and Regional Research.

Hamnett, C. and Randolph, B. (1988) *Cities, Housing and Profits*, London: Hutchinson.

Holmans, A.E. (1987) *Housing Policy in Britain*, London: Croom Helm.

Holmans, A.E. (1995) 'Where have all the first-time buyers gone?', *Housing Finance*, February.

Hughes, J. (1995) 'The impact of the Business Expansion Scheme on the supply of privately rented housing', *Journal of Property Finance*, 6(2), 21–33.

Jones, C. (2007) 'Private investment in rented housing and the role of REITs', *European Journal of Housing Policy*, 7(4), 383–400.

Kemp, P.A. (1987) 'Some aspects of housing consumption in late 19th-century England and Wales', *Housing Studies*, 2, 3–16.

Kemp, P.A. (1988) *The Future of Private Renting*, Occasional Monograph in Environmental Health and Housing, Salford: The University of Salford.

Kemp, P.A. (2004) *Private Renting in Transition*, Coventry: Chartered Institute of Housing.

Kemp, P.A. (2006) 'Housing benefit: Great Britain in comparative perspective', *Public Finance and Management*, 6(1), 65–87.

Kemp, P.A. (2007) 'Housing Benefit in Great Britain: a troubled history and uncertain future', in P.A. Kemp (ed.) *Housing Allowances in Comparative Perspective*, Bristol: The Policy Press.

Malpass, P. (2000) *Housing Associations and Housing Policy*, Basingstoke: Macmillan.

Milner Holland Committee (1965) *Report of the Committee on Housing in Greater London*, Cmnd 2605, London: HMSO.

Nevitt, A.A. (1966) *Housing, Taxation and Subsidies: A Study of Housing in the United Kingdom*, Nelson.

Paley, B. (1978) *Attitudes to Letting in 1976*, London: HMSO.

Rhodes, D. and Bevan, M. (2003) *Private Landlords and Buy-to- Let*, York: Centre for Housing Policy, University of York.

Rugg, J. and Rhodes, D. (2008) *The Private Rented Sector: Its Contribution and Potential*, York: Centre for Housing Policy, University of York.

Rugg, J., Rhodes, D. and Jones, A. (2002) 'Studying a niche market: UK students and the private rented sector', *Housing Studies*, 17(2), 289–303.

Scanlon, K. and Whitehead, C. (2005) *The Profile and Intentions of Buy-to-Let Investors*, London: Council of Mortgage Lenders.

Stafford, B. and Doling, J. (1981) *Rent Control and Rent Regulation in England and Wales 1915–1980*, Centre for Urban and Regional Studies Occasional Paper No. 2, New Series, Birmingham: University of Birmingham.

Thomas, R. (2006) 'The growth of buy-to-let', *Housing Finance*, 9, September, 1–14.

Todd, J.E., Bone, M. and Noble, I. (1982) *The Privately Rented Sector in 1978*, London: HMSO.

Whitehead, C. and Kleinman, M. (1989) 'The private rented sector and the Housing Act 1988' in M. Brenton and C. Ungerson (eds) *Social Policy Review 1988–9*, London: Longman, 65–84.

Whitehead, C.M.E. (2008) Presentation to the ENHR Workshop on Private Rented Markets, Dublin, 21–22 January.

Whitehead, C.M.E. and Kleinman, M. (1986) *Private Rented Housing in the 1980s and 1990s*, Cambridge: Granta Publications.

Wilcox, S. (2007) *Can't Buy: Can Rent*, London: Hometrack.

8 Home ownership – where now?

Peter Williams

Over the last 40 years, home ownership has come to dominate the housing landscape in the UK in a variety of different ways, including government policy, household tenure and personal finances. Its progression to that position has not been without interruption or difficulties but the reality is plain to see, in terms of the size of the sector, debt, assets and the scale of housing and mortgage markets. Against this backcloth of 'success' we have a number of issues surrounding the rise of home ownership – some very obvious, others rather more hidden – and the purpose of this chapter is to explore how the sector has evolved, the role it now plays and how it might change in the future. Without doubt it is now poised on the cusp of change and it is important we understand future dynamics and how these might play out both within the sector itself and in the wider polity and economy.

There is a nice irony in writing this chapter for this book. When Alan Murie, Ray Forrest and I published our book *Home Ownership: Differentiation and Fragmentation* in 1990 (Forrest *et al.*, 1990) it had been in gestation for some years. We had begun writing it in the boom years leading up to 1988, at which point the market began to trend down to 1992. Here we are again, with a book conceived in boom times being completed in the wake of the downturn in the market that began in the summer of 2007. Observing markets and policy through these kinds of changes is instructive in terms of our behaviour as consumers, the activity of the market's institutions and, not least, how governments react.

As the chapter title suggests, the aim is to consider the future of home ownership in the UK. Partly this requires going wider than the tenure itself to consider its wider effects around wealth and inheritance. It is clear that the Westminster government, having championed home ownership, especially over the last 5 years, has been concerned about its wider effects on inequality in the UK. The initial response to this has been to seek further ways of extending ownership, to whatever degree, to an ever wider group of people; but in changed circumstances that drive now seems to be abating or about to change, at least in some quarters of government. The chapter will explore these tensions. Finally, writing in the eye of a market storm, we have to consider how current pressures will play out over time and what impact this will have on home ownership, the policy framework and the institutional structure. All the evidence points to a fundamental reworking of policies and structures and the assumptions which have underpinned them. If this is correct, then a significant unwinding is under way.

Looking backwards

In many respects home ownership has been transformed in the last four decades. At the time of the mid-1970s Housing Policy Review the sector could broadly be characterised as follows (DoE 1977; data is for 1976):

- 10 million homes in England, or 55 per cent of the total, were owner-occupied.
- There were 731,600 new loans (£6 billion), of which 92 per cent were from building societies.
- There were 273 building societies (1980).
- Around 45 per cent of owners owned their homes outright (4 million).
- While 76 per cent of heads of household categorised as professional were owners in 1971, only 48 per cent of skilled workers and 27 per cent of the unskilled heads were in that category.

Some 30 years later:

- 70 per cent of homes in England in 2006, or 14.5 million, were owner-occupied.
- There were 1,016400 new loans (value £154 billion), 14 per cent of which came from building societies.
- There were 59 building societies, though four of these have since announced mergers.
- Around 45 per cent of owners owned their homes outright (6.7 million).

The changes are striking. Underneath this – and partly explaining it – has been a major shift in the ways of funding home ownership and government's relationship to this tenure. When Malpass and Murie (1990) characterised the phases of housing policy, 1979 was seen as the break-point, with a new focus on home ownership under the Conservative government. Although it was the Conservatives who much later began the process of scrapping a central prop – mortgage-interest tax relief, MITR – there was no doubt this tenure sat at the heart of their housing programme and, in terms of the promotion of the tenure itself, the right to buy was the flagship policy. The Labour government continued this focus, after a slightly uncomfortable start when they cut back support for low-cost home ownership and completed the phasing out of MITR in 2000; depending upon the calculation made, the subsidy balance shifted from positive to negative through this period. However, by 2005 Labour was very clearly committed to home ownership and its expansion, as much for reasons related to widening the distribution of wealth and opportunity as for the tenure itself (ODPM, 2005). But as we all know now, that forward march came to a rapid halt over the next three years.

And in part the reasons for that were other major changes which had under-pinned the growth of home ownership over the last two decades. Central to the expansion of home ownership in the UK was the reduced cost and increased supply of mortgage credit. From 1987 onwards the UK began to exploit the power of the capital markets through securitisation (by 2007 some £257 billion had been raised by this method, roughly 25 per cent of the total loan book of £1.2 trillion (Crosby, 2008a)). Indeed, in the report evaluating English housing policy over the period 1975 to 2000, Stephens and colleagues (2005) identify deregulation and liberalisation (including privatisation) as one of the three most important policy clusters over the period and central to the growth of home ownership.

Our approach to home ownership has also changed fundamentally, from being a tenure sought primarily for the reasons of stability and security to one where, while those remain important, other features such as its investment potential have been fully recognised and exploited. This change has had far-reaching conse-quences. This has happened despite what some would say are dramatic changes in its tax-favoured status.

Relevant to this chapter, not least in terms of future directions, there is also the rise of the private rented sector and its transformation from a residual and declin-ing sector, largely unloved by local authorities and tenants alike, to something which, though still very varied, is more modern, of better quality, more accessible and more competitive. And it is growing and competing with home ownership and social housing as a tenure of choice (see Chapter 7).

However, although we can point to huge changes, even transformations, there are a number of areas where change has been slower and more limited than many might have demanded or expected. Examples include:

• The home-buying and home-selling process: although we have seen mergers and take-overs in the estate-agency industry (and a short-lived invasion by lenders buying up firms), the move to conveyancing factories, the arrival of HIPs (Home Information Packs) and the use of Web-based property search/ listing companies and automated valuations, the market still has many of the features long associated with it – high levels of consumer detriment and anxi-ety. Housing chains remain, as do gazumping and 'gazundering'. The Carsberg Review, sponsored by the industry trade bodies RICS, ARLA and the NAEA, and published in June 2008, made a number of recommendations for improving the performance of the sector from a consumer perspective, largely based around tighter self-regulation (Carsberg, 2008).

- House-building: again, though changed in a variety of ways in terms of the processes of construction and the use of components assembled off-site, we have continued to suffer from output of low volume output and still modest – even if somewhat better – quality. The independent Callcutt Review, published in late 2007, provided a more detailed assessment of the industry than Barker had been able to achieve, although the report was largely descriptive. Callcutt, the former chief executive of a house-building firm and subsequently CEO of the government quango English Partnerships, emphasised the need for local authorities to adopt a partnership approach with developers and their role as 'value' managers in relation to the areas they administered. Callcutt argued against action by government against land banks and against imposing requirements concerning the use of specific building methods. In reality Callcutt, like so much else, has been overtaken by events, and to a degree by the Office of Fair Trading report published in September 2008 (OFT, 2008), although this also reaffirmed the view that there was little evidence of anti-competitive behaviour.
- Like both the industries above, the mortgage industry too could demonstrate substantial change, but in terms of products the market is still dominated by short-term fixed-rate and variable-rate mortgages, as Miles made clear in his review (2004).

And there are continuities. Although it is 20 years since the first major building society demutualised (Abbey National BS), to be followed in the next decade by Halifax, Cheltenham & Gloucester, Alliance & Leicester, Northern Rock, Woolwich and Bradford & Bingley among others, the building-society sector continues to play an important and potentially resurgent role in housing finance. And this sector is so well embedded in the psyche of the British borrower that many still refer to all the firms listed above as building societies! Indeed, what is striking about recent events is that none of the mortgage banks created by demutualisation has survived – effectively all have gone within this 20-year period.

Home ownership, too, has continued to enjoy first ranking in terms of the tenure aspirations of the majority of the population, and that has been an important conditioning factor in the politics of housing policy. Certainly there have been periods when its popularity declined, notably during and after cyclical downturns in the market, but it is a tenure in which, surveys still suggested, there was unmet demand (so too with social housing – in terms of waiting lists).

As a sector, and despite becoming more heterogeneous in terms of the social class of its occupants, home ownership continues to have features which are quite distinct from other tenures (though the blurring has increased). These include housing type (detached houses and bungalows), location (suburban and rural) and income (both high and low – reflecting the many older outright owners).

And finally, some surprises. Although there was a notable lobby against MITR, few would have expected in 1975 that it would be scrapped (although it was on the agenda for the Housing Finance Review). Indeed, in most other countries where it exists, informed observers remain incredulous that any party or government could ever take away such a privilege without being voted out of existence. In many respects the withdrawal of MITR is an exemplar of successful policy implementation (although one might argue that it did not anticipate what the consequences would be in a falling market and, for a period, rising interest costs).

Following the same theme, the removal of the cartel arrangements for setting mortgage rates and the move to full market pricing was again surprising, given the vested interests that were being protected. The mortgage market is now fully exposed to interest-rate movements, hence the renewed interest in fixed-rate loans. Despite the rhetoric about Britain being obsessed with home ownership, the overall rate of home ownership has been going down in recent years (Halifax, 2008), as has the number of mortgaged owners (Williams, 2007), and the UK is not out of line with the EU average (see HM Treasury, 2003). As these trends suggest, the inflow of households into home ownership is slowing. While we have continued to have a booming mortgage market, the reality is that this has been built around the growth of new sectors such as Buy to Let (and the rise of the older and often outright home owner seeking to boost retirement income through property-related earnings).

Given that trend it was an even bigger surprise that government expressed an aspiration to go to a home-ownership rate of 75 per cent. This had been tried in Wales in the 1980s under the Conservative administration but was quietly abandoned. As Prime Minister, Gordon Brown, was known to favour home ownership, not least for its wealth and mobility effects and the strong link between mortgage-holding and employment (and in part this flowed out of Brown's support of the asset-based welfare approach he had admired in the USA and introduced in Britain). In 2005 Brown, then Chancellor of the Exchequer, and the Deputy Prime Minister, John Prescott, set out a desire to expand home ownership, and in the Government's response to the Barker Review (2004) the ambition to take it to 75 per cent was set out (HM Treasury and ODPM, 2005a and b). In reality this aspirational target was less ambitious than some have suggested – subject to inflows, the demographics were such that this higher level would have been delivered simply by the steady replacement of older renters with younger owners that had been building for several decades through the age bands.

This commitment to ownership was then supported through government regulation of the mortgage market, an expanded low-cost home ownership programme, a rather modest adjustment to stamp duty and inheritance tax and the introduction of home information packs (and energy measures) through which buyers were to be better informed about the homes they were purchasing. Certainly for many the Labour government was seen to be steadily abandoning its commitment to social rented housing and to be building a housing system in which private provision became ever more dominant.

With rising prices and transactions, alongside falling interest rates, Britain moved forward on what seemed to be a remorseless march towards its home ownership future. This was reflected in the creation of innumerable television programmes devoted to house purchase (in Britain and abroad) and to home improvement – all sealed by pointed reminders on how much money people had made from their homes, or how much value they had added to them. A few statistics from 1997 to 2007 highlight the growth, but also the changes that were working through:

- Gross mortgage lending in 1997 was £77 billion. In 2007 it was £364 billion; this nearly 500 per cent growth over the decade was almost uninterrupted (apart from a slight dip in 2005) and is indicative of the situation that firms and the market experienced.
- Gross lending on Buy to Let was £3.1 billion in 1998 (there were no 1997 figures). By 2007 it was £45 billion.
- Average UK house price was £69,889 in 1997 compared to £213,807 in 2007 – up over 200 per cent.
- In 1997, mortgaging for house purchase was £61 billion (79 per cent), compared to £14 billion (18 per cent) for remortgages. In 2007, £155 billion went on the former (43 per cent) and £129 billion on the latter (35 per cent). As this suggests, remortgaging became the new reality, with constant churning of mortgages.
- There were 501,500 first-time buyers in 1997, 45 per cent of the total number of purchasers. Median advance was 95 per cent, multiple of income was 2.37 and mortgage payments took up 14 per cent of total income. By 2007, there were 357,800 first-time buyers (down 29 per cent) with a 90 per cent median advance, the multiple of income was 3.36 (up 42 per cent) and mortgage payments took 19.4 per cent of income (up 39 per cent). Again we can see a market moving backwards – shrinking and changing.

From the early 2000s a number of commentators began to draw attention to the rate of house-price increase on an annual basis. With annual house price inflation in 1988 at 27.6 per cent, we then saw four years of house-price falls (1990–3), followed by a period of low house-price inflation. However, by 1997 annual house-price inflation (as measured for the UK by the government) was 8.8 per cent. It then climbed to 14.9 per cent in 2000, before briefly dropping back to single digits in 2001, and then rose strongly over the next 3 years (16.2, 15.7 and 11.9 per cent) before slowing in 2005 to 5.5 per cent and then rising again to 10.95 per cent in 2007. What we can observe is that through the eight-year period

2000–7 we had five years of double-digit house-price inflation. Actual average UK house prices went up from £69,889 in 1997 to £96,340 in 2000 and £213,807 in 2007 – a 206 per cent increase since 1997 and a 122 per cent increase since 2000. Little wonder that there were increasing numbers who said it could not continue. The UK was not alone in experiencing sustained and high house-price increases, but it was argued (OECD, 2005) that here and in Ireland and Spain, these price increases were not in line with fundamentals but were due to 'over-valuation' and therefore quite vulnerable to change.

The question then was what governments should do about it. In the UK, as in the USA, the government had not moved to curb house prices through higher interest rates or other measures. Indeed, in the UK interest rates stood at 6 per cent in February 2000 and were successively cut until reaching 3.5 per cent in July 2003, before climbing again to 5.75 per cent in July 2007. The Bank has no specific remit regarding the housing market (and it is not directly captured in its inflation measures) and government was not unduly uncomfortable with rising house prices, because they helped promote a 'feel-good factor'.

This is not to suggest government was blind to the effects. What is striking about the Labour government is the effort to tackle a range of housing issues and most notably housing supply. The government and many others had constantly questioned: Why, when house prices were rising over a period, did we not see an increase in supply as well? Indeed, housing supply in the UK had remained doggedly well below what demand implied, as Bramley argues in Chapter 9 of this volume. When Labour came to power in 1997 there were 200,000 starts in the UK and 191,000 completions. That fell to 189,000 starts in 2000 and 178,000 completions before slowly rising again to 231,000 starts and 212,000 completions in 2006 (and much of the increase was due to public-sector activity – private-sector completions were 161,000 in 1997, 154, 000 in 2000 and 185,000 in 2006).

In 2003 Kate Barker, a member of the Bank of England Monetary Policy Committee, was commissioned to undertake a review of housing supply. In her interim report (Barker, 2003), it was noted that in 2001, around 175,000 homes were built in the UK – the lowest level since the Second World War – and that over the past decade, the number of new dwellings built was 12.5 per cent lower than in the previous decade. Reflecting the limited supply, house prices had gone up by 2.4 per cent a year in real terms over a 30-year period, compared to the European average of 1.1 per cent (Germany 0 per cent, and France 0.8 per cent). The report suggested that as a result of these price rises first-time buyers in 2001 paid on average £32,000 more for their homes, and that in 2002 only 37 per cent of new households in England could afford to buy a house, compared to 46 per cent in the late 1980s.

She also rightly made the connections between house prices and consumption and macro-economic volatility. In her final report, Barker (2004) stressed that weak supply added to instability. She argued for an increase in supply to bring down price pressures with an additional 70,000 to 120,000 private homes a year (on top of the 140,000 starts and 125,000 completions). Although the report pointed to some weaknesses in the house-building industry and the need for higher stand-ards and better quality, the main focus of her criticism was the planning system, which was seen as both increasing costs and reducing the responsiveness of supply (major developments often taking three to four years to get planning permission). She argued for more land release, better infrastructure provision and more incen-tives for local government. Perhaps most contentiously she proposed a Planning Gain Supplement (PGS), a tax which would largely fall on land-owners.

Though government responded positively to the Barker report, in reality progress has been slow, and the PGS was abandoned, to be replaced by a Community Infrastructure Levy (CIL), which seems to have been largely neutral-ised. Politically difficult and now economically problematic, expectations for CIL are very low. Nevertheless, housing supply did edge up to over 210,000 (including conversions and reuse of empty homes), but this trend has been reversed as the market downturn and then the credit crunch impacted the UK housing market. Expectations are that private-sector housing supply in 2008 might prove to have been as low as 100,000 homes. Sites are being mothballed and development curtailed. House-builders, like mortgage-lenders, are facing a few bleak years.

The downturn

With successive years of record borrowing and continued growth the mortgage industry in the middle years of the decade was in celebratory mood (Zhang, 2006). New firms continued to launch, new products emerged and funding continued to be plentiful. However, in reality the tensions were mounting. Affordability was being squeezed, with the consequence that more first-time buyers were having to rely on parental contributions (Tatch, 2006 and 2007) and more were being excluded from the market (Wilcox, 2003). Home ownership was coming under serious strain (Williams, 2007) and it was changing (Samter, 2008).

House-price inflation in the UK peaked around the middle of 2007 (depending on the index used and on the region). It was followed very shortly afterwards by the beginning of the sub-prime crisis in the USA, when Bear Sterns, a major bank, got into difficulty in terms of the quality of its assets and the ease with which it could raise funds. This prompted a major re-assessment of all securitised loan books and the family of derivative products linked to them. As the scale of the problem in the US grew, so housing markets around the world, which had partly been funded by the sale of mortgage-asset-backed securities to investors, steadily began to see a contraction and re-pricing of credit. Both these added pressure to a market that had peaked, and began to drive it down with a pace and intensity that had not been anticipated.

In the UK, Northern Rock became the first victim of this contraction of funding and loss of confidence in mortgage-backed assets. The bank relied on securitisation to generate around 70 per cent of its funding requirements. Having adopted an aggressive growth strategy, Northern Rock simply began to run out of money as depositors began to withdraw funds and investors refused to buy securitised assets (Brummer, 2008). Having failed to find a buyer in the marketplace at a price it deemed acceptable, it sought help from the UK government and was 'nationalised'. Although the general reaction was to focus on the failure of a specific firm, its model of funding and its management, the reality was that pressure was placed on all mortgage-lenders, whether capital market- or deposit-funded. This was partly because of the closure of the secondary mortgage market, through which around 25 per cent of UK mortgage funding was derived. This then forced many lenders to seek to increase their funding inflow from savings, as well as to limit the amount of wholesale funding they were prepared to offer to other lenders. Savings rates were pushed up, which then had to be reflected in mortgage pricing.

The effects rippled around the market. All quoted lenders saw their share prices fall, weakening their capital base and thus their capacity to manage through the crisis. The regulator, the Financial Services Authority, stepped in and required firms to rebuild their reserves; firms therefore had to undertake rights issues and or/seek new partners. In 2008, Alliance & Leicester merged with Santander; the Derbyshire and Cheshire Building Societies merged with the Nationwide; the Scarborough Building Society merged with the Skipton Building Society; the Barnsley Building Society merged with the Yorkshire Building Society; Bradford & Bingley abandoned a rights issue; while HBOS and RBS failed to secure the level of backing they desired – RBS sold less than 1 per cent of its issue and became 60 per cent state-owned as a consequence. Subsequently HBOS was forced by market pressures and concerns about its capacity to raise funds into a take-over by Lloyds TSB. Nationwide Building Society took steps to gain access to European Central Bank funding by opening up operations in Ireland.

In April 2008, the Bank of England opened up a temporary special liquidity scheme (Bank of England, 2008) aimed at providing a vehicle for the bigger deposit-taking banks to exchange existing mortgage-backed assets (pre-2008) for treasury securities; these could then be swapped for cash which in turn could be on-lent. The Bank has subsequently extended the life of the scheme (its fixed October 2008 date was one of the causes of pressures on HBOS, a major user of the scheme) and it is proposed to make it a permanent feature of the market. It will however need to be open to new mortgages and to non-banks.

In the same month, and having undertaken its own internal review of possible measures, the government asked Sir James Crosby, the former Chief Executive of HBOS and Deputy Chairman of the FSA, to undertake a review of mortgage finance. His interim report was published in July (Crosby, 2008a) and his final report in November (Crosby, 2008b).

The interim report provides valuable background information on the nature of the UK mortgage market and its funding. Of the £1.2 trillion at the end of 2007 roughly £500 billion was funded from wholesale sources – Residential Mortgage-Backed Securities (RMBS), Covered Bonds and senior uncollateralised debt. Within that total RMBS stood at £201 billion and Covered Bonds (effectively more secure on balance-sheet RMBS) £56 billion. Since August 2007 there have been only two small RMBS issues (HBOS and Alliance & Leicester), with the external market effectively closed. So the UK market has lost access to around 25 per cent of its external funding requirement and the Bank of England is now providing the only real source of funding as it buys in RMBS in exchange for government gilts. Typically bonds require repaying within one to three years, so in addition to not being able to raise new debt lenders now need to pay back this existing debt (roughly £70 billion per annum). With no new issuance, those payments have to be made from existing resources, thus squeezing further the funds available for lending.

There are strong opinions as to what can or should be done regarding restarting the securitisation market and easing the funding constraints in the mortgage market. These range from the view of the Governor of the Bank of England, who said that nothing should be done to ease funding and that lenders should revert to using savings only, to the view of the industry, which has issued strong calls for intervention, without which, they say, there will be a serious housing-market downturn, which will trigger a wider recession.

Rumours abounded, casting doubt on whether the final Crosby report would make any serious recommendations and suggesting that it had been overtaken by the government's own actions in the Pre-Budget Report of November 2008 and in other packages. However, the report in reality offered a chilling assessment of the problem, pointing towards negative lending in 2009 (that is, repayments would exceed new lending), and it made the case for a major new intervention in providing government guarantees for new RMBS issuance by any lender up to a value of £100 billion for 2 years; it also made other recommendations concerning improving the transparency of the UK RMBS market. The government moved quickly to accept the core recommendation, indicating it would now go to the EU commission to seek agreement to implementing it under the state-aid rules. Market reaction was positive but lenders underlined the need for urgent action and for the guarantees to cover existing assets as well as new ones.

Fundamentally there is a choice between a slow work-out of the current position, with a longer and more painful recession in the housing market or even more widely, or intervention to achieve a shorter version of that recession. Both will impact upon home ownership and its wider roles, but while intervention might mean that recovery is under way in 2009–10, the non-intervention alternative will mean that it lasts until 2010–11, with an appropriately longer recovery time of up to six years.

This will also be conditioned by what happens in the USA. With the US government's take-over of Fannie Mae and Freddie Mac (the secondary institutions in the mortgage market that hold around 50 per cent of US mortgage debt) and then AIG, the largest US insurer, together with other interventions, the situation there is far from stable and it is likely to be some months and possibly years before the market recovers. The collapse of Lehman Brothers and AIG have implications for recovery in that they have caused the price of RMBS assets to fall further and thus set new lows in the market, undermining current assessments of value and the new issuance.

We are thus left with a downturn under way with no immediate sense of when the market will settle or where it will settle. Realistically that could be up to two to three years away and with prices, on average, at least 25 per cent down from the peak and possibly closer to 30 per cent down. The Pre-Budget Report fiscal-stimulus package in November 2008, the earlier housing-market package in England and the most recent announcements of a home-owner mortgage-support scheme are useful and relatively well coordinated exercises, but such is the scale and speed of the downturn and the complexity of the issues underlying it that we must still question their likely impact in terms of limiting the damage and speeding the recovery (CLG, 2008; HM Treasury, 2008a,b).

The transition

Depending on the macro-economic situation, the regulatory response to the credit squeeze and house-price bubble and the reworking of the mortgage-funding market, we will see a rather different home-ownership market emerge. There are two issues. First there is the transition problem – how we get from where we are to where that new market will be – and second, what that new market will be like. The market was already in transition, reflecting on the one hand the slowing growth in home ownership followed by its contraction, and on the other the reshaping of mortgage lending, involving the growth of new specialist markets.

The transition is from a market driven by a surplus of capital and strong demand to one where there is a shortage of capital and weaker demand. It could be quite painful. Significant parts of the market – for example, the sub-prime part – will be largely unserved by mortgage products and mortgage-lenders, with consequences for the existing holders of such products and for those that might need them in the future. Having seen parts of the mortgage market disappear, those borrowers who for all sorts of reasons have or will have a weakened credit history, may find they have little choice but to exit the market. This will increase the number of forced or voluntary exits, with implications for the stability, size and shape of the sector.

To a degree it also suggests that at least for a period there will be a re-injection of homogeneity in the market. Murie has argued extensively that fragmentation and differentiation exist across home ownership – that it is not one tenure but many, and that there are many very different home ownership experiences. Though the contraction and reworking of the market will in some senses intensify that fragmentation – certainly in terms of the differential experience of home owners – as we go forward with tighter 'entry rules' we will see less variety in who can become a home owner. This will impact over the medium term.

With respect to the transition we can expect the following:

- There will be reduced access to the market for a period until funding and competition are restored. Risk appetite, partly conditioned by the regulatory overlay, will condition how that access develops. This is already reflected in first-time buyer numbers – in September 2008 13,400 mortgages were granted to FTBs, compared to 28,200 a year earlier, with a median advance of 84 per cent of the value of the home (90 per cent in September 2007). Though other factors are at work, such as the fall in demand, we can observe that lenders are requiring bigger deposits and have reduced their income multiples.

- It is hard to see some sub-markets returning as strongly as before. The sub-prime market is the obvious area. In 2007 this made up around 6 per cent of UK mortgage lending and there are probably around 600,000 sub-prime borrowers. The reality of sub-prime was that it offered access to the market for some who used the right to buy and LCHO (Low-Cost Home Ownership) programmes, along with other groups, such as foreign nationals and divorcees. It will also have a bearing on market renewal areas.

- The buy-to-let market has also benefited from market conditions in recent years, both in terms of the supply and cost of funds and the capital growth in the property purchased. With both much reduced, this market faces a rather different future and there will now be a period of adjustment. Market conditions vary wildly across the UK, with large numbers of owners moving to rent out their homes, thus increasing supply and depressing rents. With falling house prices, total yields are rising, but for those investors who saw buy-to-let primarily in capital-growth terms, this is now problematic for at least the short to medium term. Recent data has pointed to a sharp rise in buy-to-let arrears and possessions.

- Lenders will curb funding in any non-core areas. This has implications for any market support for what might be seen as less-than-mainstream traditional lending. 'Innovative' lending is always easier when underlying market conditions mean that rising property values rapidly erode the risk of the loan. Such conditions will no longer prevail and when this is put alongside an overall reduction in risk appetite we can expect a sharp contraction of such ventures, at least for a period.

- Forced exits mean forced sales, and these contribute to downward price pressures by setting lower prices and eroding confidence. Auction prices are reported to be coming down (a 30 per cent discount below conventional 'market' value is the minimum), which suggests volumes are building up. Clearly the numbers of arrears and possessions will increase in this transition, and especially if unemployment also rises because of wider recessionary trends.

- Government can help ease the transition by supporting those who 'fall out' and by offering backing to parts of the market from which lenders are exiting.

The longer term?

Turning to the longer term and the new market, much depends on how the adjustment process works through. If we accept that the market has been driven upwards by a speculative house-price bubble, we now have to find a new 'equilibrium' level around which the market will consolidate and rebuild. Differing views have been expressed as to what this might be. Some have suggested the overshoot might be around 30 per cent, others much less. If we look at long-term measures (Wilcox, 2008), albeit somewhat limited to average earnings rather than household earnings, the following is the case:

- The long-term average house-price-to-earnings ratio for first-time buyers in Great Britain was 3.61, as measured over the period 1986–2007. In 2007 the ratio was 5.54, that is, 54 per cent higher than the long-run average.
- Similarly, the long-term average mortgage-cost-to-earnings ratio was 25 per cent, but in 2007 it was 34.5, some 38 per cent higher.
- The average deposit-to-dwelling-price ratio was 17.6 per cent over the period. In 2007 it was 18 per cent, but we know over 50 per cent of buyers were parentally assisted.

There are many other measures which might be used. The simple income multiplier long used in mortgage interviews would have been 2.5 to 3.5 times the person's income, with a lower figure used for total household incomes where there was more than one earner. There is clearly a debate to be had regarding long-term prudent ratios, and the regulator is increasingly addressing affordability and responsible lending.

Lenders recognise the importance of first-time buyers in the market and not least in terms of their role as the long-term customer base and in buying homes released by last-time sellers and movers. Some smaller lenders will take the view that they neither like the empirically proven higher risk associated with first-time buyers and high-percentage loans (Burrows, 1998) nor have a capacity to price such loans competitively in the marketplace and thus will not offer such products. However, all larger lenders remain active in this market and the question will turn on how high the market puts the hurdle for entry into home ownership. The first reaction to the credit crunch was to set the hurdle very high – nothing above 75–80 per cent – but there has been some gradual easing, not least because there were funds to be lent and profits to be earned. The market may thus drive the ratio back up, though it is not clear at this stage how it might settle. In the interim a number of lenders have moved to offer products which link parental savings and other assets with first-time-buyer loans.

There is significant market rebuilding to take place. This is easily illustrated by the fall in the numbers of first-time buyers over the last 12 months noted above (though we need to recognise that over time the lack of supply of mortgages was added to by a fall in demand) and the reduction on first-time-buyer and low-cost home-ownership products.

The new world?

The argument has been that we will create a smaller, more exclusive home owner-ship sector and one that for the medium term is more associated with homes than with investment. In the last recession, reporting on negative equity was common-place: it was a market measure impacting an estimated 1.76 million households in 1992 and remaining as a significant overhang on the market till the late 1990s. Negative equity has now returned and we have seen estimates that around 1 per cent of households are in negative equity (compared to 15 per cent in 1992). For most households this is not a problem, since there is no need to crystallise the shortfall. As long as the household continues to service the mortgage debt there is no immediate difficulty. House prices have been falling at the fastest rate on record in recent months, but the previous boom in property values means that only a frac-tion of Britain's home-owners are in negative equity. The average UK mortgage is for 54 per cent of the value of the home. However, the ratings agency Standard and Poor's (2008) recently warned that for every further percentage point fall in house prices, a further 0.5–1.5 per cent of borrowers (between 60,000 and 180,000) could enter negative equity. Noting that the trough in the cycle would not be reached until 2009, Standard and Poor's noted 'At this point, we expect 1.7 million borrowers – around 14 per cent – would be in negative equity'. Borrowers in the buy-to-let and sub-prime sectors were most at risk from negative equity: the com-pany argued that a further 17 per cent decline in house prices could put around 24 per cent of non-conforming borrowers into negative equity, compared with only 13 per cent of prime borrowers.

Given all of the current conditions, we can assume that the potential and pro-pensity to churn mortgages and properties will decline. A brief examination of net lending (new business), the scale of remortgaging and the number of properties sold is instructive here. It shows the following:

- Concerning net lending, the difference between all new loans granted and the repayment of existing loans was £106 billion in 2007, an estimated £40 billion in 2008 and might be negative in 2009; that is, repayments will exceed the total value of new loans.

- Remortgaging has been a major mainstay of the market in recent years, rising from 25 per cent of the total value of loans in the third quarter of 1998 to 50 per cent of the total value in the third quarter of 2008. However, both the number of remortgages and their value have been falling since the third quarter of 2007, and it is quite clear that many households are now simply reverting to the standard variable rate rather than seeking to find a new mortgage.
- In October 1998 there were 119,000 residential-property transactions in England and Wales, in October 2008 there were 59,000 (133,000 in October 2006).

Clearly the market is contracting. This reduction will bear heavily upon particular groups and areas – those people and properties seen as most risky. This will affect both existing home owners and those seeking to enter the tenure.

Wealth, inheritance and mobility

This is an appropriate moment to reflect briefly on housing and wealth issues. A fall in house prices and a return to viewing homes as places to live rather than stores of wealth may be welcomed by many. At the same time we have to recognise that property assets are a significant part of many households' wealth and that a range of assumptions have been made as to how that might be used – trading down and releasing value for living and other costs, borrowing against the property's value, providing an inheritance as well as potentially meeting costs charged by government against the home – for example, care and home improvement.

The rise of house prices and home ownership have driven up the value of housing equity held by households. In January 2008, Halifax estimated that housing equity – value minus mortgages – had risen by 9 per cent in 2007 to a record £4 trillion, up from £1.3 trillion in 1997. Holmans (2008) estimates that in 2006 older households (aged 60-plus) had £1 trillion of housing equity; assuming these households retain their tenure (and house prices recover), by 2026 this figure will climb to around £2.3 trillion. But because of growing longevity the inheritance effects are surprisingly muted, with an estimated £16 billion released in 2006 rising to £19–30 billion in 2026.

This suggests a lot of equity will remain 'locked in'. The equity release market is still growing very slowly in the UK and has been running at around £1 billion a year. This begins to suggest the case for linking parental and grandparental wealth to first-time buyers, who will be facing a significant and even more pressing access problem. But, of course, this will be selective, with that process aiding particular social groups and, by extension, making it even harder for others to overcome the gap.

The problem this poses for a Labour government committed to greater social equality is that home ownership is in some ways adding to inequality rather than reducing it. The government is acutely aware of the tension – hence its efforts to offer routes into home ownership for tenants and to expand other low-cost home ownership routes. To date none of these have been particularly successful.

Conclusions

Home ownership has occupied a central place in the political economy of Britain since 1945. Its broadly continuous growth as a tenure, supported for the most part by house-price inflation, a serious undersupply of new homes and, over the years, a ready supply of cheap money and favoured-policy status, has carried the tenure onwards and upwards. The size and characteristics of the sector were significantly changed in the 1980s and 1990s by the right to buy and by the growth of local authority mortgage schemes in the 1970s. By the mid-1990s growth had slowed significantly, but it was still edging up, reflecting the rise of the non-prime market. All of this has now come to an end (though local authorities are looking again at entering the mortgage market).

Having said this, the appetite for home ownership continues, tempered by a degree of caution and reduced expectations plus considerable constraints, at least for first-time buyers and for those with weaker credit histories. None of this suggests we will see a retreat from home ownership in the same way we saw the 20th-century march from private renting. However, the tenure is contracting and changing at the margins. This will pose new challenges in terms of managing the transition from where we are to where we will be in relation to the reduced scale and scope of home ownership.

If home ownership in the UK shrinks from 71 per cent (it is 75 per cent in the South-East of England) to, say, 65 per cent over the next five years, the number of home-owners will fall by around three-quarters of a million. This would be a combination of a reduced inflow – this is already the case with 25- to 44-year-olds – and an increased outflow (last-time sales plus forced exits).

Earlier in the chapter the funding for owner occupation was discussed. Funding via deposits would support a smaller mortgage market than we had in 2007, 25 per cent of which was funded via securitisation. Assuming we can increase savings by around £70 billion per annum (previous annual growth), it might take five years to build up the flow to counteract the loss of capital-market finance. There are complex questions here which must remain unexplored at present, including the issue of the propensity to save in a low-interest-rate environment.

We simply don't know how all of this is going to work through. What does seem very clear is that we will have a smaller funding market, a smaller home-ownership market and a more exclusive one. This has huge implications for other tenures and creates considerable opportunities for landlords in both the public and private sectors.

Government, too, will have to negotiate stepping back from its 75 per cent aspiration and opening up new avenues, not least around sustainable home ownership and a more flexible interplay between tenures. We have reached the limits of what the market is capable of at present. Clearly government could choose to help it to do more, as is the case in other countries. It will also have to choose whether to do more to boost private renting, social renting or both. All of this should be looked at in the round, suggesting it is now time for another strategic review – this time informed by a better understanding of the capacity of markets and recognising that cyclical behaviour has not been eradicated, as was long claimed. There is a real case for some quite radical rethinking regarding housing policy, informed by evidence and analysis, although it is not at all clear this is where the government is going. Although it will be interesting to see where we go, the stakes are very high!

References

Bank of England (2008) *Special Liquidity Scheme*, London: Bank of England.

Barker, K. (2003) *Review of Housing Supply: Securing Our Future*, Interim Report – Analysis, London: HM Treasury.

Barker, K. (2004) *Review of Housing Supply: Delivering Stability: Securing Our Future*, Final Report – Recommendations, London: HM Treasury.

Brummer, A. (2008) *The Crunch: The Scandal of Northern Rock and the Escalating Credit Crisis*, London: RH Business Books.

Burrows, R. (1998) 'Mortgage Indebtedness in England: An Epidemiology,' *Housing Studies*, 13(1), 5–21.

Callcutt Review (2007) *The Callcutt Review of the Housebuilding Industry*, London: Communities and Local Government.

Carsberg, B. (2008) *Carsberg Review of Residential Property: Standards, Regulation, Redress and Competition in the 21st Century*, London: RICS.

CLG (Department for Communities and Local Government) (2008) *Facing the Housing Challenge: Action Today, Innovation for Tomorrow*, London: CLG.

Crosby, J. (2008a) *Mortgage Finance: Interim Analysis*, London: HM Treasury.

Crosby, J. (2008b) *Mortgage Finance: Final Report and Recommendations*, London: HM Treasury.

DoE (Department of the Environment) (1977) *Housing Policy: A Consultative Document*, London: DoE.

Forrest, R., Murie, A. and Williams, P. (1990) *Home Ownership: Differentiation and Fragmentation*, London: Unwin Hyman.

Halifax (2008) *Record Fall in Owner Occupation in England*, Press Release 13 February, Halifax: Halifax/HBOS

HM Treasury (2003) *Housing, Consumption and EMU*, London: HM Treasury.

HM Treasury (2008a) *Pre-Budget Report 2008: Facing Global Challenges – Supporting People Through Difficult Times*, November, London: HM Treasury.

HM Treasury (2008b) *The Homeowner Mortgage Support Scheme*, Press Notice 135/08, London: HM Treasury.

HM Treasury and ODPM (2005a) *Housing Policy: An Overview Statement*, London: HM Treasury.

HM Treasury and ODPM (2005b) *The Government's Response to Kate Barker's Review of Housing Supply*, London: HM Treasury and Office of Deputy Prime Minister.

Holmans, A. (2008) *Prospects For UK Housing Wealth And Inheritance*, London: CML Research, CML.

Malpass, P. and Murie, A. (1990) *Housing Policy and Practice*, Third Edition, London: Macmillan.

Miles, D. (2004) *UK Mortgage Market: Taking a Longer-Term View*, London: HM Treasury.

ODPM (Office of the Deputy Prime Minister) (2005) *Extending Home Ownership*, London: ODPM.

OECD (Organisation for Economic Cooperation and Development) (2005) *Recent Role of House Price Developments: The Role of Fundamentals*, Chapter 3, Paris: OECD Economic Outlook 78, OECD.

OFT (Office of Fair Trading) (2008) *Homebuilding in the UK: A Market Study*, London: OFT.

Samter, P. (2008) 'Fuzzy Households, Fuzzy Tenures,' *Housing Finance*, London: CML.

Standard and Poor's (2008) *Negative Equity*, London: S&P.

Stephens M., *et al.* (2005) *Evaluation of English Housing Policy: Lessons from the Past, Challenges for the Future for Housing Policy*, Overview Report and 7 Themed Reports, London: ODPM.

Tatch, J. (2006) 'Will The Real First Time Buyers Please Stand Up,' *Housing Finance*, February, London: CML.

Tatch, J. (2007) 'Affordability – Are Parents Helping?' *Housing Finance*, London: CML.

Wilcox, S. (2003) *Can Work, Can't Buy*, York: Joseph Rowntree Foundation.

Wilcox, S. (2008) *Private Housing*, in Wilcox, S. (ed.) *UK Housing Review 2008/2009*, London: BSA and CIH.

Williams, P. (2007) 'Home-Ownership at the Crossroads?' *Housing Finance*, London: CML.

Zhang, P. (2006) 'A Trillion Pound Success Story,' *Housing Finance*, London: CML.

9 Meeting demand

Glen Bramley

This chapter addresses the question of housing supply and the policy problem of meeting the demand for new housing in Britain in the early 2000s. In a previous review of English housing policy since 1975 I argued that planning for new housing supply was, in retrospect, perhaps the most significant failure of housing policy in that period (Bramley, 2007; Bramley *et al.*, 2005). After 2003, housing supply was subject to a 'sudden rediscovery' after 25 years of neglect, and a major critical review (Barker, 2004) led to greatly enhanced attention from central government. However, the task of re-energising supply has been complicated by cross-cutting political priorities and, more recently, by a financial and economic tsunami, the credit crunch, which threatens to derail the necessary measures required for a longer-term solution.

Taking a broad view of housing policy in Britain, one of the key features of policy after 1975 and up to the early 2000s was that the overall supply of housing was neglected. This represented a profound reorientation of policy, which contrasted strongly with the earlier postwar period. Between 1945 and 1975 the greatest preoccupation of housing policy had been with promoting an increased supply, first to overcome postwar shortages, second to cope with demographic and economic growth, and third to replace obsolete and substandard 'slum' housing. Political parties and governments competed to claim ever-greater numbers delivered, and government used the public sector as a major agent in actually providing new housing.

The change in orientation post-1975 reflected ideological shifts and pressures on public expenditure, but it was undoubtedly facilitated by a perception (and evidence) that the fundamental shortages of the postwar period had been overcome (Holmans, 2000, 2005; Holmans *et al.*, 2007). Other policy preoccupations came to the fore within housing – subsidy distribution, choice, quality and management – but more broadly housing policy retreated from the front rank of policy sectors, displaced by social security, health and education, and reflected in relative shares of public expenditure (Bramley, 1997).

Housing supply suddenly came to the fore as a policy problem again because of the coincidence of a range of problems, notably deteriorating affordability in a booming market, dramatic regional market imbalances, problems delivering better public services in the face of 'key worker' shortages, concerns about economic competitiveness in high-growth regions, and worries about the interaction of housing with monetary and macro-economic conditions. Barker (2004) provided a convincing account of the adverse consequences for economy and society of a supply which was both low and unresponsive, and a comprehensive analysis of the factors lying behind this – notably the planning system but also fiscal arrangements, public investment (in both housing and infrastructure) and the nature of the house-building industry.

In the four years since the Barker review was published, one can see much evidence of good intentions by government, but the evidence of achievement on the ground is disappointing, to say the least. Stepping back a little, one is struck by three features of the policy system that make for difficulty, features which are perhaps more enduring and not without historical parallels. First, this is an excellent illustration of the problems of policy implementation in a complex and decentralised system. Second, it is difficult for the policy system to maintain focus on a longer-term agenda when the force of short-term market fluctuations is so powerful. Third, in a system dominated by and reliant upon markets, supply is critically influenced by demand, which itself is critically dependent upon the flow and terms of credit.

This chapter starts from the standpoint of broadly accepting the Barker (2004) diagnosis. The questions which are our main concern revolve around the apparent difficulty of actually delivering on this supply agenda:

- What are the most important things that need to happen for supply to improve significantly?
- Why does the policy system find it difficult to make those things happen, and what elements in the system's architecture are crucial?
- How far is any of this altered by the credit crunch?

I do not believe that national government in England (or Scotland for that matter) has lacked the political will to drive up housing supply in the last few years. However, yet again the gap between policy and outcome remains substantial.

What needs to happen?

Longer-term spatial planning

The planning of future housing provision, by which I mean primarily land-use planning and the associated arrangements for the provision of infrastructure such as transport, water and sewerage, education and health facilities and so forth, is necessarily a long-term process. Larger housing schemes can easily take five to seven years from initial planning consent to completion, or 10–15 years from first conception to full realisation as a 'new community'. However, the political and administrative world works to shorter time horizons, and there is always a tension here. The actual operation of the statutory planning system in England has tended in practice, until recently, to move towards shorter time horizons (Bramley, 2001; Bramley and Lambert, 2002; School of Planning and Housing, 2001); in the 1990s, typical horizons for Structure Plans were 15 year and for Local Plans only 10 years, and by the time these plans were approved much of this time had already elapsed.

It is interesting to note that in the USA, as ideas about smart urban growth and growth management have taken hold, the focus has tended to be on setting urban-growth boundaries with a relatively long time horizon, such as 25 years (Knaap, 2001). The point about longer-term spatial planning is that it represents a commitment to both the idea of growth and the direction and location of growth. It is the antithesis of incrementalist political decision-making, which tries to avoid making any decisions which don't have to be made today and which might upset some local lobby. In a longer-term framework you have to commit to larger decisions about land release – decisions, for example, about new settlements or major urban extensions, or about the redesignation or reshaping of green-belt boundaries (Bramley *et al.*, 2004). In practice, in the 1990s the system was 'muddling through' on minimal new land releases, partly dressed up in the ideology of urban regeneration or renaissance (DETR, 1999), and with heavy reliance on windfalls of land from redundant factories and the like. Longer-term plans provide the trigger and framework for necessary bigger decisions and about urban form and associated investment. They also provide a much larger pool of land which can be brought forward, sooner or later as the situation demands – a necessary condition if the key weakness emphasised by Barker (unresponsive, or inelastic, housing supply) is to be overcome. The idea of market-contingent land release is an interesting, if problematic one, but there is no question that the right planning context for it is longer-term spatial planning.

Government has gone some way towards this goal by committing to some large-scale growth areas and encouraging local or sub-regional initiatives for growth points, and by the way the planning system has been reformed. Regional Planning Guidance (RPG) was criticised in a Green Paper for being insufficiently focussed and strategic, and in particular for 'avoiding difficult decisions, for example in relation to the provision of an adequate supply of housing in the South-East of England' (DTLR, 2001, para. 4.41).

However, old habits die hard and some planners still use short-term market fluctuations as a reason for arguing that the future is 'too uncertain' to plan further ahead. In my view, that is a non-sequitur; the medium and longer term may in some respects be more certain than the short term. The people who will form households in 20 years' time have already been born, and economic growth rates over periods of this duration have not varied that much historically.

Bigger numbers

It is interesting that the housing policy debate has come to focus, again, on numbers. Numerical targets played a big part in the 1950s and 1960s, and some of the consequences attracted subsequent criticism. It is easy to criticise 'crude numbers' in planning, but difficult to escape the conclusion from a wide range of evidence that the recent supply numbers have simply been too small. Analysis in Barker (2003, p. 59) suggested an extra 70,000 (54 per cent) private-sector and 17,000 (121 per cent) social rented units were needed each year in England to bring real house-price growth down from its historic 2.4 per cent to the European average of 1.1 per cent. This drew on a national macro-economic model of the housing market developed by Geoff Meen, and subsequently developed further into a regional 'affordability model' (ODPM *et al.*, 2005). Bramley and Leishman (2005) suggested, using a different economic model, that a private-output increase of 39 per cent might be sufficient to achieve the same goal.

The body set up specifically to promote this issue following Barker, the National Housing and Planning Advice Unit (NHPAU), has worked with more developed versions of the Meen affordability model, as well as with more traditional demographic approaches to housing need and requirements, to produce broad guidance to regional planning authorities (NHPAU, 2008). This argued that the regions should 'test' supply scenarios in the range 240,000–300,000 p.a. 'net additions', which may be compared with actual levels of output in the mid-2000s of about 170,000. Even these high numbers were not expected to do much more than stabilise affordability or enable more than a very gradual reduction in backlogs of need.

It can be argued that, in some senses, even these big-looking numbers are not enough. Under the mainstream private-development model followed in Britain, new building decisions are essentially made by private actors: the house-builders and, in some instances, the landowners. The planning authorities have a strong negative regulatory role, in that they can refuse planning permission, but they do not have any equivalent positive power to make a developer actually build houses on a permissioned site immediately, rather than at some time in the future; nor to bring forward an allocated site for permission and immediate construction. The planning system is pushing string as far as private development is concerned. Clearly, market conditions and expectations will be dominant influences on these decisions, as will be the particular strategies and tactics of particular developers.

The upshot of this is that, in general and at the margin, you have to release more land through planning (in terms of plots or number of housing units) than you will get back in the short term in terms of extra completions.

In a more recent version of the Bramley and Leishman (2005) model we specifically tested what extra numbers of permissions would be needed to generate certain output increases. Typical findings were as follows:

- the elasticity of total output with respect to permissions flow is only between one-third and one-half (0.34 overall, 0.45 in some southern regions)
- the elasticity of *private* output in 2016 with respect to private permissions is only 0.25 (0.32–0.46 in some southern areas)

Hence, to get average annual output for England over the period 2006–21 up from 200,000 to 230,000 – that is, by 30,000 or 15 per cent:

- the flow of new (private) planning permissions must rise by 85,000 or 43 per cent
- *and* the flow of social-housing permissions must be raised by 10,000 by 2016 (20 per cent)

These increases would improve affordability (ratio of house price to income) by 10 per cent in 2016.

The issue of whether and why developers might hold back on developing sites with planning permission was rehearsed in some lively debates following Barker (Kliman, 2008). However, two official inquiries (Calcutt, 2006; OFT, 2008) failed to find clear evidence of anticompetitive behaviour, and tended to conclude that house-builder behaviour was rational in the face of a constrained and uncertain land supply.

Plans in place

The 1990s planning system was supposed to be distinguished from the 1980s system by being more 'plan-led'. This required up-to-date local plans to be in place in all areas. However, the process of getting these plans into place was slow, dogged by cumbersome and conflictual local inquiry procedures and scarcity of human resources in local planning departments. Even in 2001, 13 per cent of authorities still had not put in place a Local Plan, and 214 other plans were out of date (DTLR, 2001, para. 2.4). Reform of this system was foreshadowed in the Planning Green Paper (DTLR, 2001) and given effect through the Planning and Compulsory Purchase Act of 2004. The centrepiece of the reforms is the creation of new-style 'Local Development Frameworks'(LDFs) containing a clear set of policies and criteria for decisions and more detailed Area Action Plans for key areas of development. The statement of core policies in the LDF should be frequently updated to maintain consistency with national and regional policies, with a modular form of plan rather than a single document.

Yet despite the clear intentions, recent data suggest that local authorities are struggling to achieve coverage with these new-style LDFs. According to official research 'The majority of local authorities are experiencing delays in implementing the reforms and getting plans in place, and overall, progress has been slow' (Baker Associates *et al.*, 2008, para. 1.7). Reasons given for this include the system transition itself, understanding the new approach, uncertainty over changing national policies, underestimation of resource requirements and, in some cases, lack of local corporate or political leadership.

Lack of approved LDFs does not necessarily prevent housing being built, but it does not help, creating greater costs and uncertainties for developers and reinforcing the previous reliance on windfall and *ad-hoc* site releases.

Infrastructure funding

The issue of infrastructure requirements to meet new development, and the cost involved, has been as neglected an issue as housing supply itself in recent years. Suddenly, it appears to have become *the* key issue in the debate/negotiation between local authorities, regional planning bodies (RPBs) and government (IPPR, 2005).

Traditionally much of the major infrastructure required for larger-scale development would have been funded through local-authority capital programmes, but these were disproportionately cut back after 1975. At the same time the institutional framework for provision was fragmented, with the abolition of higher-tier local authorities in metropolitan and other areas and the privatisation of water, energy utilities, rail and bus transport, while some elements are controlled by national single-purpose agencies (for example, the Highways Agency for trunk roads). Where local authorities owned a lot of the land they could coordinate the development, including the infrastructure provision, and pay for it from the development profits, but local authority land holdings have been greatly reduced.

Barker recommended mechanisms whereby these requirements should be taken into account in the spending programmes of relevant departments, while the key agencies should be involved in the planning process at an early stage. However, recent evidence indicates continuing problems with the Highways Agency over roads and the Environment Agency over flood risk assessment and prevention. English Partnerships (or development corporations) could be given a lead role in assembling key sites, in partnership with other agencies, and Barker recommended that a Community Infrastructure Fund should be established, which regions could bid into.

It is difficult to get a reliable estimate of the necessary cost of essential infrastructure. In a recent study (albeit for an interested party, the South-East Counties), Roger Tym and Partners (2004) suggested that the cost per extra dwelling in the South-East would be of the order of £38,000 (including affordable housing subsidies). In recent negotiations around a shared tariff in certain growth areas, figures of the order of £15–20,000 per house have been bandied around. Potentially the most costly elements relate to transport, and these would seem to be 'as long as a piece of string', in the sense that meeting aspiration levels for high-quality public transport services might cost far more than the minimum cost of a connection to the existing road network. Here, cost depends on standards (of congestion, and environmental pollution). Some arguments about infrastructure costs are spurious, insofar as the people will be living somewhere and consuming water, electricity, telecoms and so on anyway, regardless of the number and location of new houses.

How will this infrastructure be funded? Certainly the announced special funds (for example, 'Growth Points') will not go very far, although they may help politically. Some of the funding may be found within the budgets of national departments and agencies, some of which have been greatly expanded recently and include enhanced capital programmes. In Scotland, serving a given quantum of new housing development has been written into the regulator-determined capital programme for Scottish Water. However, it is difficult to resist the broader conclusion that the Government is moving towards the position where much of the infrastructure to support new development is to be funded by the development itself. This could be through the existing Section 106 planning-agreement mechanism, through beefed-up versions of this (for example, Barker's proposed 'Planning Gain Supplement', now dropped) or some other form of 'development impact fee' (for example, the proposed 'Community Infrastructure Levy', or (where applicable) through the special-purpose development vehicles (discussed further below).

As pointed out below, this may be seen as a return to a recurrent issue of urban and planning history, the so-called betterment taxation problem.

Public housing investment

Another, perhaps more obvious, 'back to the future' idea is that maybe the public sector should invest in building a lot of housing. As Figure 9.1 shows, public investment in new housing, whether directly through local authorities and similar bodies (for example, new-town development corporations) or indirectly through grants to housing associations, fell dramatically after 1975 and never returned to comparable levels. Historically, the only way England was able to build more than 200,000 houses per year was when the public sector built around half of them.

Although there is probably close to a consensus that the government should encourage the provision of more new housing in the broadly 'affordable' category (Bramley and Karley, 2005; Fitzpatrick and Stephens, 2008; Holmans, 2000), there is less consensus about the form this should take. The idea that local authorities should again be given *carte blanche* (and subsidies) to build large numbers of houses to rent would probably not find wholehearted support from the main political parties, although there are clearly groups within them who might support this. As a longer-term policy this raises concerns about sheer cost, its misalignment

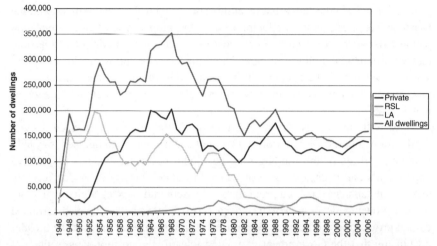

9.1 Housebuilding: permanent dwellings completed, by tenure, England.
Source: Crown Copyright, DCLG live table 244; last updated Dec 2008.
Key: *RSL*: Registered Social Landlord; *LA*: Local authority.

with popular preferences and aspirations, the damaged reputation and image of council housing (often most associated with the products of high-volume mass provision, but also with paternalistic and bureaucratic management), and the need for socially mixed communities. A more cost-effective strategy for the medium term would arguably be to rely more on housing associations (RSLs), with their access to private funding, to mix social rented with low-cost home ownership and mid-rent provision, and to maximise the use of (Section 106) planning agreements.

However, at the time of writing (autumn 2008), in the depths of a credit crunch and the early stages of a recession, the idea of simply building quite a lot of council housing rather quickly has much to commend it, on straightforward Keynesian economic grounds (see below).

A supply of credit

The housing industry is peculiarly dependent upon the supply of credit. Policy thinking over the last decade or so has perhaps been guilty of assuming a ready, competitively priced supply of credit for more or less anything. This was not always the case historically. When private finance for housing associations was introduced in the late 1980s, there was much doubt about whether it would be possible to obtain such lending, and on a sufficient scale. A generous supply of mortgage finance and other financial products at the going rate of interest has been more or less taken for granted since the mid-1980s. Similarly, it has been assumed that house-builders would be able to obtain finance to undertake viable developments. Unfortunately, in the midst of the current credit crunch most of these assumptions do not hold. The implications and prospects following on from this are discussed below.

Localities and regions not in denial

The last item under the heading of what needs to happen is more in the realms of politics and administration. It is very difficult to make local planning authorities allocate land and grant planning permission for new housing if they really don't want to, and doubly so if they can get their Regional Planning Body to agree with them. This is unfortunate, since the nature of the regional structure of England's housing markets is such that the regions which, from an affordability and need point of view, probably have most to do in terms of raising supply are the regions where the local political opposition to increased house-building is most vociferous.

London has the worst affordability and the highest housing needs on most measures, but London is already striving to build as much as it can on limited (almost entirely recycled) land resources. The South-East largely surrounds London and is the natural overspill area for excess demand from London, and indeed this region has always acted as a commuting hinterland for London, with a closely connected economy. This region tends to have the second-worst affordability scores after London and relatively high needs associated with housing short-age. However, its RPB has proposed levels of new housing provision well below those suggested by Government, based on previous household projections. The NHPAU (2008) advice on supply ranges suggested the South-East should look at numbers in the range 39,000–55,000, compared with the South-East's proposed 27,000. The South-East is particularly trenchant in its criticism of NHPAU and the underlying arguments and models, and argues that it does not have the environmental or infrastructure capacity to take this number of new houses (although it seems to be happy enough to take a similar number of new jobs). It is true that the South-East has a lot of green-belt areas and Areas of Outstanding Natural Beauty (and a new National Park), but these are man-made designations and cover by no means all of the region.

The East of England region is rather similar in its situation and attitude. The South-West, although similar to the East of England in several respects, displays a more mixed attitude towards development. Particular (attractive, potentially high-growth) localities can be resistant to new housing, but other areas are willing to contemplate more development if given some help with infrastructure, as demonstrated by responses to the Growth Points initiative. Generally, the further north you go, the less strong the housing market, the less acute the need for extra supply, but the more willing the regions and local authorities are to support growth.

Although there are difficult balances to be struck in some of these regions between, on the one hand, suburban, town and greenfield locations and, on the other, urban brownfield regeneration, there is less of a sense of blanket denial of the issue.

Architecture of the policy system

A new numbers game?

The most important Barker recommendation was that the government should set affordability targets, nationally and regionally, and that planning should determine numerical trajectories for new housing supply which would be geared to achieving these affordability targets. This represents a fundamental shift in the mode of operation of the planning system, placing affordability outcomes rather than trend-based household projections at the centre of the system.

Forward planning for housing had previously operated largely on a basis of projecting household numbers and then allocating enough land to accommodate these numbers, without much margin. This so-called 'predict and provide' approach can be criticised for emphasising the demographic, rather than any economic, drivers of demand (Meen, 1998), and for being a somewhat 'circular' process, insofar as the trend-based household-growth numbers reflect any past restriction on supply (Bramley and Watkins, 1995).

Affordability targets are currently expressed in terms of the ratio of lower-quartile house prices to earnings. Thus, house prices become the key driver of the proposed new system. This ratio might be criticised as a rather simplistic measure of affordability, but it is robust and can be shown to be a reasonable predictor of payment problems (Bramley, 2006).

One may speculate that the underlying thinking was that the system would operate in a somewhat iterative fashion, 'learning by doing'. If the price and affordability numbers did not respond exactly as expected, the supply targets will be subject to further adjustment. In the real world, of course, lots of other things change and it may be difficult to discern the effects of supply on affordability among all the other factors which may be changing.

Evidence and advocacy

Barker recommended certain institutional changes, including strengthening regional planning for housing by combining existing bodies and setting up an independent unit to advise on the technical evidence relating affordability to planning. This unit, the National Housing and Planning Advice Unit (NHPAU), was finally established at the end of 2006, with an independent Board and a core staff of analysts based at the Office of National Statistics (ONS) site in Titchfield, Hants. The core task of the Unit is to advise Regional Planning Bodies on the implications of planned housing numbers for affordability, but it also commissions research on a range of topics relating to affordability – early reports have dealt with such issues as Buy to Let, second homes, and the implications of worsening affordability for social housing needs.

The unit's most important output so far has been a document which proposes 'supply ranges' which should be tested in the regional planning and review process (NHPAU, 2008). Planning guidance requires the regional planning bodies to have regard to this advice. The methodology used to inform these ranges employed two independent approaches, the econometric 'affordability model' developed by Reading University under Geoff Meen for the CLG, and a more traditional demographic approach based on household projections and estimates of 'constrained demand' (for example, potential households unable to form). Both methods supported the promulgation of numbers ranging from above the current government target of 240,000 net additions per year up to 300,000.

It remains to be seen how far this advice will be reflected in future reviews of regional planning numbers, because most regions had gone too far through their current round of Regional Spatial Strategies (RSSs) for it to have been fully reflected. In particular recent instances where Strategies have come up for response from central government, the general tendency has been to increase numbers. However, by this stage the credit crunch was beginning to affect the market in a serious way; this has created a further credibility problem in terms of the gap between likely output in the immediate future and these ambitious targets.

We can only speculate about the prospects for the NHPAU in the longer term. Regions like the South-East remain opposed to this approach and are likely to lobby the political system to sideline the Unit, hoping perhaps for a sympathetic hearing from a future government of a different hue. At the same time, it is clear that regional and local authorities would benefit from authoritative technical advice and data on a number of issues relating to affordability. These include, for example the appropriate geographical basis for subregional assessments; modelling approaches which can link demographic and economic factors to housing market outcomes; detailed measures of affordability; the private rented sector; and the relationship of housing markets to labour markets and economic growth. The planning inspectorate would also welcome more guidance on these matters, as they often have to adjudicate on conflicting claims supported by a range of consultancy studies of varying quality.

Spatial (regional) mismatch

A dominant and persistent feature of the housing market in England has been the marked disparity between regions in housing-market performance and the associated outcomes in terms of affordability and need. Arguably, this reflects a systematic mismatch between regional economic performance and housing supply.

While both of these are theoretically subject to 'planning' in the broad sense, there is a marked difference of 'regime' in the treatment of economic development versus housing. The bodies charged with economic development responsibilities (Regional Development Agencies, RDAs) are broadly developmentalist in outlook and local authorities tend to be supportive of most types of economic development (except, in some instances, retail). Therefore the planning system is generally accommodating to economic development, even in regions where employment is high and housing markets are overheating (Bramley and Kirk 2005; Bramley and Lambert 2002). The Regional Planning Bodies dealing with housing, and the local authorities they represent, are much more likely to adopt a more restrictive stance – justified on grounds of environmental sustainability and infrastructure capacity, although perhaps reflecting an underlying NIMBYist political climate. This is particularly true in the southern regions, which have the highest rates of economic and employment growth.

The present system does not seem to have the capacity to challenge this structural imbalance. Central government has no real regional policy for England as a whole and is reluctant to be prescriptive about the regional location of economic activity, fearful probably of the potential international mobility of capital and jobs in an era of globalisation. Tentative proposals in the South-East to exercise restraint on economic development in certain areas were struck out in the 1999 Panel Report for that region, on the grounds that this was inconsistent with national policy. NHPAU might develop its technical role in pointing up the inconsistency of economic and housing plans, but evidence alone may not be sufficient to overcome these persistent structural imbalances.

Regional and sub-regional governance machinery

The government carried out a 'sub-national review' of regional governance structures in 2007. Regional governance had been a somewhat rudderless area of policy following the failure of a referendum on regional devolution in the North-East. The main proposal was to give the RDAs a leading role in RSSs. This can be seen as an attempt to couple the economic and housing agendas and inject a more developmentalist perspective into housing planning. However, RDAs have attracted criticism from the Opposition and might be abolished or curtailed if there were a change of government.

Meanwhile, there has been growing interest on the sub-regional scale of government. It can reasonably be argued that the most appropriate spatial unit for planning of housing provision and responses to problems of affordability is in fact a sub-regional scale, based around the concept of Housing Market Areas, which very often would tend to be city regions, including their commuting hinterland. Sub-regional housing partnerships have been established in quite a few areas, and local housing need and affordability studies are increasingly organised on a joint sub-regional basis. Several housing initiatives have emphasised the importance of partnership working (for example, Housing Market Renewal, Growth Points and Areas).

Having undertaken analytical work for a couple of sub-regional partnerships, I would observe that joint working at this level is still at a fairly rudimentary stage. Sub-regional partnerships lack a strong central body with adequate professional staffing and rely on borrowed inputs from member authorities. Even more importantly, they lack a statutory basis for joint decision-making and rely on a fairly weak consensus model.

A solution to the betterment issue

When discussing infrastructure funding above, it was pointed out that this inexorably led to the proposition that new housing development would in future be expected to pay for much of the infrastructure required to support it, and that this inevitably meant engaging with the long-standing issue of betterment taxation. Three previous top-down attempts at reforming this since 1947 all failed to secure consensus support which would survive a change of government. The bottom-up solution, which has shown a greater survival capacity despite its very uneven performance, has been the use of planning agreements. In addition to infrastructure, this mechanism has played an increasingly important role in the delivery of 'affordable' housing, such that by 2006 a majority of new affordable housing in England was coming through this route (Crook et al., 2002; Monk et al., 2005; CLG HSSA data).

In 2001 government proposed a reform of planning agreements entailing the establishment of a so-called 'tariff' system, with locally determined and variable, but comprehensive and standardised, tariffs. This was debated at some length, but then overtaken by a proposal in the Barker (2004) review for a 'Planning Gain Supplement'. This would have been a standard betterment levy (possibly at 20 per cent of the gain in land value), with the proceeds partly retained locally and partly redistributed regionally. This was debated at length, and finally rejected. It has been superseded by proposals for a Community Infrastructure Levy, still subject to consultation. One might observe that if the earlier 'tariff' proposals had been implemented we might have had something in place a good deal sooner.

Meanwhile, authorities in major growth areas continue to try to use the existing system, improvising ad hoc arrangements to apply a common approach across different developments in the same area, enforced through planning agreements. Use of Section 106 for affordable housing has become the mainstream approach and would operate alongside the infrastructure-related charges, although this mechanism too has been badly disrupted by the credit crunch.

173

Incentives

Barker's analysis drew significant attention to the structural issue of the incentives which local authorities face when considering options for new housing development. Other authors have also drawn attention to contrasts between different national contexts in this regard, and the apparently greater willingness of local authorities to allow or promote housing development in some other countries or regions which is argued to derived from this (Evans and Hartwich, 2005). The main incentives involved are financial and relate to the fiscal regime under which local authorities operate. British local authorities derive most of their funding from a system which does respond in part (and in arrears) to population numbers. Equalisation arrangements tend to ensure that they do not get a direct benefit from the additional local tax base *per se* (namely, the council tax and non-domestic rate). Government response on this issue has been muted, with some fiddling around at the margins on business development incentives but a reluctance to tamper too much with council tax.

The planning-gain mechanism can be said to create some incentive to permitting development, or at least to provide a compensatory mechanism to lessen the disincentive. That is part of the justification for retaining this as a bottom-up and partially negotiated mechanism. In the recent period government has also used specific grant mechanisms to encourage a more positive approach: (a) through the Growth Points initiative, which invited bids for supporting infrastructure funding associated with significant new housing allocations; and (b) through the use of a specific grant to the planning service linked to housing targets. These may help at the margins – one can certainly observe some positive examples of (a) above inducing local authorities to put their heads above the parapet and offer new growth opportunities. At the same time, the volume of funding involved has been modest, and these specific grant mechanisms are vulnerable to periodic moves to consolidate them into general block grants to authorities. Such consolidation moves tend to be favoured by the collective representatives of local government, and tend to be adopted in periods (such as the present) of increasing public-finance stringency.

A proactive development arm of the state

One can bring several of these strands of argument together by considering the case for having a more proactive development arm of the state engaged in promoting new housing development. When discussing 'bigger numbers' we pointed to the historical record, which underlines the major role played by the public sector in past eras of high housing output. We also pointed to the more specific and recent evidence that trying to promote higher housing supply is like pushing a piece of string, when most of the development is done by private house-builders. British planning generally lacks a strong capacity for 'positive planning', for actually making things happen. This can also be related to infrastructure funding, because a publicly sponsored development vehicle can pay for infrastructure up front and recoup its outlay downstream as prepared sites and houses are sold on. There are also potential gains in terms of urban design through master-planning.

Historically, the new town development corporations were the archetypal model for this kind of vehicle, although some developmentalist local authorities with large land banks managed to play a similar role (for example, Swindon). In the late 1970s and early 1980s, existing NTDCs were rapidly run down and asset-stripped. Short-life Urban Development Corporations operated in the 1980s and 1990s, although with a primary remit for urban regeneration, including a lot of commercial property. The successor body to these enterprises is English Partnerships, which is in the process of merging with the Housing Corporation investment function to become the new Homes and Communities Agency. This is clearly the national body which could take on this role, although there is also room for local-authority sponsored bodies, which might be constituted as joint-venture companies.

Large scale (re)development is a longer-term business, like planning. However, given appropriate public funding, such bodies could also play a countercyclical role. Following the credit crunch, there is an early opportunity to demonstrate this.

Political grandstanding versus consensus

Planning and housing policy sits at the interface between space, politics and markets. Planning for new housing is a necessarily long-term enterprise, and has an internal logic that rests on rationality and consensus. Yet both politics and markets operate to a shorter tempo and time horizons, and follow rationalities that differ in their perspectives and key drivers. This presents quite a conundrum for designing a policy architecture for achieving broader societal goals through housing planning, such as sustainable communities and affordable housing for all (goals to which most people would sign up, in a general sense).

There are certainly plenty of examples where oppositional party politics and democratic electoral processes seem to confound sensible measures to promote housing supply, such as those derived from the Barker review. At local and regional level, different political parties garner support by pandering to NIMBYist sentiment. The difficulty in getting plans in place stems in part from a reluctance of local politicians to commit to growth strategies. The regional governance structure is weak, divided, and overshadowed by opposition proposals to abolish or emasculate key agencies. The planning system remains substantially decentralised, and this is perhaps a necessary price for obtaining consent, but the logic of the problem of supply and affordability is one which requires a concerted response. There is a collective-action problem, because it is undoubtedly true that an individual local authority cannot have much impact on market affordability however much it builds within its administrative boundaries.

This discussion could lead to quite pessimistic conclusions about the prospects for policy to increase housing supply in the coming years. However, one should not despair, as there are elements in the picture which give more ground for hope. In particular, one should focus on those elements which still provide positive motivation for actions in the right direction. One example is economic development, the promotion of enterprise and job opportunities, and the greater awareness of competition between cities and regions and the consequent need for cooperation within interdependent parts of these functional areas. Arguments and evidence about the links between housing and economic progress will appeal to local and regional actors across the political spectrum. A second example is the promotion of affordable housing for manifest local needs, particularly younger generations struggling to enter the housing market. Even in the South-East there is strong support for significant affordable-housing provision. It is not difficult to demonstrate that the only way to meet this need in the medium term is to build more housing of all kinds, using Section 106 powers but in a context of mixed and balanced communities. A third example is infrastructure – for example, public-transport improvements or new schools which people want to see in their area. The way to get these will be to capture development gains through planning agreements and/or CIL, together with attracting grants from government which will be linked to growth promotion.

The credit crunch

What happened and why?

During 2007 the 'sub-prime' part of the US mortgage market began to give concern. As the US housing market weakened, losses began to mount in parts of the market and defaults on sub-prime lending escalated rapidly. It then emerged that many of these loans had been 'securitised' – bundled up with other loans and sold on to third parties, including many banks in Europe and elsewhere. Suddenly many institutions found that they had 'assets' on their books which were of very uncertain worth. The chain reaction this started initially involved banks and other financial institutions ceasing to be willing to buy mortgage-backed securities. This dealt a mortal blow to banks heavily reliant on this mechanism, notably Northern Rock in the UK, which experienced a bank run, leading to rescue efforts and government guarantees to savers and ending in full nationalisation. The crisis widened as banks became increasingly unwilling to lend to each other, for any purpose. This reluctance stemmed from a loss of confidence in the solvency, as well as the liquidity, of banks, resulting from the write-down of mortgage-backed securities and other complex derivative products. The crisis deepened as more institutions had to be rescued, nationalised, or in one key case (Lehman Brothers) allowed to go under. The crisis culminated (one hopes!) in October 2008 with concerted international bank-rescue moves by a range of governments, entailing massive lending and in some cases partial nationalisation of banks.

The economic repercussions of this crisis are now spreading rapidly. Mortgage lending has fallen to a fraction of its previous level. Therefore, although transaction numbers have fallen, inevitably house prices are now falling. House-builders are struggling to sell their stock in hand and cutting back new build numbers drastically. Jobs are being lost or threatened in the previously dynamic financial-service industries. Bank lending to business has also been curtailed, leading to cutbacks in investment or expansion plans across a wide spectrum of industries. Consumer confidence and retail spending are falling, and the economy is falling into a recession – the first for the UK since the early 1990s.

Why did this happen? The short answer is 'financial deregulation'. The US in particular, but also the UK and other countries to a considerable degree, followed a deliberate policy of deregulation in the financial sector, with an emphasis on 'light touch' approaches by regulators where they did exist. Deregulation plus low interest rates was a recipe for the promotion and rapid expansion of credit of all kinds, mortgage, consumer and business. In the mortgage sector, lenders and other intermediaries fell over themselves to promote products on ever more generous terms, so one saw the rise of loan-to-income ratios and the spread of 'interest-only' mortgages and other relatively risky products, with secondary secured consumer lending also increasingly piled on top of basic mortgage loans. In the USA there is much evidence of fraud and bad practice (for example, fictitious income information on mortgage applications), encouraged by the on-selling and packaging of loans, and failures by intermediary bodies such as the credit rating agencies to act as any sort of check. In the investment-finance field, this low-interest, low-regulation regime encouraged a lot of activities (private equity investment, hedge funds) aimed at making a lot of money on the back of a very highly geared or 'leveraged' model involving lots of borrowing. Much of this activity now has to be unwound, with the unwinding process driving down stock-market share values and further compounding the problems of solvency of key companies.

Getting out of it

This financial crisis threatens to cause a very serious recession in the 'real economy'; indeed some have likened it to the1929 slump, which led to the Great Depression of the early 1930s. There are, however, important differences, notably that there is much greater awareness of the potential roles of government in countering recession through fiscal and monetary policies to stimulate activity. The international context is in some respects even more threatening, because of today's greater global inter-connectedness and because of some major structural imbalances (for example, large deficits in the US and the UK, large surpluses in China). However, there seems to be a greater readiness to engage in concerted international action, although the formal machinery for this (the IMF, etc.) is semi-moribund.

The situation calls for an almost classic Keynesian policy of reflation – more public spending, less taxes, lower interest rates – even if that makes the public finances look even worse in the short term. The most important thing that needs to happen for things to get back towards a form of normality is that banks start lending to each other again on a significant scale. Until that happens, mortgage lending will remain very limited and the housing market will continue to fall. The housing market was arguably over-inflated – opinions vary on by how much – and therefore a downward 'correction' in prices is necessary and desirable, but in the short run painful for some and problematic for the operation of the market. Some owners get stuck with negative equity, while many potential buyers are deterred by the prospect of immediate capital losses, and lenders will continue to deny high loan-to-value mortgages. The market needs to bottom out, but there is some danger of an 'undershoot' because of these processes.

Sustainable credit and regulation

Looking to the world beyond the immediate crisis, it does appear that the credit crunch has changed not just the economic context but also, critically, the political *Zeitgeist*. One can say, with some confidence, that the high era of free-market liberalism and the belief in the unbounded benefits of unregulated free markets has run its course and been shown to have been wanting. In that sense, the parallel with 1929–33 may prove to be apt.

Credit is the lifeblood of a successful economy but you can have too much of a good thing. Somewhere between 1995 and 2005 things got out of hand. The mortgage market had no statutory regulation until 2004 and it is not clear that the FSA was fully policing the new mortgage code (MCOB) even after that. Consumer credit was regulated, but with some glaring gaps, and money was cheap anyway. The more esoteric investment products of the city were probably not fully understood by anyone, and not effectively regulated, owing to the obsession with maintaining the competitive edge of London in financial services.

Currently there is particular policy attention upon mortgage repossessions and measures to prevent or ameliorate the expected spike in these numbers. It is unlikely that repossessions in the UK will in any way approach the scale of this phenomenon in the US (measured in millions), and the announced restoration of the income-support safety net to pre-1995 terms, MCOB-13 regulation and new court protocols could serve to keep things in check. A mortgage rescue scheme has been announced in England, somewhat similar to one operating in Scotland since 2003 – a relatively marginal, and expensive, initiative.

Of more general interest for the medium term is what the typical terms and conditions of mortgage lending will be, once the new 'normality' is established. One may speculate that loan-to-income ratios will be curbed somewhat, with more attention to actual outgoings and other commitments. There is a particular concern that high loan-to-value ratios may not return, and that consequently the deposit constraint will become the major issue in access to home ownership. This in turn may lead to pressure on government to develop subsidised saving/bonus schemes and/or adaptation of LCHO mechanisms to address this issue. Also of interest will be how the Buy To Let sector emerges from all of this – there will, after all, be lots of demand for private renting from people who can't get into home ownership.

Implications for affordability and access

House prices have fallen and will fall further, and so have interest rates. On a simple view, that surely means housing is becoming more affordable, and therefore home ownership may become more accessible again. The government's target ratio, the ratio of lower-quartile house price to income will have fallen. That view is, of course, too simple. At the time of writing (late 2008) it is very difficult to get a mortgage at all. We may hope or expect mortgages to be more generally available in a year's time, but the terms will certainly be more onerous in certain respects than they were two years ago. The maximum loan-to-value ratio may be 85–90 per cent rather than 95–100 per cent. The effective interest rate will be well above the Bank of England minimum lending rate, especially for those a high loan-to-value ratio. The maximum amount lent may well be a lower multiple of the borrower's income. This all assumes the borrower is still in a job, but unemployment is clearly going to rise substantially.

This suggests that the flow of new, younger households into home ownership may continue to be at a low level, and the aggregate size of the tenure may continue to decline. New homebuyers will rely where they can on gifts and loans from parents and relatives to pay for deposits. The 'family circle' of finance, relatively neglected in Britain until recently because of the ready availability of mortgages, will become more important. This seems likely to reinforce wealth inequalities from generation to generation. It raises interesting questions about whether and how government should apply tests of wealth or assets in giving housing subsidies or assistance, and how practical this is.

There will be even greater competition for access to both social and private rented sectors. This is good news in the short term for social landlords in former low-demand areas, but in the medium term they may experience a higher turnover as these households later exit. In pressured areas it puts even more of a squeeze on groups at the bottom of the heap – for example, homeless people in temporary accommodation. Rents in the private sector may well rise further, despite the fall in prices, and, given the Local Housing Allowance reform, more households will be exposed to unaffordability problems in this sector. One may anticipate a further growth in sharing.

Implications for investment

The credit crunch has disrupted some aspects of Government plans to expand investment in affordable housing. In particular, Section 106 schemes delivering affordable units on the back of private sales may be forced to slow down, delay or restructure in a market situation where it is difficult to sell new units. Secondly, it has become increasingly difficult to market low-cost home ownership units, as part of the general mortgage famine. Therefore, it appears to make more sense in the short term to build units for rent, although these need not all necessarily be social rent units – they could be on an intermediate rental basis intended for middle-income working households.

In an earlier section the comment was made that, whatever the merits of public housing as a long-term provision strategy, it may have considerable merit as a short-term Keynesian economic booster. It would do more to increase employment and income circulating in the economy than most other mooted fiscal measures, including tax cuts, would meet an obvious need using a pre-existing structure, and does not commit anyone to that mode of provision in the longer term. The scheme could be set up as a competition between LAs and RSLs for access to grant, the main objective being spending quickly (many LAs may have lost the professional and organisational capacity to act as a housing developer, and may find RSLs are simply quicker and readier to do this). As noted above, much of the housing built could be let to people on middle incomes, who would be encouraged to buy it later, so generating capital receipts which compensate for the initial borrowing.

A concluding thought: marrying the economic and environmental agendas

In examining the issue of housing supply in this chapter, one is struck very forcibly by the tensions and contradictions between the short term and the medium-longer term. The post-Barker agenda was very much about the longer term, with a central focus on planning. The credit crunch is essentially about the short term, although it will leave a longer-term legacy of some sort. It is difficult to keep a policy focus on the longer-term supply agenda when the headlines are all screaming about market collapse, repossessions and the like. Those in the policy system (some local and regional planners, politicians and pundits) who have been in denial about the longer-term supply issue may find this a good opportunity to try to get parts of the longer-term post-Barker agenda spiked.

As should be clear from the earlier part of this chapter, I would consider that to be an unfortunate outcome. Nevertheless, it is worth paying some attention to issues which those who have been critical or sceptical of the Barker agenda are concerned about. A lot of their concerns relate, indirectly at least, to environmental issues. As someone who grew up in the 'leafy' South-East I can confirm that, comfortable and wealthy as many are in that region, the environment and quality of life has been considerably degraded, notably by traffic congestion and associated pollution (including light and noise), intensive air transport, and the like. There is popular concern about past major housing developments (public and private) that were 'plonked down' without proper services or measures to integrate communities.

Professional planners are concerned about protecting environmental assets and promoting more sustainable living and travel patterns.

More broadly, many would regard the environmental challenges facing us in the twenty-first century (of which climate change is currently the most prominent aspect) as being the most important issues to address. There is scope to tap into a lot of motivation and enthusiasm by being able to promote policies and programmes which clearly reflect longer-term environmental goals. That in a sense is what the 'Sustainable Communities Plan' (ODPM, 2003) was attempting to do. Coming at it from an economic direction, one may arrive at a similar or compatible position. After the smoke clears from the credit crunch, what should we be looking at as areas for economic expansion, investment and innovation? With 'financial services' clearly not the answer to this question, many are suggesting that environmentally-related sectors, such as renewable energy, should be a major focus.

Thus, in conclusion, I would argue that meeting the demand for new housing is a very worthwhile challenge in its own right, but that to do so in a way which is environmentally sustainable is the right way to go to motivate action in the current crisis. Good planning at regional and local levels is part of the answer to more responsive housing supply but is also essential to sustainability. We need good evidence and analysis to help move beyond sterile 'numbers' arguments, and the interests of local communities in economic development, affordable housing and better infrastructure and services should be recruited in support of a more positive approach. The public sector should invest now to lead the economy out of recession, while playing a more proactive and coordinating role in land and infrastructure development for the long term.

References

Adams, D. and Watkins, C. (2002) *Greenfields, Brownfields and Housing Development*, Oxford: Blackwell Science, in association with RICS Foundation.

Baker Associates, Terence O'Rourke, University of Liverpool, University of Manchester and University of the West of England (2008) *Spatial Plans in Practice: Supporting the Reform of Local Planning*, Planning Research Report: Communities and Local Government (CLG). ISBN: 978-1-8511-2974-4 http://www.communities.gov.uk/publications/planningandbuilding/spatialplanfinal

Barker, K. (2003) *Review of Housing Supply: Securing our Future Housing Needs, Interim Report – Analysis*. London: TSO/H M Treasury.

Barker, K. (2004) *Review of Housing Supply: Delivering Stability: Securing our Future Housing Needs,* Final Report and Recommendations. London: TSO/H M Treasury.

Bramley, G. (1997) 'Housing policy: a case of terminal decline?', *Policy and Politics*, 25(4), 387–407.

Bramley, G. (2001) 'Monitoring and managing urban growth in the United Kingdom: What have we learned?', in G. J. Knaap (ed.) *Land Market Monitoring for Smart Urban Growth*, Cambridge, Mass: Lincoln Institute of Land Policy.

Bramley, G. (2006) 'Affordability comes of age', in P. Malpass and L. Cairncross (eds) *Building on the Past: visions of housing futures*. Bristol: Policy Press.

Bramley, G. (2007) 'The sudden rediscovery of housing supply as a key policy issue', *Housing Studies* 22(2), 221–42.

Bramley, G. and Watkins, C. (1995) *Circular Projections: Household Growth, Housing Need and the Household Projections*, London: Council for the Protection of Rural England.

Bramley, G. and Lambert, C. (2002) 'Managing urban development: land use planning and city competitiveness', in I. Begg (ed.) *Urban Competitiveness: Policies for Dynamic Cities*, Bristol: Policy Press.

Bramley, G. and Karley, N.K. (2005) 'How much extra affordable housing is needed in England?', *Housing Studies*, 20(5), 685–715.

Bramley, G. and Kirk, K. (2005) 'Does planning make a difference to urban form? Recent evidence from central Scotland', *Environment and Planning A,* 37, 355–78.

Bramley, G. and Leishman, C. (2005) 'Planning and housing supply in two-speed Britain: modelling local market outcomes', *Urban Studies,* 42(12), 2213–44.

Bramley, G., Kirk, K., Prior, A., Raemaekers, J., Robinson, R. and Smith, H. (2004) *Review of Green Belt Policy in Scotland*, Edinburgh: Scottish Executive/ Government.

Bramley, G., Fitzpatrick, S., Karley, N. K., Monk, S. and Pleace, N. (2005) *Evaluation of English Housing Policy Since 1975. Theme 1 Report: Supply, Need and Access.* London: ODPM.

Calcutt, J. (2006) *The Calcutt Review of House-building Delivery*, London: CLG.

Crook, A., Curry, J., Jackson, A., Monk, S., Rowley, S., Smith, K. and Whitehead, C. (2002) *Planning Gain and Affordable Housing: Making it Count*, York: Joseph Rowntree Foundation.

DETR (Department of the Environment, Transport and the Regions) (1999) *Towards an Urban Renaissance. Final Report of the Urban Task Force under the chairmanship of Lord Rogers of Riverside*, London: TSO.

DTLR (Department of Transport, Local Government and the Regions) (2001) *Planning: Delivering a Fundamental Change*, Planning Green Paper. London: DTLR.

Evans, A. W. and Hartwich, O. M. (2005) *Bigger Better Faster More: Why Some Countries Plan Better Than Others*, London: Policy Exchange Limited. www.policyexchange.org.uk

Fitzpatrick, S. and Stephens, M. (eds) (2008) *The Future of Social Housing*, London: Shelter.

Government office for the South-East (1999) *Regional Planning Guidance for the South-East of England,* Public Examination, May–June 1999. Report of the Panel. Guildford: Government Office for the South-East.

Hills, J. (2007) *Ends and Means: The Future Roles of Social Housing in England*, CASE Report 34, Centre for the Analysis of Social Exclusion and London School of Economics.

Holmans, A. (2000) 'Estimates of future housing needs and demand', in S. Monk and C. Whitehead (eds) *Restructuring Housing Systems: From Social to Affordable Housing*, York: York Publishing Services.

Holmans, A. (2005) *Housing and Housing Policy in England 1975–2002: Chronology and Comments*, London: ODPM.

Holmans, A., Stephens, M. and Fitzpatrick, S. (2007) 'Housing Policy in England since 1975: an introduction to the special issue', *Housing Studies* 22(2), 147–62.

IPPR (Institute for Public Policy Research) (2005) *The Commission on Sustainable Development in the South-East: Final Report,* London: IPPR.

Kliman, A. (2008) *Opening up the Debate: Exploring Housing Land Supply Myths,* London: Royal Town Planning Institute.

Knaap, G. J. (ed.) (2001) *Land Market Monitoring for Smart Urban Growth.* Cambridge, Mass.: Lincoln Institute of Land Policy.

Meen, G. (1998) 'Modelling sustainable home ownership: demographics or economics?', *Urban Studies*, 35, 1919–34.

Monk, S., Crook, T., Lister, D., Rowley, S, Short, C. and Whitehead, C. (2005) *Land and Finance for Affordable Housing: The Complementary Roles of Social Housing Grant and the Provision of Affordable Housing Through the Planning System,* York: Joseph Rowntree Foundation.

NHPAU (National Housing and Planning Advice Unit) (2008) *Meeting the Housing Requirements of an Aspiring, Growing and Prosperous Nation: Advice to the Housing Minister About the Housing Supply Range to be Tested by the Regional Planning Authorities,* Titchfield, Hants: NHPAU.

ODPM (Office of the Deputy Prime Minister) (2003) *Sustainable Communities,* London: ODPM.

ODPM (Office of the Deputy Prime Minister) with Allmendinger, P., Andrew, M., Ball, M., Cameron, G., Evans, A., Gibb, K., Goody, J., Holmans, A., Kasparova, D., Meen, G., Monk, S., Muellbauer, J., Murphy, A., Whitehead, C., and Wilson, I. (2005) *Affordability Targets: Implications for Housing Supply.* London: ODPM.

OFT (Office of Fair Trading) (2008) *New House-building*, London: OFT.

Roger Tym and Partners (2004) *Costing the Infrastructure Needs of the South East Counties.* Final Report. Guildford: Government Office for the South-East.

RTPI (Royal Town Planning Institute) (2000) *Green Belt Policy: A Discussion Paper*, London: RTPI.

School of Planning and Housing (2001) *The role of the Planning System in the Provision of Housing.* Edinburgh: Scottish Executive.

10 Competitiveness and social exclusion

The importance of place and rescaling in housing and regeneration policies

Peter Lee

The themes of this book concern the transformation of housing policy and its increasing complexity within the context of the crises affecting the British state and economy during the mid-1970s; and the processes of liberalisation, privatisation and individualisation of welfare and economic policy that emerged out of the transition from Keynesian demand management to neoliberal supply-side policies. Previous chapters have looked in detail at the transformation in the role and function of tenures and the organisational changes in the delivery of housing policy in the UK. In the next chapter Rob Rowlands considers the meaning of the role of community and housing in delivering sustainable communities. This chapter adopts a wider spatial focus and emphasises how housing policy and, more specifically, the spatial aspects of housing strategy development have evolved in response to changes in the discourse affecting housing. Central to this changing discourse are issues of distribution and access to housing and how this has altered over the past 20 to 30 years.

Different interpretations of social exclusion and how this relates to housing and regeneration are of relevance, as they have implications for changes in the narrative of social exclusion for housing and the direction of policies designed to tackle neighbourhood disadvantage. Central to the argument developed in this chapter is how the competitiveness and economic efficiency agenda has demanded a greater understanding of the function of housing and its relationship across space; this is characterised as a process of *rescaling*. Associated concepts such as 'place-making' and 'place-shaping' have evolved as inclusion and sustainability have been framed within a broader competitiveness agenda. This chapter, therefore, examines the way in which housing and strategies designed to tackle spatial manifestations of housing and social exclusion have changed. It considers how the neighbourhood and estate (that is, the physical embodiment of 'community') have been *rescaled*, spatially, so that they are understood not only within the context of the city and region, but also in ways that engage with a more comprehensive agenda of improving competitiveness to deliver social inclusion. These developments have been for the purpose of inserting people into the labour market, reconnecting the economic and housing-market function of places and delivering competitiveness as a mechanism for tackling social exclusion. This reflects the importance of place, social exclusion and the rescaling of housing in regeneration and renewal policies.

Social exclusion and housing, differentiation and complexity

From the late 1960s, the framework within which housing and regeneration professionals operated had to adapt to increasing complexity resulting from the changing role of housing tenures and economic restructuring. The sale of council housing (see Chapter 4) had contributed to a highly differentiated pattern of owner occupation and the residualisation of social housing (Lee and Murie, 1997, 1999). The policy of right-to-buy together with a decline in private renting and an expansion of home ownership from the mid-1960s onwards changed the characteristics of those entering the social rented sector. As a result council housing (and social housing more generally) increasingly became a sector for the elderly, the unemployed, female-headed households and those with no housing choice. The trend was evident from the 1960s and resulted both from policy changes and wider social changes. The extent to which the social rented sector took on a residual role was not simply a result of sales and the decline of the private rented sector but reflected widening social inequality and unemployment from the early 1970s. The process of economic restructuring, from this period, therefore resulted in increased levels of worklessness, long-term unemployment and a growth in social inequality. This had a major impact on the spatial pattern of inequality and patterns of residence in British cities, which began to surface in the 1970s. The end of the Keynesian welfare state (with consequent increased unemployment, resulting in the expansion and prolonged use of subsistence benefits) signalled the demise of the social contract between state and individual. This changed the assumptions of welfare and resulted in a profound and prolonged effect on the spatial distribution of outcomes mediated principally through housing and economic policy. Liberalisation of financial markets changed the role of housing and its consumption altered the dynamics of housing tenures, estates and neighbourhoods.

Whereas the post-war era can be generally characterised as a period in which housing was dominated by supply-related issues, from the mid-1970s onwards economic and tenure restructuring meant that housing was dominated by consumption-related issues. How housing contributed to the experience of poverty is therefore a story of changing narratives: *social* as well as *material* aspects of deprivation became important aspects of describing and understanding poverty dynamics.

185

Poverty is primarily defined by a focus upon distributional issues: 'the lack of resources at the disposal of an individual or a household' (Room, 1995a, pp. 5–6). The empirical traditions of British social researchers and commentators such as Rowntree (1901, 1941) and Townsend (1979) relied upon an analytical framework that was highly dependent on empirical measurement of the distribution of resources (incomes and wealth) at household level. There was no explanatory or descriptive potential for differentiated experience of poverty across space.

During the late 1980s the term 'social exclusion' began to be used to highlight the epistemological tensions in poverty studies and how the experience of poverty at household and individual level could be best represented and measured. 'Social exclusion' referred to the dynamic process of 'being shut out, fully or partially, from any of the social, economic, political and cultural systems which determine the integration of a person in society' (Walker, 1995, p. 8). It was distinguished from poverty in that it 'goes beyond economic and social aspects of poverty and embraces the political aspects such as political rights and citizenship which out-line a relationship between individuals and the State as well as between the society and the individual' (Rodgers *et al.*, 1995, pp. 6–7). Social exclusion examined the underlying barriers that contributed to the denial of social rights, premised on a primarily relational focus: ' . . . in other words inadequate social participation, lack of social integration and lack of power' (op. cit pp. 5–6). Four key 'symptoms' of social exclusion were identified by Room (1995a, 1995b):

- concentration: social deprivation and poverty are concentrated in parts of the city and these disadvantaged groups or areas are cut off from the mainstream, contributing to social exclusion;
- persistence: social exclusion is experienced when there is a long-term exposure to poverty and social deprivation;
- compounded: the persistence of social exclusion is reinforced by processes that interlock and reinforce one another; for example, through the 'poverty trap' or the failure of services to coordinate or cut across one another; and
- resistance: traditional policy solutions are not effective as the welfare system – designed under different assumptions of household formation and the role of citizens – is not sufficiently flexible to respond adequately (Room, 1995b).

Social exclusion as a framework for understanding the dynamic processes of disadvantage had significant implications for housing, including the need to broaden the spatial focus (see Table 10.1 for a summary of the implications for housing of the social-exclusion approach to disadvantage). The four dimensions summarised above the way in which social rights and access to housing was changing and was giving rise to spatial consequences of social exclusion. Somerville (1998) and Lee and Murie (1997) provide an overview of 'direct' and 'indirect' measures of housing-related social exclusion. The emergence of associated concepts such as social cohesion (Cantle, 2004) was a response to

Table 10.1 Defining characteristics of poverty and social exclusion, and implications for housing

Defining characteristics	Poverty	Social Exclusion	Implications for housing
Scale and the role of place	Poverty resides at the level of the household or individual; participation standards (Townsend, 1979) define thresholds below or above which households or individuals are in poverty.	Individuals could be said to be experiencing social exclusion where they do not enjoy full citizenship rights or are not integrated into the market (employment), community (reciprocity) or welfare (access to services and welfare) (Kesteloot, 1997). While the focus is on the individual, the role of place and space in contributing to experiences of exclusion broadens the scope and scale of influence.	Housing investment needs to be seen in a broader spatial context – for example, the relationship between housing and the economy and existing distributional patterns of housing consumption and aspirations. The role of place and neighbourhood have important defining characteristics.
Distribution vs. process	Poverty is traditionally defined in absolute or relative terms. Relative deprivation is ultimately concerned with the distribution of resources and incomes within society. Logically, absolute poverty must result in death and therefore the relative concept must be employed, as there must be a relative judgment about the minimum intervention necessary to sustain life.	While there are contested definitions of social exclusion (Levitas, 1997), with some arguing that social exclusion remains exclusion from work and resources, it is the process of exclusion which in itself provides a lens through which to explore inequality in action.	The focus for housing should combine distributional (needs-based) approaches with process-driven accounts of housing production and consumption – for example, the role of planning and the development industry in processes of social exclusion.

(Continued)

Table 10.1 Defining characteristics of poverty and social exclusion, and implications for housing *Cont'd*

Defining characteristics	Poverty	Social Exclusion	Implications for housing
Relative vs. relational	Citizenship is dependent on participation. Theory of poverty suggests that as income goes down deprivation rises exponentially and participation rates decrease.	Social exclusion is concerned with citizenship rights, but whereas some definitions parallel a traditional poverty approach, it is the role of kinship and social interaction which differentiates a social exclusion approach.	Outcomes at an individual and aggregate level require planning and housing monitoring to provide cross-classification of spatial and household data to address the question of whether the same areas are deprived over time or whether people and households move over time.
Dynamics vs. cross-sectional	Viewed as cross-sectional and static. Measurement is at one point in time; 'official' measures such as the HBAI measure the proportion of households below 60% of median household incomes. This does not capture the proportion of households that have remained within this threshold over time.	The interaction between places and displacement (REF) effects or additionality (EP, 2004) of housing investment is a central concern for the analysis of social exclusion and the delivery of sustainable communities.	

problems of social conflict arising from increasing segregation between groups of 'difference' (that is, ethnic groups), which has grown in importance as a 'visible' marker of social polarisation and growing spatial inequalities. This comes at the expense of a class analysis, which is highlighted by the absence of concern over income and wealth inequalities in 'community cohesion' policies.

Social cohesion is a relatively new concept, but reflects a concern with the consumption of space and how this impacts on social outcomes. Booth's identification of the feckless classes related to concerns over the 'miasmic' effects of the working classes (Booth, 1891); the 'culture of poverty' thesis (Lewis, 1961), as well as interest in how the concentration of poor households was affected by the outward migration of middle-class role models (Wilson, 1987), reflects a concern for the effects of concentrated disadvantage. More recently a growing literature on the dynamics of place and poverty reflects the importance of this topic for the broader policy community concerned with tackling disadvantage arising from spatial inequalities (so-called 'neighbourhood' effects: see Friedrichs *et al.*, 2005). Much of this research has been stimulated by the policy imperative of mixed, balanced and sustainable communities. The conclusions to be drawn from this literature concerning the benefits from social mix are, however, ambiguous. Using a quantitative, survey-based approach to test neighbourhood effects and cumulative disadvantage, Buck and Gordon (2004) concluded that it is 'better to be deprived in a deprived area'; whereas a more qualitative approach led to the conclusion that ' . . . it is worse to be poor in a poor area than one that is socially mixed' (Atkinson and Kintrea, 2003, p. 437). Partly this grows out of a geographical literature, but it is also influenced by communitarian ideas and thinking, most noticeably through the work of Pierre Bourdieu (1984), Perri 6 (1997) and Robert Putnam (2000), who have emphasised the role of social capital and the importance of social networks. This large body of work identified important defining characteristics between households and individuals dependent on the strength and geography of networks in determining experiences of social exclusion.

The contested nature and role of place in mediating disadvantage and social exclusion illustrates the difficulties for policy-makers in responding and designing appropriate interventions to tackle 'place-based' exclusion. In his review of segregation and area-based policies designed to tackle segregation and social exclusion, Cheshire (2007) is ambivalent about the effectiveness of area targeting, arguing that national 'people-focused' policies on inclusion are more effective. These contributions demonstrate the way in which social exclusion has opened up the debate; the term 'social exclusion' allowed politicians to escape the politically polarising effect of discussing 'poverty' while facilitating the recognition of something new happening within society that needed to be captured by the political process. It therefore provided the opportunity to explore the relationship between *poverty* and *place* without the moral opprobrium of the *culture of poverty* thesis. What can be concluded from this body of literature is that the role of 'place' and 'space' in experiences of social exclusion and the incorporation of relational and social dimensions (that is, not just distributional and material disadvantage) into our understanding of poverty dynamics, has grown in importance over the past 20 to 30 years and has shaped policy approaches and objectives.

New Labour and social exclusion

However, the question remained: Exclusion from what? In an early critique of New Labour, Levitas (1996) identified three versions of social exclusion: a traditional poverty approach, an underclass perspective and an economic or labour-market definition of exclusion. Levitas argued that only a traditional poverty approach could be effective in determining social policy and preventing extreme forms of poverty and exclusion. The other two versions tended to marginalise the problem of poverty: the underclass perspective defined the problem as behavioural, while New Labour's adoption of exclusion as concerned with 'exclusion from the labour market and insertion into the world of work' was a narrowly defined policy variation which marginalised non-economically active households. Policies on housing and neighbourhoods that are designed to tackle social exclusion need therefore to be understood in this context. During and after the 1997 general election the social exclusion discourse ran through New Labour policy and the newly elected government quickly established the Social Exclusion Unit, located within the Cabinet Office to consider the causes of exclusion and how to tackle it. Its first reports emphasised populist notions of social exclusion which reflected a cultural explanation of social exclusion (for example, rough sleepers and teenage pregnancy, and resonating with earlier 'cultural' accounts of poverty), or were highly endogenous and focused on the 'partial' outcome of a process rather than on the process itself and its wider impact. This tendency towards an endogenous focus on the manifestation of problems rather than causes was prevalent in New Labour's commitment to tackling the 'worst estates'.

The identification of the 'worst estates' attributed problems of exclusion to geographically discrete boundaries, somewhat ignoring the process and dynamics of how the estates became the 'worst'. Aiming policies at the visible manifestation of problems appealed, however, to an electorate that wanted to see change, and this populism was reflected in the decision to launch the new government's position on social exclusion on a council housing estate in the largely deprived South London borough of Southwark. The method used to identify the 'worst estates' relied heavily on a study for the Department of the Environment (DoE, 1997), which defined the worst estates as predominantly local-authority-run areas. This method identified over 1,300 estates meeting this definition in England; the estates ranged in size from just 50 households to 5,000 (SEU, 1998). It was hardly surprising that the worst estates were identified as mainly council housing estates when the methodology used the proportion of dwellings in council ownership as the criteria for inclusion. The identification of the worst estates reflected two tendencies within public policy related to housing and area regeneration:. First, equating housing-related poverty and disadvantage with council housing (Lee and Murie, 1997); and second, an endogenous focus highlighted by the desire to address spatial manifestations of social exclusion with 'place-specific' interventions. Such interventions generally failed to understand the dynamics and interdependencies of spatial policies and to locate these within a broader spatial context; examples included City Challenge, the Single Regeneration Budget (REF) and New Deal for Communities (NDC) (Cheshire, 2007).

The NDC policy, launched in 1998 by New Labour, was a direct result of the previous Conservative government's interpretation of the 'worst estates'. While the policy was targeted at discrete communities – the NDC estates were neighbourhoods of between 3,500 and 4,000 households – they were not 'single-tenure' estates and there were no strict guidelines to local authorities on how to select NDC neighbourhoods. The launch of the New Deal for Communities emphasised the competitive element of regeneration policy, which had been a feature of City Challenge and SRB, in effect creating a competition between 'poorest neighbourhoods' for investment. Pathfinders were chosen on the basis of their ability to develop partnerships and deliver solutions, but there was also a broad geographical spread in order to provide a seemingly equitable distribution of resources. The NDC programme initially targeted £800 million to the most deprived neighbourhoods over the period 1999–2001. To ensure a 'geographical spread of [NDC] Pathfinder districts across England' (SEU, 1998), DETR identified at least one local authority area in each region of England. In regions with disproportionate shares of deprivation, additional authorities were awarded 'Pathfinder' status (SEU, 1998). Initially, 17 Pathfinder Local Authorities were chosen: Newcastle-upon-Tyne and Middlesbrough (NE); Liverpool and Manchester (NW); Bradford and Kingston upon Hull (YH); Nottingham and Leicester (EM); Birmingham and Sandwell (WM); Norwich (E); Bristol (SW); Brighton and Hove (SE); Newham, Hackney, Tower Hamlets and Southwark (L).

The neighbourhoods chosen by each local authority across the NDC programme reflected a diverse set of housing and socio-demographic circumstances. The area chosen in Birmingham (Pool Farm), for example, was a broadly single-tenure neighbourhood, dominated by council housing. It had no significant ethnic minority population, was located on the south-west periphery of the city adjacent to the green belt and therefore was a significant distance from the inner-city neighbourhoods where the main BME populations had tended to live and moved into from the 1950s onwards (see Rex and Moore, 1967). In Sandwell the area chosen as the Pathfinder (Greets Green) was an inner-city neighbourhood of mixed tenure, with a significantly high proportion of ethnic minorities. Largely 'single tenure' council housing estates were selected in Hull and Norwich, while the majority of the remaining NDC areas outside London were mixed-tenure areas reflecting the 'differentiation' of housing tenure. In Beswick (East Manchester) the area chosen had evidence of new housing that had been abandoned and the strategy for NDC in that area was closely linked to the economic development potential of the area.

After 1998 there was a marked shift in language away from 'worst estates' and increasing reference to 'poorest neighbourhoods'. The publication of the National Strategy for Neighbourhood Renewal and subsequent government statements aimed to improve the life chances and opportunities in the most deprived communities through the launch of the Neighbourhood Renewal Fund (NRF). Meanwhile, the Beswick NDC Pathfinder demonstrated the importance of a growing literature on low demand and abandonment of housing suggesting that the physical condition of housing stock (that is, *distributional* aspects of housing and social exclusion) will not always be a predictor of the popularity of an area (Lowe *et al.*, 1998; Murie *et al.*, 1998) and that relationships among a whole series of other factors, at a variety of spatial scales, were resulting in low demand.

Low and changing demand: the rescaling of housing

The popularity and market appeal of different neighbourhoods was a theme that was developing in the literature to differentiate *between* deprived neighbourhoods and to demonstrate how areas with similar levels of deprivation differ in their popularity and crime levels and their function and trajectory (Burrows and Rhodes, 1998; Lee and Murie, 1997). The literature began to argue the need to demonstrate the coincidence of social exclusion with popular and sustainable neighbourhoods and understand the changing demand and aspirations for housing within a broader spatial context and how the market for housing operated across tenures and across administrative (local authority) boundaries. Problems of social exclusion needed to be viewed within a broader spatial context. The phenomenon of changing demand for low-income housing was a major housing policy issue at the end of the 1990s and shaped a great deal of the subsequent policy landscape concerning the strategic role of housing, its fit with the governance of planning at the regional and sub-regional level, the delivery of sustainable communities and the role of regeneration. The government estimated that nearly one million homes were affected by low demand in England with the main concentrations in the North-West and North-East of England (DTLR, 2002).

The characteristics of low demand were outlined in a series of papers and reports between 1997 and 2003, which identified a growing volatility in tenancy turnover as residualisation of council housing contributed to a polarisation in the age structure (that is, older tenants and younger tenants) (Pawson and Bramley, 2000) and significant falls in waiting lists for social housing (Nevin *et al.*, 2001). Murie *et al.* (1998) used house prices and vacancy rates to measure housing-market weakness in the late 1990s, to identify spatial concentrations of multi-tenure neighbourhoods which appeared to have low demand, across parts of the northern and midland regions of England. Keenan (1998) carried out micro-analysis of turnover and demand in the West End of Newcastle, demonstrating how the speed of residential abandonment undermined comprehensive regeneration initiatives. Webster (1998) and Holmans and Simpson (1999) added to the debate by emphasising regional economic decline and inter-regional shifts in population as major causes of low demand. Murie *et al.* (1998) noted that while economic restructuring was an important factor in explaining change, other considerations such as differential migration within the region, changing aspirations, the growth in two-income households, and the increasing affordability of owner occupation were also likely to impact upon the older industrial settlements. These assumptions have tended to be supported by more detailed research into changing housing markets at the regional level (Lee *et al.*, 2002, 2003; Nevin *et al.*, 2001).

In England the work of the Social Exclusion Unit in relation to neighbourhood renewal included a Policy Action Team concerned with unpopular housing. The Report emerging from this team (Policy Action Team 7) concluded that the problems of low demand needed to be understood locally and that no single model of causality would apply in all cases; a combination of factors at local and regional level were responsible. These findings influenced the shape of the Housing Market Renewal (HMR) programme in England and the avoidance of a nationally prescriptive set of interventions. Low-demand or unpopular housing was defined as occurring in social housing where there was a small or non-existent waiting list, tenancy offers were frequently refused, high numbers of empty properties were available for letting and there was high tenancy turnover (DETR, 2000). But the significant thrust of the analysis during this period (1997–2003) was demonstrating the interdependencies of places operating at different spatial scales and how time lags between areas of policy affected outcomes and timing of outcomes. Secondly it was indicating that inter-related demographic, social and cultural trends pointed towards the need for a new methodology for housing studies and for better strategy development that cut across administrative boundaries and created greater shared understanding of how investment at regional and sub-regional level interacted. The experience of extreme forms of social exclusion experienced as a result of abandoned housing and low demand on a quite unprecedented scale in some northern towns and cities demonstrated these sets of processes; this was most apparent in the case of Liverpool, as highlighted in a number of reports on dimensions of low demand and the housing market during the period 1998–2002 (see, for example: Groves *et al.*, 2001; Lee and Nevin, 2002; Nevin *et al.*, 2001) and can be summarised as follows:

- *Diversification of the economy*: during the 1970s and 1980s Liverpool had a high dependence on manufacturing and low-skilled employment within the motor- and shipping-related industries, giving rise to a tight relationship between housing and the economy. The failure of the city to diversify its economic base alongside housing-market interventions would have repercussions for changing demand in future waves of development.

- *Decentralisation*: during the 1950s and 1960s, the city experienced a decentralisation of population through the creation of new towns such as Runcorn and the growth of housing in the Wirral and Skelmersdale. This had the effect of providing housing opportunities for migrating households out of the city.
- *Impact of national welfare policies*: the expansion of higher education during this period created the first generation exposed to mass higher education and opportunities to move out of the city and develop career trajectories and educational outcomes outside the city; the failure to diversify the economy or consolidate the housing-market offer in the city compounded future problems of low and changing demand.
- *Concealed effects*: a range of household responses to restructuring and unemployment during the 1970s and 1980s, such as retirement and redundancy payments used to invest in housing, did not result in housing disinvestment or a collapse in the housing market; the problem was concealed.
- *Reinvention of housing markets*: the expansion of higher education in the city served to redefine and reinvent parts of the housing market through the housing of students in inner-city terraced housing areas. This housing reflected a different economic era, and student housing ensured reinvention, to concealing the longer-term trends towards low demand.
- *Fragmented governance*: the political instability of the early 1980s, signalled by fractures in the local Labour party and embodied in the influence of the 'Militant Tendency', reflected a dissonance between local politics and the structure of economic capital and national economic policy. The city council pursued a policy of investment in additional social-housing provision for the working classes. This compounded the problem of over-supply and created further instability in the market. Housing Associations operating in the inner city failed to provide an integrated strategy and adopted differential speeds of investment and disinvestment.

The overall impact of the failure to accommodate these key signals resulted in cumulative disadvantage and social exclusion by creating a highly volatile housing market affected by national and global economic pressures, the failure of sub-regional planning and a failure to interpret sub-regional housing market dynamics. The fractured political and governance infrastructure delivered further contradictions which added to the endemic problems of low demand.

Competitiveness and rescaling

The response to low demand in England was the publication of the *Sustainable Communities Plan: Homes for All* (ODPM, 2003). This five-year plan sought to deliver affordable housing and balanced growth in the South-East through the designation of growth points, while in the Midlands and North changing demand was tackled through Housing Market Renewal Pathfinders. This was followed by the creation of Regional Housing Boards to oversee Regional Housing Strategies (RHSs), to co-ordinate investment and determine needs. In England, the HMR programme represented an attempt at designing an intervention that located the spatial manifestation of the housing problem within a broader spatial context which understood the dynamics and interdependencies of spatial policies. The Pathfinders were tasked with developing comprehensive approaches to neighbourhood renewal through major changes to the housing stock and tenure, in order to encourage income mix and choice in the housing market alongside improvements to the environment. The government set Pathfinders ambitious targets to reduce low demand and abandonment and narrow the gap in house prices between the Pathfinders and the sub-regional average.

This intervention coincided with a complementary and parallel series of reports and policy developments concerned with competitiveness and prosperity of cities in the North and Midlands. In 2003 and 2004 reports for the Office of the Deputy Prime Minister (ODPM, 2003, 2004) compared English Core Cities (Birmingham, Bristol, Leeds, Liverpool, Manchester, Newcastle, Nottingham and Sheffield) with European comparators. These studies identified skills gaps, the need for a more decentralised economic development pattern to take pressure off London and the South-East and improved governance mechanisms to coordinate activities across local authority boundaries. 'Critical' characteristics such as economic diversity, a skilled workforce, connectivity, innovation and quality of life (see ODPM, 2004, p. 5) were seen as crucial aspects of competitiveness, which need to be tackled to improve productivity and gross value added (GVA). Part of the strategy, influenced by Florida's thesis on the creative and knowledge class (Florida, 2004), was to target knowledge-intensive industries and promote housing, planning and regeneration policies to attract and retain knowledge-intensive workers and the creative class.

The Barker Review of Housing (ODPM, 2004) tackled competitiveness and the competitive advantage of English cities and regions by proposing a review and overhaul of the planning system; it recognised that competition for investment will increasingly force planning to respond in a way that allows business and capital to flow to those economies and nation-states that can offer the most attractive and barrier-free conditions for business development. In order to compete, the UK needed a more responsive planning system:

> Rapid changes in the global economy, technological advances and ease of travel are transforming the way we do business. Globalisation implies a significant intensification of cross-border economic competition. Many potential new markets and job opportunities have opened up. But this also means that there is increased competition, including from high growth economies such as China and India. Planning is critical to ensuring that we can respond to these

challenges. We need a planning system that is responsive and efficient and which positively supports vital economic development and encourages greater investment. . . . (CLG, 2007, Planning White Paper, p. 111, paras 7.36–7.37)

The role of housing and planning in nurturing competitive neighbourhoods and markets for a knowledge clientele means that statutory (local) authorities will increasingly have to work strategically across boundaries to develop the most effective mechanisms for attracting business to invest and providing the right environment in order to retain and attract a knowledge-based and skilled labour market. These relationships and cross-boundary alliances will be cemented through multi-area agreements and various other proposals as part of a Sub-National Review of Economic Development and Regeneration (CLG, 2007c). The proposals represent a rescaling and integration of housing into the broader canvas of the city-region in order to achieve competitiveness; the policies for housing as recommended in the SNR in July 2007 include:

* developing proposals for Multi-Area Agreements to allow groups of local authorities to agree collective targets for economic development issues;
* moving to a single integrated regional strategy which sets out the economic, social and environmental objectives for each region and places housing within this integrated approach;
* giving Regional Development Agencies the executive responsibility, on behalf of the region, for developing the integrated regional strategy, working closely with local authorities and other partners and abolishing Regional Housing Boards and the regional assemblies established under the 2003 Sustainable Communities Plan.

The government department in England responsible for spatial planning and regeneration policies and for the development of communities and policies designed to combat social exclusion and promote social cohesion re-badged itself as a department of economics, setting out the relationship between economics and housing and spatial planning:

Economics is at the heart of what we do in the Department. We need to understand – and be capable of thinking rigorously about – the choices and trade-offs that people make in reaching decisions, what can incentivise behaviour, and how markets operate and change' (CLG, 2007b, p. 4)

and:

spatial disparities are often simply the spatial manifestation of non-spatial policies or processes . . . we need to be clear about the rationale for spatial policies in terms of the three basic rationales for intervention [efficiency, equity and the environment] . . . we intervene where spatial market and government failures undermine economic performance and welfare. Addressing these failures will enable places to identify their role in the global economy and if spatial disparities at least partly reflect market and government failures they represent a drag on economic performance and welfare. (CLG, 2007b, p. 34)

The New Labour 'project', starting from a genuine but narrowly drawn and populist approach to housing and regeneration policies designed to tackle social exclusion (namely, 'worst estates', New Deal for Communities and rough sleeping), broadened and rescaled housing to engage with a more comprehensive agenda of improving competitiveness to deliver social inclusion. The Sustainable Communities Plan (responsible for urban renaissance, housing market renewal and regional housing strategies) and the competitiveness agenda (influencing the designation of city-regions and regional economic policy) presented a pivotal role for housing and neighbourhood as focal points for reinserting housing into the wider sub-regional economy for the purpose of competitiveness. Subsequent reports from ODPM presented arguments for a city-region approach to planning, economic development and housing. Meanwhile, the mood was reflected by the launch of the Northern Way by a coalition of partners: it was designed to produce a coordinated response to closing the gap between the prosperity of the eight city-regions across the North of England and the UK average.

Conclusions

This chapter has looked at the changing context and policy responses to housing and strategies designed to tackle spatial manifestations of housing and social exclusion. The incorporation of relational and social dimensions alongside distributional and material accounts of poverty has added a dynamic place-based context to understanding housing-related disadvantage over the past two to three decades. This has shaped a number of policy approaches and objectives and broadened the spatial focus of housing. Populist and narrow assumptions of housing's role in social exclusion and mechanisms designed to tackle it, such as the 'worst estates' approach, have been rejected in favour of a more sophisticated and spatially embedded approach with competitiveness as a key driver. The neighbourhood and estate – the physical embodiment of 'community' – have been *rescaled* so that they are understood within the context of the city and region. This reflects the importance of place, social exclusion and the rescaling of housing in regeneration and renewal policies.

This emphasis has carried through into strategic housing and planning and the development of regional housing strategy-making and single integrated strategies.

The emphasis on social exclusion and place has also used an increasingly abstract set of geographies in order to pursue housing policies that maximise profit and competitiveness. While social exclusion has elevated the role of place in contributing to disadvantage, over the past decade processes of rescaling as they relate to housing have seen the strategic role of housing become more aligned to that of the economy. A number of important developments have signalled the way in which the economy and economics are at the heart of integrationist strategies for housing designed to deliver social inclusion and sustainable communities: the emergence of sub-regional housing strategies, Strategic Housing Market Assessments (SHMAs) and integration with regional economic and spatial strategies; proposals to integrate the strategic housing function at regional level in England within RDAs under proposals set out in the Sub-National Review of Economic Development; and the positioning of CLG as an 'economics department' (see: CLG, 2007b). Housing in this context has moved away from questions about the distributional impacts of housing shortage on experiences of social exclusion to pose questions about the role of housing in competitiveness and the economy. These developments have been for the purpose of inserting people into the labour market, reconnecting the economic and housing-market function of places and delivering competitiveness as a mechanism for tackling social exclusion. And so where residualisation has been the housing manifestation of structural economic change, the response to the problems which emerge from this are seen to be best addressed through continued restructuring and economic development.

The interaction of economic change and neighbourhood change had profound effects on the spatial distribution of life chances and outcomes. The role of place and space in shaping households' and individuals' experience of social exclusion was heightened after the mid-1970s. Economic restructuring and globalisation had dramatic influences on the organisation of work, reducing the significance of the role of the workplace in defining and shaping social relations. Sennett (2006) has argued that place is a defining attribute of what he calls the new age of capitalism: as places increasingly reflect the fragmented and polarised nature of global capitalism, place will become a defining characteristic of welfare and inclusion. Changes in the consumption of housing and growing spatial inequalities changed the assumptions about the role of place and how the state should intervene. Understanding the narrative of the city through the lens of housing consumption has become more difficult. The Post-Fordist city, defined by economic relations of class and mass consumption and production, has given way to post-modern forms of niche consumption and expressions of individualism (Forrest and Kennett, 1998). Understanding, or 're-reading', the city in the context of these changes to the urban form and the signs and signifiers that the urban housing form represents is increasingly complex. 'The "simple suburbs", these unremarkable places, have begun to be transformed as processes of commodification, decommodification and deregulation have penetrated residential space. Reading the suburbs has become more complex as "traditional" employment has been replaced by high-tech areas on the fringe of cities in which employment opportunities range from highly paid managerial to low-paid, predominantly female, disorganised workers. Flexibility and mobility, unemployment and unpredictability, impact on households in different ways. There is a growing dissonance between the built form, the symbols of the Fordist hierarchy, and who lives there.' (Forrest and Kennett, 1998, p. 74)

The changing nature of place and the complexity of interactions between households, places and the economy indicate that we have entered into a new phase of policy development. One of the policy responses has been to create new layers of information exchange such as Strategic Housing Market Assessments and Single Integrated Regional Strategies (CLG, 2007a). These take the form of information inventories and information indexes to handle strategic decision making on housing and the economy. The drivers of this have generally been competitiveness and productivity, rather than social sustainability and social inclusion. The dramatic housing market volatility experienced over the period 2007–8 following the collapse of the US sub-prime financial market in 2007 and continuing through the banking crisis in the autumn of 2008, which further restricted loans and mortgages, indicates the need to build in more comprehensive strategic policies around housing and inclusion and resilience in response to a narrative of housing and spatial policies which in England were designed to tackle social exclusion in the mid- to late 1990s but progressively championed abstract spatial scales in pursuit of competitiveness. Building in resilience means that sustainability as a goal and inclusion policies related to housing and neighbourhood are ongoing processes. Ironically, while politically the qualitative concept of social exclusion has been accepted, in England there has been a tremendous shift towards a positivist methodology in predict-and-provide, highlighted by the Barker Review and the move towards Communities and Local Government as a department of economics. Therefore, while there has been increasing sophistication in the intelligence-gathering and understanding of place, housing strategy development and policy formulation must be resilient to short-term shocks and must take an extensive view of market outcomes and the relationship to place; this must balance goals of competitiveness with those of inclusion and goals of abstract scale (city–region) with that of the community.

This journey from residualisation and social exclusion to economic restructuring and shared prosperity would seem on the face of it to be a positive story: the discourse is of development and, through integrated strategies and the insertion of strategic housing into planning and economic development policy-making, inclusion. But the reliance on the free market to deliver a significant share of this change and the emphasis on owner occupation and a more responsive, development-led planning system will ultimately lead to differential outcomes at the local level. As Rowlands outlines in the next chapter, at a neighbourhood level delivering such goals can be difficult and complex.

References

6, P (1997) *Escaping Poverty: From Safety Nets to Networks of Opportunity*, London: Demos.

Atkinson, R. and Kintrea, K. (2003) 'Opportunities and despair, it's all in there: fractured experiences and explanations of area effects and life chances', *Sociology*, 38(3), 437–55.

Booth, C. (1891) *Labour and Life of the People of London*, London: Williams and Norgate.

Bourdieu, P. (1984) *Distinction: A Social Critique of the Judgment of Taste*, translated by Richard Nice, London and New York: Routledge and Kegan Paul.

Buck, N. H. and Gordon, I. (2004) 'Does Spatial Concentration of Disadvantage Contribute to Social Exclusion?', in *City Matters*, Edited by Boddy, M. and Parkinson, M., Policy Press, 71–92.

Burrows, R. and Rhodes, D. (1998) *Unpopular places? Area disadvantage and the geography of misery in England*, Bristol: Policy.

Cantle, T. (2004) *Community Cohesion: A New Framework for Race and Diversity*. Basingstoke: Palgrave Macmillan.

Cheshire, P.C. (2007) *Segregated Neighbourhoods and Mixed Communities: A Critical Analysis*. York: Joseph Rowntree Foundation.

CLG (2007) *Planning for a Sustainable Future*, Planning White Paper May 2007, London: Communities and Local Government.

CLG (2007a) *Strategic Housing Market Assessments, Practice Guidance Version 2*, London: Communities and Local Government, August 2007.

CLG (2007b) *Communities and Local Government Economics Paper 1: A Framework for Intervention (Communities and Local Government as an economics department)*, London: Communities and Local Government, September 2007.

CLG (2007c) *Taking Forward the Review of Sub-National Economic Development and Regeneration*, CLG and Department for Business Enterprise and Regulatory Reform (DBERR). London: CLG.

DETR (2000) *Unpopular Housing, Report of Policy Action Team 7*. London: Department of Environment, Transport and the Regions.

DoE (1997) *Mapping Local Authority Estates Using the 1991 Index of Local Conditions*, London: Department of Environment.

DTLR (2002) *Report of the Empty Homes Inquiry*, Department of Transport, Local Government and the Regions Select Committee: London: HMSO.

Florida, R. (2002) *The Rise of the Creative Class: And How It's Transforming Work, Leisure, Community and Everyday Life*. New York: Basic Books.

Forrest, R. and Kennett, P. (1998) 'Re-reading the City: Deregulation and Neighbourhood', *Space & Polity* 2(1), 71–83.

Friedrichs, J., Galster, G. and Musterd, S. (2005) *Life in Poverty Neighbourhoods: European and American Perspectives*, London: Routledge.

Groves, R., Lee, P., Murie, A. and Nevin, B. (2001) *Private Rented Housing in Liverpool: an Overview of Current Market Conditions*, Research Report No. 3, Liverpool: Liverpool City Council.

Keenan, P. (1998) 'Residential Mobility and Low Demand: A Case History from Newcastle', 35–47 in Lowe, S., Spencer, S. and Keenan, P. (1998) *Housing Abandonment in Britain: Studies in the Causes and Effects of Low Demand Housing*, York: Centre for Housing Policy.

Leather, P., Lee, P. and Murie, A. (2002) *North East England: Changing Housing Markets and Urban Regeneration: Final Report*. Birmingham: University of Birmingham, Centre for Urban and Regional Studies.

Lee, P. and Murie, A. (1997) *Poverty, Housing Tenure and Social Exclusion*, Bristol: Policy Press.

Lee, P. and Murie, A. (1999) 'Spatial and Social Divisions within British Cities: Beyond Residualisation', *Housing Studies*, 14(5), 625–40.

Lee, P. and Nevin, B. (2002) *Renewing the Housing Market of Liverpool's Inner Core*, Research Report No. 8, Liverpool: Liverpool City Council.

Lee, P., Barber, A., Burfitt, A., Collinge, C., Ferrari., Hall, S., Murie, A. and Roberts, J. (2003) *The Housing Market and Economic Function of the Eastern Corridor of Birmingham and Solihull: Interim Report to Birmingham City Council and Solihull Metropolitan Borough Council*. Birmingham: University of Birmingham, Centre for Urban and Regional Studies.

Levitas, R. (1996) 'The Concept of Social Exclusion and the New Durkheimian Hegemony', *Critical Social Policy*, 16(46), 5–20.

Lewis, O. (1961) *The Children of Sanchez: Autobiography of a Mexican family*, New York: Random House.

Murie, A., Nevin, B. and Leather, P. (1998) *Changing Demand and Unpopular Housing*, Working Paper 4, London: Housing Corporation.

Nevin, B., Lee, P., Goodson, L., Murie, A. and Phillimore, J. (2001) *Changing Housing Markets and Urban Regeneration in the M62 Corridor*, University of Birmingham: Centre for Urban and Regional Studies.

ODPM (Office of the Deputy Prime Minister)(2003a) *Sustainable Communities Plan: Homes for All*, London: Office of Deputy Prime Minister.

—— (2003b) *The Cities, Regions and Competitiveness*, The Second Report from the Working Group of Government Departments, London: ODPM.

—— (2004) *Competitive European Cities: Where do the Core Cities Stand?*, London: ODPM.

Pawson, H. and Bramley, G. (2000) 'Understanding Recent Trends in Residential Mobility in Council Housing in England', *Urban Studies*, 37(8), 1231–59, July 2000.

Putnam, R. (2000) *Bowling Alone: The Collapse and Revival of American Community*, New York: Simon & Schuster.

Rex, J. and Moore, R. (1967) *Race, Community and Conflict: A Study of Sparkbrook*. Institute of Race Relations. Oxford: OUP.

Rodgers, G., Gore, C. and Figueiredo, J.B. (1995) *Social Exclusion: Rhetoric, Reality and Responses*, Geneva: International Institute for Labour Studies, United Nations Development Programme.

Room, G. (1995a) *Beyond the Threshold: The Measurement and Analysis of Social Exclusion*, Bristol: The Policy Press.

—— (1995b) 'Poverty in Europe: competing paradigms of analysis', *Policy and Politics*, 23(2), 103–13.

Rowntree, B. S. (1901) *Poverty: A Study of Town Life*, London: Macmillan.

—— (1941) Poverty and Progress, London: Longmans, Green.

Sennett, R. (2006) *New Age of Capitalism*, Yale: Yale University Press.

—— (2001) *A New Commitment to Neighbourhood Renewal: National Strategy Action Plan*, London: Cabinet Office.

Somerville, P. (1998) 'Explanations of Social Exclusion: Where Does Housing Fit in?', *Housing Studies*, 13(6), 761–80.

Townsend, P. (1979) *Poverty in the United Kingdom*. London: Allen Lane.

Walker, A. (1995) 'The dynamics of poverty and social exclusion', in Room, G. (ed.) *Beyond the Threshold: The Measurement and Analysis of Social Exclusion*, Bristol: Policy Press.

Webster, D. (1998) 'Employment change, housing abandonment and sustainable development: structural processes and structural issues', in: Lowe, S., Spencer, S. and Keenan, P. (eds) (1998) *Housing Abandonment in Britain: Studies in the Causes and Effects of Low Demand Housing*, 47–60. York: University of York, Centre for Housing Policy.

Wilson, W. J. (1987) *The Truly Disadvantaged: The Inner City, the Underclass, and Public Policy*, Chicago: University of Chicago Press.

11 Sustainable communities

Housing, dogma and the opportunities missed

Rob Rowlands

Sustainable communities have gained an important place in public policy from an environmental, social and, importantly, an economic perspective. The UK government's announcement of a Sustainable Communities Plan in 2003 and subsequent inclusion of the term in all planning policies has placed this notion at the heart of policy and strategy. Housing, as a central component of urban and planning policies, has been brought into the mix of sustainability. As the foundation of most neighbourhoods, housing should be an integral part of any strategy to deliver sustainable communities. Several questions arise from this: How is housing integrated into this strategy and what role does it play? Does the role cast for housing achieve the aims of a sustainable community? Is housing's role overplayed? Even more importantly, what have been the failings of this approach and what is missing from the mix to make communities more sustainable?

This chapter reflects on the place of housing in the pursuit of sustainable communities. It provides a critical overview of the sustainable communities concept and its implementation as a policy. The chapter presents evidence from a range of research projects and argues that the focus on housing is misplaced and misguided.

What is a sustainable community?

Sustainable communities are inherently a good idea; and Who would argue against them, faced with the myriad of social, economic and environmental challenges of today? Despite this, this term is fraught with difficulty, and the different usages of the term make monitoring the achievement of a sustainable community difficult. With this in mind it is useful to unpack what a sustainable community means in definition and in policy and how it has come to be articulated in practice. From a theoretical perspective we need to draw on the definitions of the two concepts which make up the notion of a sustainable community: sustainability and community.

Let us start with how we define community. Community is seemingly everywhere, yet the definition of a community remains unclear. An important element of this definition is whether community is spatially defined. The *Oxford English Dictionary* definition of community emphasises both a dimension based around place and a notion of collectivity or commonality (OED, 2008). Evidence from the Housing Corporation's Existing Tenant Survey highlights the fact that tenants relate community to concepts including locality, the notion of everyone living together and the feeling that people support each other (BMG, 2008). The idea of neighbouring and neighbourhood is significant within this and is a point which we will return to. In a variation on this theme, Robertson *et al.* (2008: 101) highlight how community is seen by residents of neighbourhoods as 'often rooted in this realm of the familiar but mundane and everyday interactions'. These interactions are seen to be based in a locality and around focal points within the community which facilitate everyday life – the post office, the shops, the school gates. But of course community is not always neighbourhood-based and can be aspatial, based around a commonality of identity. Sometimes the two can overlap – for example, where immigrant communities become spatially concentrated and can be identified by both common identity and concentration of residential pattern. Equally, the two can be poles apart.

With regard to public policy, the concept of community has undertaken something of a boomerang course. Twenty years ago Margaret Thatcher famously said there was 'no such thing as society'. Her emphasis was that individuals should not expect government to bail them out without first demonstrating their own attempts to improve their situation. While there is some debate about the implicit individualism of the sentiment, the present Labour government is outwardly committed to community as the basis of decision-making and delivery of public services:

> The next step in service delivery is empowering local communities with the freedom to agree for their own public services their own local performance standards. (Brown, 2003)

Community it seems is unavoidable. Ironically, it is the role of individuals in making this community a reality which is most prominent. Although the veneer of community concern appears collective, there are many who have identified the underlying individualism of these statements, the responsibilisation and even regulation of the citizen and the continuing shift of the welfare state from government to individual. This responsibilisation is highlighted by the National Curriculum's provision for citizenship teaching at Key Stage 3. Such teaching clearly enshrines the responsibilities expected of members of a community and highlights the communitarian focus in the use of the idea of community by government in recent years (DfES, 2008), a theme returned to below.

As Walker *et al.* (2000) indicate, the tendency is to look for measurable outputs rather than softer outcomes. This focuses the attention on demonstrable community formation, participation and benefits rather than the implicit and hidden successes. However, ultimately we should always bear in mind Pahl's (1970) assertion that 'community' has become an unhelpful term which hinders academic analysis, and which, as Farrar (2001) suggests, 'serves more to confuse than to illuminate'.

The second dimension to consider is that of sustainability. Sustainability is universally defined after the Brundtland Commission's report as 'the ability to meet the needs of the present without compromising the ability of future generations to meet their own needs' (Brundtland, 1987). This definition has three dimensions to it, often referred to as the '3 Es', namely economic vitality, equality of opportunity and environmental quality. These three facets address the social, economic and environmental dimensions of sustainability. Indeed, planning policy reflects this need for balance and places on local planning authorities the responsibility for the social, economic and environmental well-being of their areas (ODPM, 2005).

The reality is often that when talking about sustainability, as with community, the focus is on measurable outputs – for example, the pursuit of carbon reductions – over and above softer, more effective, behavioural changes. Again this misses the more delicate and intangible outcomes and the potential impacts (both positive and negative) of such actions. A further problem is that, rather than being balanced, people often refer to only one of the three elements – they say 'sustainable' but they only mean economic sustainability or green development. As with community, sustainability is so often reduced to measurable indicators, of which economics often becomes the primary goal (Darby and Jenkins, 2006). As economic concerns have been prioritised, any balanced approach to sustainability is lost: arguments begin to revolve around being unable to be more sustainable because the perceived outcome is a drop in material living standards. With the prioritisation of economics through the Treasury's ever growing role in regulating, it is not difficult to understand the trajectory of policy to meet sustainable aims.

With the two concepts of community and sustainability in mind, What then does a sustainable community look like? Of course, the idea is not a new one but has been described by different names over time. There have been numerous attempts to plan and develop 'model communities' which are sustainable. Ebenezer Howard's vision of the garden city is an obvious precursor to the sustainable community and has formed a basis for today's planning system. This model attempted to link the benefits of the rural and the urban, to be self-sustaining and to offer social mix. Earlier attempts by philanthropic industrialists such as Robert Owen,

Titus Salt and later Cadbury and Lever demonstrated the idea of self-sufficiency, accessibility of employment, good-quality housing and open space and social facilities. The early co-partnership housing movement created neighbourhoods which were initially self-sustaining and policing and owed much to the vision of Howard's idea. These examples are still held up as examples of how communities should be developed, and Bourneville in particular is seen as an exemplar of the sustainable community.[1] The municipal 'fathers' of Britain's Victorian cities thought through a more comprehensive development of the settlements, with the provision of services for both housing and industry. Chamberlain's Birmingham is often upheld as an example of this Victorian planning. Yet it is fair to say that the majority of cities, neighbourhoods and communities have become less sustainable as we have entered the twenty-first century, whether in economic, social or, increasingly, environmental respects.

What does the government want a sustainable community to be? The government definition of a sustainable community reflects the accepted notions of sustainability as balancing the present and future needs of communities, locally and further afield. Its definition of 'sustainable communities' is of places where:

> . . . people want to live and work, now and in the future. They meet the diverse needs of existing and future residents, are sensitive to their environment, and contribute to a high quality of life. They are safe and inclusive, well planned, built and run, and offer equality of opportunity and good services for all. (CLG, 2008)

As a result of the Bristol Accord and the Leipzig Declaration, this definition is now widely accepted across Europe. What this means in practice is likely to differ from country to country. In the UK, Raco (2007) has summarised recent government approaches to sustainable communities and suggests that: 'a sustainable place is one in which employment, mixed housing and social facilities are co-present and available to a range of socio-economic groups'. It is the balance and, in particular, the mix which has come to shape and signify 'sustainable community' policy and it is especially the elements of mix and provision of facilities that will be picked up in this chapter.

Another question which should be asked with this definition in mind is: how will sustainable communities be delivered? Again it is important to look at the government's approach here. 'Sustainable communities' have been an implicit policy goal of the government since its election in 1997. The change of language adopted by the Blair government in its reference to social exclusion and neighbourhood renewal marked a shift towards inclusive and holistic regeneration. The Sustainable Communities Plan was launched in 2003 with a focus on accommodating growth in the South and change (both growth and decline) in the North of England in an effective and efficient way. The emphasis of the sustainable-communities policy has always been on growth and regeneration, with housing at its core. The Egan Review (2004) and the Academy of Sustainable Communities both highlight the need for a new focus to deliver on the joined-up, holistic approach, the rhetorical mantra of the Labour government. However, other elements of sustainable communities have appeared as additional straplines to the policy. These have included the Respect agenda, aimed at addressing anti-social behaviour, and more recently 'cleaner, safer, greener neighbourhoods', which in fact encompasses a myriad of diverse policies from town-centre management to allotments. While these suggest an attempt to join up a diverse range of policy aims, a lack of coordination between other government departments, and even within CLG itself, and the focus on housing and neighbourhoods of a particular type, indicate the complexity of the task faced and the improbability of reaching the required outcome.

While housing and communities are the main focus of this policy, a significant thrust of New Labour's policies has been the responsibilisation of individuals, and therefore of the community as a collective of individuals. This amalgam of communitarian approaches, highlighted by Delanty (2006) and Robinson (2008), is aimed at creating active citizens who will be co-producers of community. It is perceived as the responsibility of citizens to take on this role. In turn, those who become active will have an influence over non-active citizens, with the intention of their becoming active too. This process relies on the creation of dominant discourses within communities about how they should evolve and, importantly, how citizens should behave. This process of normalisation was identified by Foucault (1991) and used by others to demonstrate how control can be implicitly implemented (Flint and Rowlands, 2003; Gurney, 1999; Rose, 2001); in this case it is intended to deliver sustainable communities through coercion. The outcome of this process is the improvement not only of places but also of people. Raco (2007) suggests that citizens will exercise choice in selecting areas where there are already active citizens and where by definition neighbourhoods are better. But this choice implies that those neighbourhoods without active citizens will continue to decline while affluent citizens will continue to exercise choice through the housing market. The outcome is likely to be further rather than less segregation if allowed to continue unchecked. If the sustainable-communities policy is reliant on self-help by resourceful active citizens, it is unlikely to meet its aims of sustainable cities.

The prominent role of housing policies is clear in this strategy. Housing is an essential anchor of residential communities and there is a need to offer both quality and choice, as indicated by the Housing Green Paper in 2000 (DETR, 2000). But housing is also a sphere which government has utilised for the responsibilisation of citizens. For some time, tenure prejudices have been a means of normalising home ownership and ensuring a majority of ordinary citizens are ever more tied into the operations of the economy.

The approach to monetary policy adopted by the Thatcher governments utilised increasing levels of home ownership as a means of making citizens responsible consumers by exposing them to the outcomes of monetary policy. Perhaps now the credit crunch is another realisation of this policy. Yet in the last 10 years housing has become a means of direct social control and social housing has been placed in the forefront of the recent Respect agenda (Flint, 2002; Flint and Nixon, 2006). In the government's eyes, responsible citizens are likely to be home owners, as this will create greater place attachment. As Raco (2007: 314) states:

> Good, sustainable citizens are those who have made the active choice of acquiring their own property through the market and have therefore purchased a direct stake in the quality and character of their neighbourhoods.

Housing, both its consumption and its connection to the neighbourhood, plays a key role in the creation of responsible citizens and therefore contributes to the development of sustainable communities.

The next part of this chapter looks at how housing is a part of the problematic of neighbourhoods and its role in sustainable communities policies; it emphasises the perceived importance of tenure in explaining the problems and of mix in providing the solutions.

The role of housing tenure and the housing market

What is the problem with communities today? This is a question asked by politicians, academics and newspaper journalists alike. The demise of society, so succinctly described by Margaret Thatcher over 20 years ago (Marr, 2007), is arguably at the root of this and in part can be blamed on the increased materialism and individualism which has underpinned the development of the UK. Clearly housing has played a role in this trend since the mid-1970s, with a notable increase in home ownership and latterly a return to property ownership, particularly through buy-to-let type arrangements in the last 10 years. As part of this pattern of change tenure itself has played a role in the explanation of the differential development of communities and neighbourhoods as the housing market does its job.

The role of tenure in the analysis of these problems is sometimes presented as a straightforward split between public renting and property ownership. For some time now there has been a clear focus by researchers on the residualisation of public housing and a subsequent concentration of poverty (Cole and Furbey, 1994; Forrest and Murie, 1983, 1995; Forrest et al., 1990), even if government ministers have only awoken to this issue some 25 years later (Flint, 2008). Residualisation has been a long-run trend, a process aided by two main housing policy strands. These have gone hand in hand, more by accident than by design, and have resulted in the shifting role of housing as part of the welfare state (Malpass, 2008).

Housing has become increasingly commodified beyond its role in providing shelter and is increasingly demanded as an investment, both by owner-occupiers and more recently by a new landlord class. As such the role and function of social housing have changed. Though never a universal good under the welfare state, council-built housing met the needs of a wider social class. Now housing is an essential component of what is becoming a two-tier welfare state, with asset-based welfare providing a higher level of security and care for those with such tradeable assets. As home ownership has risen and become more attainable, so the better tenants and properties have left the sector. The sale of social housing, primarily through the right to buy, together with a building programme which has failed to keep up with losses, has seen the worst properties and estates remain in the social sector and used to house those households in highest housing need. The result is a growing polarisation both between places and between those who own and those who rent. The emerging debate about the new sandwich class, those who 'can work, can't buy' (Wilcox, 2003), highlights how this polarisation in asset ownership is growing beyond the traditional tenure divides.

The policy analysis has concluded that there is a need to break up the spatial polarisation that occurs and has been concerned with developing and delivering mixed communities. Focus has been on delivering mix through the mechanism of mixed tenure. Underpinning this policy is the transfer of state support to the individual as a means of providing opportunity rather than the barrier which previous institutionalising benefits have delivered. Therefore tax credits and new forms of benefits 'vouchers' have been developed to facilitate individuals and to enable them to exercise choice. The latest changes to housing benefit highlight this extension of choice to impoverished housing consumers. Furthermore, mixed communities are seen as liberating, offering opportunity and mutual benefit. However, this solution has raised questions about the efficacy of poverty dilution, with a continued concern over whether it is better to be poor in a poor area or poor in a mixed area (Buck *et al.*, 2005; Lee and Murie, 1997), and a review of mix policies in both the US and Europe reveals that mix alone is insufficient in producing the desired outcomes (Galster, 2007a, 2007b; Galster *et al.*, 2003; Popkin *et al.*, 2006). Viewed from the alternative perspective, it is very hard to see what benefits there are for the better off from living in a mixed neighbourhood, and obvious reasons for not wanting to do so, not least the perceived negative effect on property values. There remains no clear evidence to support either side in this debate to date (Atkinson, 2005; Cheshire, 2007), yet policies of mix remain enthusiastically advocated (Berube, 2006; Holmes, 2006).

But too strong a focus on tenure can lead us down the wrong path. Tenure is part of the explanation of the position we are in today, but the housing system has become more complex over time and a new means of analysis is required. Murie (2006) has suggested that the tenure-based analysis of the housing system which identified partitioned patterns of control and finance has become less appropriate in today's fragmented housing system. Rather, a more stratified and complex system exists, in which there is competition between tenures and less direct bureaucracy governing allocation and access, but in which there now exists a wider range of stakeholder influences. Processes that were once tenure-specific have now spanned tenures. For example, the recent tightening of the credit market has highlighted this through the squeezing of credit availability for both individual households and housing associations alike, an indication of the wider influences on the housing system and the competition between sectors for resources.

In respect of residualisation, the picture is more complex than tenure alone and again highlights the need for a better explanation. Council-built housing was once a favoured and popular tenure, social housing as it is today is now in a minority, with a residualised client base. This is not to say that the social sector houses all of the most deprived households. There exist high levels of deprivation and social problems in parts of both the private rented sector and in owner occupation. But because the concentrations are less visible as a part of the whole and form only a part of the sector, they escape the easy labelling attached to social renting. It is the spatial homogeneity of poverty which is seen as the problematic in these analyses and which government is concerned with breaking. Although tenure, often based on historic tenure patterns, has been used as a label, it is misplaced. While mono-tenure social housing is clearly seen by policy-makers and some researchers as problematic, this concern is only tenable in this form if social-housing estates are truly mono-tenure today. The pattern and process of change in the sector (high turn-over, using voids to rehouse those in most housing need, and so on) would almost certainly result in socio-economic patterns which would continue to concentrate deprivation in specific locations (Bramley *et al.*, 2007).

As demonstrated elsewhere (Murie and Jones, 2006) these estates are rarely mono-tenure: older estates have seen the process of change through sales, newer estates are mixed by design. Nor does this explain the levels of deprivation found in non-social-housing areas. The lack of housing opportunity in the social-housing sector, even for households in acute housing need, means that neighbourhoods with private renting are now as deprived as some social-housing estates. For example, recent research by the author shows that the West End of Morecambe has witnessed a high proportion of benefit-dependent single-person and predominantly male households in subdivided properties, partially as a result of a limited supply of social housing and partly as a result of their exclusion from access to the supply that exists, either by a lack of priority need or through their behavioural history. Therefore we cannot blame tenure solely for the concentrated deprivation we see – it is merely one of a series of explanations. The role of the housing market is overlooked in the analysis of these patterns, yet its more complex operation is more important for understanding the outcomes for sustainable communities than the demarcation lines that tenure conveniently provides.

The response to this situation is equally challenging because of the misplaced analysis of tenure as the root of the problem. The main policy tool for addressing deprivation is to develop 'mixed communities' with an assumption that this will provide social and economic benefits for low-income households. This policy is applied to break-up deprivation and social housing. The means of delivering these mixed communities is through a policy of mixing tenure, assuming that social housing alone is bad and that 'market' housing offers a panacea. It is a simplistic solution to provide the anticipated complex outcomes. The development of mix assumes two things: that proximity leads to interaction which is in some way beneficial to both parties and that localised economic multipliers can be created through some form of trickle-down. It assumes that there is a substantive difference between households.

The question which should be asked (but seldom is) is whether these assumptions are actually fulfilled. As I have demonstrated elsewhere, the picture itself is mixed (Rowlands et al., 2006). Using household income as a proxy for social mix, new mixed-tenure estates are mixed but this mix is limited by the form of the property (size and type), the difference in this between tenures and the market segment at which market properties on the development are aimed. These factors work together in delivering a particular outcome, as demonstrated below. But whether this proximity of residence and social mix leads to any form of social interaction is yet to be proved with any certainty. The studies that have taken place have demonstrated that: mix does not automatically result in interaction and mutual support (Jupp et al., 1999); that where interaction takes place it remains internally stratified by tenure (Atkinson and Kintrea, 2000); that the narrower the income mix is, the wider people perceive the social mix to be (Rowlands et al., 2006); and that ultimately cross-tenure social interaction takes place most in areas which have developed this mix organically (Beekman et al., 2001).

Why is this the case? The market operates in such a way that mixed communities create a partial mix within a certain section of society. Income mix may appear broad but it captures those within a certain part of the market. The crucial element here is that the housing market operates to facilitate and form the mix created. What do I mean by this? Cole and Goodchild (2001) have said that the terms 'sustainable', 'balanced' and 'mixed' have been conflated but remain conceptually distinct and, while they may overlap, this should not be taken as proof that one leads to another. Using two different examples of mix, the outcomes of tenure mix are demonstrated below.

The right to buy, as with other social-housing sales policies, is often justified as creating mixed estates. However, does this policy actually do this? Murie and Jones (2006) have demonstrated that in the early phases of the policy in the early 1980s, purchasers tended to be older and had an intention to remain on the estate in the house. This creates tenure mix and aids the maintenance of a form of balance within the community. However, the social mix that occurs remains the same and all that has altered is the tenure of the property. Over time these estates become more mixed. The resale of properties brings in new households, some of whom will have different social characteristics than the remaining social tenants. Social mix starts to alter only after the resale of properties as new households move into the estate. However, this process and any social mix that results is a product of the housing market. The type of buyer of these properties will depend on the local housing market, affordability levels and the place of the relevant estate in that local market. Analysis of right-to-buy sales in Birmingham highlights the situation that has emerged (Murie *et al.*, 2008). The sales process does not break the continuity of the historical position of these estates within the housing market hierarchy within the city and moderating factors which may have been in place as a result of a more bureaucratic allocations system are removed, exacerbating differences between estates and making polarisation greater. The analysis suggests that, while those estates with a better reputation may have an upward trajectory and command a better housing market position, sales policies are unlikely to improve the position and condition of the worst estates.

Therefore, resale is no guarantee of attaining a social mix or improvement of estates. As demonstrated in a range of locations (Ireland, 2005; Murie and Jones, 2006; Murie *et al.*, 2008) resale into private renting can replicate the same client base – or an even more residualised one – as households in social housing. And not only is social mix undermined by this process, but the estates themselves can become less stable as a result of the continual churning of tenancies on both tenures. Ultimately it is important to ask ourselves whether this is sustainable. I would contend that the operation of the market has placed these estates in a particular segment and worked against stability. The estates may still perform a function in the housing market and meet housing needs, but the wider reputation of the neighbourhood may suffer as a result, and it may become less attractive as a place to live. Considering this within the policy context already outlined, continued sales policies are likely to address a desire for home ownership among a declining proportion of tenants, but the processes which have been created are likely to end in less sustainable communities and increasing polarisation.

In new-build housing estates the picture is slightly different. Here, mix is a factor incorporated in the design. Planning policies now require the inclusion of mixed tenure in new developments (CLG, 2006), off-site provision is increasingly disallowed and some planning authorities are imposing high levels of affordable housing on development (for example, the Greater London Authority's now rescinded 50 per cent quota for new developments). The outcome is evidenced by recent work for the Joseph Rowntree Foundation which illustrates the outcomes of policies aimed at creating new mixed communities (Rowlands *et al.*, 2006). The evidence shows that by mixing tenure, planners can create varying degrees of income mix on new estates. In the case of those with a broader tenure base, the income mix itself can be quite broad. But this mix does not always translate into a balanced or sustainable community.

Certainly, the research indicates that the narrower the income mix is, the more socially mixed residents perceived it to be, and while this in itself may be counter-intuitive, it provides residents with a comfortable degree of otherness in similarity (Rowlands, 2008), as explained below. But it is the fact that the mix perceived by planners ignores the reality of what actually occurs which is of most significance in the use of this tool. One estate in the study, developed on a brownfield site in a town in the south of England, illustrates this. The tenure mix agreed by planners was 75 per cent housing for sale, 25 per cent affordable housing.

Herein lies the first problem. Because the planning mechanism cannot easily accommodate affordable housing, it usually ends up as social rented housing. However, the broader category of 'housing for sale' is assumed to be owner-occu-pied housing. This blend created an income mix which was broad, yet skewed towards both ends of the income range. The mix was dictated by the tenure. Important in this was the emergence of a significantly large private rented sector. This was not anticipated by the planners: at approximately 30 per cent of the prop-erties, it was larger than the level that might have been expected. This outcome is a product of the development's position in the local housing market, and its form, which makes it attractive to investment purchasers. Yet the outcome for a sustain-able community is questionable. Private renting can have a destabilising effect on neighbourhoods as a result of high turnover, low place attachment and poor man-agement by landlords. The results of this research indicated that private renters often had a more transitory housing history and most were not intending to remain in these locations beyond a year. Therefore, while these estates are mixed, are they balanced or sustainable? A recent revisit to one estate indicated that poor planning and the impact of these dynamics was now starting to become a liability for the future of the area.

The pursuit of mix as a panacea for urban poverty can be considered a new technological short-cut to social change (Murie and Rowlands, 2008). This is based on ideological assumptions about the power of mix underpinned by an eco-nomic imperative to deliver more for less state input. Therefore not only is mix assumed to deliver social benefits but through the planning system it is assumed to enable the delivery of more affordable housing for the same or less subsidy. But does either of these contribute to a sustainable community?

'Sufficient range, diversity, affordability and accessibility of housing within a balanced housing market'

A crucial element of the UK government's stated sustainable communities policy is the provision of opportunity to access housing within a balanced market. As Cole and Goodchild (2001) have previously noted, the terms 'sustainable' and 'balanced' have been used interchangeably but without recognition of their distinct differences. While the policy aims for a mixed market which provides opportunities for all, the market only delivers balance across a wide geographic scale through varying degrees of localised homogeneity of both product and price. Despite planning policies, this localised homogeneity has increased in recent years. Therefore the housing market operates in a skewed way so that opportunities to move locally within a narrow radius and within existing neighbourhoods remain limited. Arguably, the ladder of opportunity is broken, if it ever existed at all. How does this contribute to a sustainable community?

Housing choices are constrained. It has been clear over time that people cannot always live where they want to and, more importantly, where they need to at a price that they can afford. Mobility has enabled this to be increasingly overcome, leading to a greater separation of work and residence. For those on lower incomes, and especially as we move into a post-peak-oil phase of development, this disjuncture is of significance. Yet the government appears to overlook much of this in its housing policies and seeks a utopian vision of a balanced housing market. Its own response has been initially through targeted intervention in supply: for example, through the Key Worker Living Initiative, and latterly endorsing the necessary increase in supply proposed by the Barker Review by imposing higher housing targets on all regional housing boards across England, and not just in the pressured South-East (NHPAU, 2007). The success of this intervention is patchy. For example, the Key Worker Living Initiative was most successful in retaining rather than recruiting essential staff and often those in more senior positions (Battye *et al.*, 2005), and therefore, it could be argued, underpinned the growing asset divide rather than facilitating access.

The increasing limitation of opportunity is important if the idea of sustainable communities is based on stability and familiarity. Communities that are mixed are increasingly micro-polarised internally and are externally polarised from more affluent private housing neighbourhoods. This is the result of the operation of the housing market and the position of these neighbourhoods within it. But while mixed opportunities may be expected to offer a range of housing opportunities which enable mobility locally, the reality is that there are few opportunities within the estates and neighbourhoods. To move up the housing ladder even marginally often means a move away from the existing neighbourhood to another. Low-cost home-ownership products lack sufficient flexibility and choice to provide an adequate alternative to the status quo of housing offer. In most situations, to get onto the housing ladder and climb it, it is often necessary to leave the neighbourhood, highlighting the lack of balance achieved through these policies. HomeBuy products facilitate initial affordability and upward staircasing for the current household but in practice do not retain affordability for future households, nor do they offer flexibility and security downwards should household circumstances change. Indeed, it is market-based solutions provided by some private house-builders which appear to offer greatest satisfaction for purchasers (NAO, 2006) and develop somewhat better levels of blind, albeit narrow, mix between market and sub-market housing. The credit crunch is unlikely to result in a market slow-down, which helps those locked out of the market – rather, the credit crunch could prevent even more people entering, and prevent those already in the market at the margins facing an unsustainable future as home owners. Without sustained government intervention, either through subsidised development or personal subsidy (grants or loans), the levels of housing demand already stated will continue to remain unmet in the short to medium term.

Underlying these problems would appear to be the government's continued pressure to make an even greater majority of households home owners. Repeated social surveys suggest that 90 per cent of households *want* to be home owners and this is seemingly the guideline figure the government uses as a benchmark to be achieved. A recent evaluation of the Social HomeBuy scheme, which enables sitting social housing tenants to buy a part-stake in their home, showed that not all tenants are in a position to buy even a 10 per cent stake in their property, and even if they do their current home is not seen as a realistic option (Rowlands and Murie, 2008). So in essence the opportunities for everyone have boiled down to opportunities within one tenure, if households have the necessary resources. Those who do not are increasingly isolated, financially and socially. This is a reflection on the policy of promoting home ownership and the benefits that government sees of it in wider society, but there is an increasing urgency to address the question of what happens to those with few choices. This is no longer a case of just the poor in residualised housing, but, as highlighted earlier in the chapter, now involves an increasing proportion of middle-income households who would previously have been in a position to buy. The analysis indicates that housing processes are increasingly unsustainable, divisive and segregating, but the policies in place by government seem not to recognise this.

More than housing

A focus on housing alone is misplaced. Housing's role is simultaneously under- and overestimated in analyses of the problems faced in creating sustainable communities. Above I have highlighted the under-reliance on a housing explanation. However, housing on its own does not recognise two factors that are key in realising sustainability in neighbourhoods: wider social counter-trends working against the policy intentions; and a lack of joined-up thinking in the planning of housing and the needs of neighbourhoods and communities.

Wider social trends and other policies work against sustainable communities. Robertson *et al.* (2008) has interesting findings about the 'everyday interactions' that promote community by local facilities such as post offices and schools. These are two areas where sustainable-communities policy has not penetrated beyond the areas of immediate concern, planning and housing. Recent announcements of policy arc likely to work in the opposite direction to those being developed around sustainable communities. For example, local post offices are under threat of closure in some areas and school admission policies have highlighted perverse patterns of disconnection between where people live and the schools their children attend. Planning policies have favoured development patterns which require mobility over accessibility and localism. Although out-of-town shopping centres have been limited in recent years, the continued trend for shopping has focused on large-scale development with a wide hinterland best served by car. Take, for example, the development of supermarkets in the UK and the power they wield. As highlighted by critics (Simms, 2007) and regulators (Competition Commission, 2008) alike, consumers have been increasingly forced to focus their shopping on a few big players. This has reduced choice and, through the power of their market position, supermarkets have been able to squeeze out local competition. Ultimately this means a demise of choice and a drain on local communities. Supermarkets are often also a drain on local economies and do not provide as large a multiplier as some local schemes can (Simms, 2007, p. 160). We have been familiar with food deserts for some time: now we need to think about how the way we shop fits with policies for housing and sustainable communities, and how better coordination, investment and support could work to prevent these and offer more besides – for example, jobs. Cheapest isn't always best. These policies highlight the short-term, economic focus of policy-making. Times are clearly different from those of the Victorian place-makers, who made things happen despite cost.

A focus for this has been a perceived trend for individuals to search out similarity, or 'people like us'. While the extent of this may have been overstated, it is clear that households seek out areas which do not have dramatic differences from themselves, and are guided by appearance, reputation and prejudice. Therefore people don't mind narrow mix. The under-researched realm of suburbia is perhaps the telling evidence of this trend towards a bland normality. Processes of social privatisation, the increased consumption at home of what used to be communally consumed goods and services, such as alcohol and films, further compound the sense of a loss of active community, or at the very least communal experience. For policy-makers this challenges the traditionally perceived notion of 'community', particularly in deprived neighbourhoods, and is seen to make the process of developing sustainable neighbourhoods more difficult. At the heart of this concern is a lack of interaction which, as highlighted above, is important for the responsibilisation process.

If sustainable communities are to be realised there is a need to expand our focus. Sustainable communities need to provide opportunities in three areas: social, economic and political.

Social opportunities require the creation of space within which interaction can take place. Little consideration is given to these spaces in the development and remodelling of neighbourhoods, and other arenas in which interaction may take place locally are under threat from the whims of both the market and government policy, as highlighted above. But open space is often seen as unproductive and facilities for interaction are often underused because of poor planning and a lack of flexibility. Interaction arenas need to be considered and created in the design phase of development and intervention and, most importantly, thought through with people who live there. The informal rather than the formal is the key to participation. There needs to be better thought of what interaction arenas can be created and supported, and in this thinking there needs to be more scope for innovation in their design and delivery to ensure that sustainable utilisation and benefit are derived from them. For example, a housing association developing a new site in the rural West Midlands is currently considering how the struggling local pub could be supported to provide more community facilities.

The 'trickle-down' approach to economic development has been shown not to work on a large scale (Imrie and Thomas 1999; Lupton and Tunstall, 2008; Robson *et al.*, 1994; Thornley, 1999), and these lessons should be heeded at a localised level. Galster (2007a, 2007b) shows that the benefits of mix policy thus far are equivocal and that there is only a tentative yes to the question of whether it is beneficial – the results depend on other factors. His conclusions are that mixing high-income groups with low-income ones is more detrimental than beneficial. Mixed-tenure policies do create a narrow income mix in the UK and therefore may be beneficial. But without the means of economic capture it relies on the proximity approach of good behaviour rubbing off on a feckless population. What is needed is more means of local economic capture through the development of locally rooted businesses and real opportunities for endogenous growth. This could also see the development of potential for new business and services which meet the needs of local residents. Local resources will grow in importance as we reach peak-oil and move beyond it – it is important to start planning for it now.

Communities are increasingly being perceived as apathetic to politics in general and local politics in particular. Yet most residents have genuine concerns about the state of their neighbourhoods and the services they receive. The problem is then perhaps more in the methods used to enable political engagement than a general apathy among the population. Engagement in more deprived areas is seen as a challenge, yet less so in affluent neighbourhoods. It is also seen as something which should exist in deprived areas, when it doesn't elsewhere. Yet as Kingsnorth (2008) highlights, affluent communities rarely participate day-to-day – rather, they do so when there is a problem to rally around. Instead we should be changing the perspective through which we view the challenge. In all cases, the means of engagement are often formulaic and formalised to the extent that they can become the very barrier to better participation (Mullins *et al.*, 2004). Burrows *et al.* have highlighted roles for the Internet and other electronic forms of participation in community governance, and a growing literature documenting the rise of the virtual community's power indicates the role it plays in creating mass movements of the twenty-first century (Leadbetter, 2008; Shirky, 2008; Tapscott and Williams, 2007). The crucial challenge is how best to capture the soft elements of participation in a way that is meaningful to residents. Local governance and services need to be more responsive and meaningful to the communities that they serve. Although this was recognised by the Prime Minister in 2007 (Brown, 2007), the continued central control over targets and resources makes meaningful engagement problematic. New structures and greater freedom are needed if engagement and participation are to be meaningful and productive.

These elements are ultimately lacking from the present approach. A focus solely on the market to deliver forgets that the market will only provide those things which deliver a guaranteed and instant return. Earlier in this chapter I highlighted the fact that the form of mixed-tenure developments becomes a product of development economics. This is where the state, in partnership with others, could play a crucial role in realising the value of place. This is nothing new, and more enlightened projects have provided a model for what might be achieved, even if they themselves have some way to go in delivering on all of their aims.

The first priority is embedding communities by providing better anchorage for individuals and households. This requires the development of better outcomes from the planning system rather than systematic outputs. Ultimately reasons must be provided to keep people within neighbourhoods and communities, reasons to want to live there and means to stay there when their circumstances change.

The question at the end of this critique is: What might this new mode look like? The answer is not straightforward, but there are clues to the components that should be considered in developing the solutions: they include better interaction arenas, planned by the people who use them, and a range of goods and services available locally which would provide opportunities for employment and enterprise. One model may be the development of a coherent system of 'community trusts'. These would be organisations charged with the development and management of neighbourhoods and the services provided within them. The trusts would be small enough to foster an improved attachment to place and to facilitate interaction with residents. They would ensure a range of housing which has affordability built in, through an improved model of flexible tenure utilising elements of the co-operative and community land trust models already employed in housing in the UK and further afield. The trust would provide seamless neighbourhood management, developing the idea proposed by the Callcutt Review of Housebuilding of an ongoing interest by developers in the management of new estates (Callcutt, 2007). The trust could also have a role in fostering economic development which facilitates local service provision and negates the need to travel. As we move into a paradigm of sustainability in general, the policy of sustainable communities needs to reverse the mantra of globalisation and become Local:Global – acting locally to have a positive impact globally.

Utopian dream or realistic fatalism?

The charge which could be levelled at this vision is that it is too utopian. Without intervention by government, and where societal trends of privatism and individualism outcompete mutual gains, this likelihood is greater. Yet the challenges we now face require a new vision, a shift in the direction of societal trends and a step change in intervention to make them achievable. We have reached a crossroads where difficult choices have to be made and where decisions will have to be taken which will not always be popular, if we are to secure a sustainable future. Developing sustainable communities will not be a straightforward task. This chapter has highlighted the relationship between housing and communities, the disjuncture in policy and strategy between these, together with the complex challenge faced in delivering neighbourhoods that work in the face of current and future challenges. While it is not the role of the researcher alone to advocate which direction to take, the suggestions in this chapter form the basis of what may be a more sustainable route to community. However, while we blame politicians and policy-makers for a lack of coherent planning, as researchers we are often equally guilty in remaining in our own silos and comfort zones. In doing so the opportunity to cross boundaries and provide a more sophisticated analysis of the problem is lost. Furthermore our attention to policy-based evidence often limits our scope for fresh thinking. Ultimately the potential for a positive contribution is gone.

If we are to regain our supposed lost communities, rebuild neighbourhoods that work or develop a better-functioning urban fabric, it is vital that the various yet complex strands needed to realise the vision are brought together. While recent attempts to join up policy should be acknowledged, the balance between the social, economic and environmental concerns is not yet in equilibrium. Nor will these changes be brought about through laissez-faire actions. Disparate and disjointed policies together with a need to satisfy dominant beneficiaries amount to less sustainable communities. Only if politicians and policy-makers are prepared to take hard, serious decisions which change the present trajectories of individuals and households will sustainable communities be delivered. This might be described as realistic fatalism, yet it represents one of the most significant opportunities to plan today the communities we want and need in the medium and long terms.

Notes

1. Bourneville is often referred to as an exemplar of community – for example in Holmes (2006). But as Groves *et al.*, (2005) have identified in recent research, the success of Bourneville owes as much to the ongoing management of the estates as it does to the original planning, and perhaps even less so to any tenure mix.

References

Atkinson, R. (2005) *Neighbourhoods and the Impacts of Social Mix: Crime, Tenure Diversification and Assisted Mobility*, CNR Paper 29, ESRC Centre for Neighbourhood Research, http://www.bristol.ac.uk/sps/cnrpaperspdf/cnr29pap. pdf – accessed 6 May 2009.

Atkinson, R. and Kintrea, K. (2000) 'Owner-occupation, social mix and neighbourhood impacts', *Policy and Politics*, 28(1), 93–108.

Battye, F., Harris, P., Murie, A., Rowlands, R. and Tice, A. (2005) *Evaluation of Key Working Living Initiative*, London: ODPM.

Beekman, T., Lyons, F. and Scott, J. (2001) *Improving the Understanding of the Influence of Owner Occupiers in Mixed Tenure Neighbourhoods*, Edinburgh: Scottish Homes.

Berube, A. (2006) *Mixed Communities in England: A US Perspective on Evidence and Policy Prospects*, York: Joseph Rowntree Foundation.

BMG (2008) *Housing Corporation Residents Panel Survey 4*, Cambridge: Housing Corporation (http://www.housingcorp.gov.uk/upload/doc/SURVEY4_FINAL_REPORT.doc).

Bramley, G., Leishman, C., Kofi Karley, N., Morgan, J. and Watkins, D. (2007) *Transforming Places: Housing Investment and Neighbourhood Market Change*, York: Joseph Rowntree Foundation.

Brown, G. (2003) Speech at the opening of the Millennium City building at the University of Wolverhampton, http://www.hm-treasury.gov.uk/press_16_03. htm – accessed 6 May 2009.

Brown, G. (2007) Speech to the National Council of Voluntary Organisations on politics, 3rd September 2007 (http://www.number-10.gov.uk/output/Page13008. asp visited 17 June 2008).

Brundtland, G. (1987) *Our Common Future: World Commission on Environment and Development*, Oxford: Oxford University Press.

Buck, N., Harding, A., Gordon, I. and Turock, I. (2005) *Changing Cities: Rethinking Urban Competitiveness, Cohesion and Governance*, Basingstoke: Palgrave Macmillan.

Callcutt, J. (2007) *The Callcutt Review of Housebuilding Delivery*, London: Department for Communities and Local Government.

Cheshire, P. (2007) *Are Mixed Communities the Answer to Segregation and Poverty?* York: Joseph Rowntree Foundation.

CLG (2006) *Planning Policy Statement 3: Housing*, London: Department for Communities and Local Government.

CLG (2008) *What is a Sustainable Community?*, http://www.communities.gov. uk/archived/general-content/communities/whatis/ – accessed 6 May 2009.

Cole, I. and Furbey, R. (1994) *The Eclipse of Council Housing*, London: Routledge.

Cole, I. and Goodchild, B. (2001) 'Social mix and the "balanced community" in British housing policy – a tale of two epochs', *Geojournal*, 51(4), 351–60.

Competition Commission (2008) *The Supply Of Groceries in The UK Market – Investigation*, London: Competition Commission.

Darby, L. and Jenkins, H. (2006) 'Applying sustainability indicators to the social enterprise business model: The development and application of an indicator set for Newport Wastesavers, Wales', *International Journal of Social Economics*, 33(5/6), 411–31.

Delanty, G. (2006) *Community*, London: Routledge.

DETR (2000) *Quality and Choice: A Decent Home for All*, London: DETR.

DfES (2008) *Citizenship at Key Stage 3*, London: DFES http://www.standards. dfes.gov.uk/schemes2/citizenship/

Egan, J. (2004) *The Egan Review: Skills for Sustainable Communities*, London: ODPM.

Farrar, M. (2001) 'Re-thinking "community" as a utopian social imaginary', Paper presented to 'Class, Space and Community – A Workshop Conference', Department of Sociology and Social Policy, University of Durham, 6th to 8th April 2001 (Available at http://www.maxfarrar.org.uk/docs/CommunityPaper Durham.pdf – retrieved on 16 May 2008).

Flint, C. (2008) Address to the Fabian Society (Available from: http://www. communities.gov.uk/speeches/corporate/fabiansocietyaddress – accessed 6 October 2008).

Flint, J. (2002) 'Social Housing Agencies and the Governance of Anti-social Behaviour', *Housing Studies*, 17(4), 619–37.

Flint, J. and Rowlands, R. (2003) 'Commodification, normalisation and intervention: Cultural, social and symbolic capital in housing consumption and governance', *Journal of Housing and the Built Environment*, 18(3), 231–32.

Flint, J. and Nixon, J. (2006) 'Governing neighbours: Anti-social behaviour orders and new forms of regulating conduct in the UK', *Urban Studies*, 43(5/6), 939–55.

Forrest, R. and Murie, A. (1983) 'Residualisation and council housing: Aspects of the changing social relations of housing tenure', *Journal of Social Policy*, 12(1), 453–68.

—— (1995) 'From privatisation to commodification: Tenure conversion and new zones of transition in the city', *International Journal Of Urban And Regional Research*, 19(3), 407–22.

Forrest, R., Murie, A. and Williams, P. (1990) *Home Ownership: Differentiation and Fragmentation*, London: Unwin Hyman.

Foucault, M. (1991) 'Governmentality', in: G. Burchell (ed.) *The Foucault Effect: Studies in Governmentality*, Hemel Hempstead: Harvester Wheatsheaf, 87–104.

Galster, G. (2007a) 'Neighbourhood social mix as a goal of housing policy: A theoretical analysis', *European Journal of Housing Policy*, 7(1), 19–43.

Galster, G. (2007b) 'Should policy makers strive for neighbourhood social mix? An analysis of the western European evidence base', *Housing Studies*, 22(4), 523–45.

Galster, G., Santiago, A., Tatian, P., Pettit, K. and Smith, R. (2003) *Why Not In My Back Yard? Neighbourhood Impacts of Assisted Housing*, New Brunswick: Center for Urban Policy Research Press.

Groves, R., Murie, A., Middleton, A. and Broughton, K. (2005) *Neighbourhoods that Work*, Bristol: Policy Press.

Gurney, C. (1999) 'Pride and prejudice: Discourses of normalisation in public and private accounts of home ownership', *Housing Studies*, 14(2), 163–83.

Holmes, C. (2006) *Mixed Communities: Success and Sustainability*, JRF Foundations, York: JRF.

Imrie, R. and Thomas, H. (1999) *British Urban Policy: An Evaluation of the Urban Development Corporations*, London: Sage.

Jupp, B., Sainsbury, J. and Akers-Douglas, O. (1999) *Living Together: Community Life On Mixed Tenure Estates*, London: Demos.

Kingsnorth, P. (2008) *Real England*, London: Portobello Books.

Leadbetter, C. (2008) *We-think: The Power of Mass Creativity*, London: Profile Books.

Lee, P. and Murie, A. (1997) *Poverty, Housing Tenure and Social Exclusion*, Bristol: The Policy Press.

Lupton, R. and Tunstall, R. (2008) 'Neighbourhood regeneration through mixed communities: "a social justice dilemma"?' *Journal of Education Policy*, 23(2), 105–17.

Malpass, P. (2008) 'Housing and the new welfare state: Wobbly pillar or cornerstone?' *Housing Studies*, 23(1), 1–19.

Marr, A. (2007) *A History of Modern Britain*, Macmillan.

Mullins, D., Beider, H. and Rowlands, R. (2004) *Empowering Communities, Improving Housing: Involving Black and Minority Ethnic Tenants and Communities*, London: ODPM.

Murie, A. (2006) 'Moving with the Times: Changing Frameworks for Housing Research and Policy', in P. Malpass and L. Cairncross (eds.) *Building on the Past – Visions of Housing Futures*, Bristol: Policy Press.

Murie, A. and Jones, C. (2006) *The Right to Buy*, London: Blackwell.

Murie, A. and Rowlands, R. (2008) 'The New Politics of Urban Housing', *Environment and Planning C*, 26(3), 644–59.

Murie, A., Rowlands, R. and Tice, A. (2008) 'The Right to Buy and Private Renting in Birmingham', Unpublished working paper, Birmingham: CURS.

NAO (2006) *A Foot on the Ladder: Low Cost Home Ownership Assistance*, London: NAO.

ODPM (2005) *Planning Policy Statement 1: Delivering Sustainable Development*, London: ODPM.

OED (2008) *Oxford English Dictionary*, Online version.

Pahl, R. (1970) *Patterns of Urban Life*, London: Longman.

Popkin, S., Katz, B., Cunningham, M., Brown, K., Gustafson, J. and Turner, M. (2006) *A Decade of HOPE VI: Research Findings and Policy Challenges*, Washington: Urban Institute (http://www.urban.org/UploadedPDF/411002_HOPEVI.pdf).

Raco, M. (2007) 'Securing sustainable communities: Citizenship, safety and sustainability in the new urban planning', in *European Urban and Regional Studies*, 14(4), 305–20.

Robertson, D., Smyth, J. and McIntosh, I. (2008) *Neighbourhood Identity: People, Time and Place*, York: JRF.

Robinson, D. (2008) 'Housing and Cohesion in England', Plenary paper presented to HSA Annual Conference: Housing and Cohesion, University of York, 2–4 April 2008.

Robson, B., Bradford, M., Deas, I., Ham, E. and Harrison, E. (1994) *Assessing the Impact of Urban Policy*, London: HMSO.

Rose, N. (2001) 'Community, citizenship and the third way', in D. Merydyth and J. Minson (eds) *Citizenship and Cultural Policy*, London: Sage.

Rowlands, R. (2008) 'Otherness in Similarity: The Scope of Mix in Urban Neighbourhoods', Paper presented to 'Diversity and plurality in the urban context' International Seminar, Katholieke Universiteit Leuven, Belgium 19–20 September 2008.

Rowlands, R. and Murie, A. (2008) *Evaluation of Social HomeBuy Pilot Scheme for Affordable Housing: Final Report*, London: CLG.

Rowlands, R., Murie, A. and Tice, A. (2006) *More than Tenure Mix*, York: JRF.

Shirky, C. (2008) *Here Comes Everybody*, London: Allen Lane.

Simms, A. (2007) *Tescopoly*, London: Constable.

Tapscott, D. and Williams, A. (2007) *Wikinomics: How Mass Collaboration Changes Everything*, London: Atlantic Books.

Thornley, A. (1999) 'Is Thatcherism Dead? The Impact of Political Ideology on British Planning', *Journal of Planning Education and Research*, 19, 183–91.

Walker, P., Lewis, J., Lingayah, S. and Sommer, F. (2000) *Prove It! Measuring the Effect of Neighbourhood Renewal on Local People*, London: Groundwork, The New Economics Foundation and Barclays PLC.

Wilcox, S. (2003) *Can Work, Can't Buy: Local Measures of the Ability of Working Households to Become Home Owners*, York: JRF.

12 Rediscovering housing policy

Back to the future?

Alan Murie

Much of the discussion in the published work on housing since the late 1970s was about the relegation of housing policy from the key political and electoral issue that it was in the early postwar period to a low-priority policy area. But in the years since 2000 government and the electorate have rediscovered housing policy. This chapter discusses some of the key dimensions of this shift in status and the discourses around it. Initially it considers the changing importance of the policy area and then goes on to refer in more detail to key elements in the recent discussion of policy and to the future direction of policy, especially towards rented housing.

The development of housing policy

Accounts of housing policy in Britain trace, in more or less detail, the development of interventions and legislation by government (see, for example, Harloe, 1995; Holmans, 1987; Malpass, 2000, 2008; Malpass and Murie, 1999; Merrett, 1979; Mullins and Murie, 2006). They conventionally refer to phases of development with distinctive characteristics. Although there is disagreement over exactly when one phase ends and another begins, there is broad agreement in other respects. There is a long period, from the mid-19th century through to the First World War, in which urban and housing problems attracted attention but generated public health rather than housing policy measures. In this period, although there were powers for local authorities to intervene in housing, there was insufficient political weight behind proposals for explicit subsidy for housing, and a reluctance to interfere with the market. The inadequacy of this situation was apparent before 1914 but the measures taken during the war and the political situation after it resulted in a major shift. Exchequer subsidy was introduced in 1919 and has continued in some form ever since. Local authorities became part of the permanent architecture of housing policy in Britain in the interwar years (Bowley, 1945). Exchequer subsidy facilitated direct provision of housing by the state, although changes in subsidy arrangements also affected the quality and types of housing built by the state (Malpass, 1990).

Many of the accounts of policy in the 60 years after 1919 refer principally to changes in exchequer subsidy and their effect on how much council housing of what type was built. Housing policy in this phase was often a numbers game – competition between parties and administrations at central and local levels to achieve the highest rates of new building and address housing supply and condition issues. This was especially true between the wars (with the shift to slum clearance in the 1930s altering the emphasis) and in the early postwar period. However, by the 1960s the decline of private renting and increasing problems of access to housing, partly associated with a much greater slum clearance programme, ushered in a period of more complex policy intervention. It was no longer sufficient to build more houses or even replace more slum properties. The older housing stock required more responsive approaches through improvement and repair. Problems of access and homelessness required different types of policy that addressed how ordinary families, as well as vulnerable groups, negotiated access to good-quality housing; and how they worked around the rules operated by local authority gatekeepers rationing high-demand council housing; and the rules operated by private-sector gatekeepers controlling access to mortgage finance in an environment where the demand for such funds exceeded the supply. The tasks given to the Housing Corporation, established in 1964, reflected the view that local authority activity was not sufficient. The Housing Corporation was initially tasked with filling a gap for middle-income groups by assisting housing associations to build cost-rent and co-ownership housing. By 1974 it had a wider remit, complementary to that of local authorities. Housing associations could also access government subsidy to contribute to the response to problems associated with homelessness and the inner city, and the need for area renewal, the improvement to older properties and building for special needs (Murie, 2008). A more complex policy architecture was emerging to address more diverse problems.

The parallel growth of home ownership and council housing, and the continuing decline of private landlordism, continued until the end of the 1970s. Both the research literature and policy switched emphasis from house condition and supply to the differential access to housing associated with tenure. The housing strategies of individual households were increasingly strategies to gain access to council housing or to home ownership, and the literature was dominated by debates about rationing, gatekeepers and managers, choice and constraint and competition for housing (for example, Bassett and Short, 1980; Henderson and Karn, 1987; Lambert *et al.*, 1978; Murie *et al.*, 1976; Rex and Moore, 1967). By the late 1970s the privately rented sector (which housed some 90 per cent of households in 1914) had declined dramatically at the expense of two tenures favoured by governments. Owner occupation housed some 60 per cent of the population, and councils and housing associations just over 30 per cent. This is the period referred to as the golden age of council housing (Harloe, 1995), when that tenure was superior to much of the private sector and there was high demand for it from a wide mix of households. While the conventional political perspective continued to highlight the subsidised nature of state housing and whether council tenants needed or deserved subsidy, alternative accounts had identified that by this stage, some 50 or more years on from the introduction of exchequer subsidy, the financial arrangements for the sector had some clear advantages when compared with home ownership (Kemeny, 1981, 1995). The debt associated with ownership of a home reflected its market value when last sold – and so increased periodically. In contrast, the debt associated with council housing was the historic debt incurred at construction, plus any major repairs or improvement costs that were capitalised. Any such debt was eroded by inflation, and the financial model for council housing enabled continuing housing construction (albeit including the often unattractive housing associated with multi-storey council housing) to be cross-subsidised by the rents generated on older properties; and this involved less call on exchequer funds than would otherwise have been the case, but with rents also remaining below market levels. Tenants of older properties were increasingly subsidising new council building and as the tenure matured the potential for this increased.

In this phase of policy there was active debate about local authorities as providers of rented housing but discussion of comprehensive housing services also blossomed. This reflected the involvement of government and local government not just in land supply and release for housing or the development and ownership of council housing, but also in: funding for housing associations and for the improvement and repair of the older housing stock, irrespective of who its owner was; the provision of mortgages for house purchase as well as improvement; the development of local rent rebate and allowance schemes; the regulation of parts of the private rented sector; the provision of housing aid and advice; the development of housing for older people and special needs groups; and the use of powers to promote home ownership, both through discretionary sales of properties to sitting tenants and through innovative schemes such as equity sharing. Building housing was no longer enough and the state was deeply entrenched in different parts of the housing market.

The abandonment of housing policy

The promise of a more complex and comprehensive housing service emerging as council housing matured was not, however, realised. The next phase of policy was one in which both the numbers game and concern about access to housing were displaced by the wider fiscal and economic preoccupations of government and the single ambition to expand home ownership. Rather than the latent financial strength of council housing being retained within that sector or channelled into wider housing policies, the era of privatisation and 'marketisation' enabled government to sell council houses at very large discounts to council tenants and generate capital receipts that were used to support non-housing expenditures and taxation changes. This was an era of disinvestment in state housing. It may have been intended by some that the enormous capital receipts generated by the sale of council housing would be reinvested in housing and in addressing urban problems, but in practice they represented a windfall gain for the Treasury and were used to fund other priorities.

Five orthodoxies can be identified at this point. The first was that the overwhelming preference of the British electorate made home ownership and its growth the central or even sole preoccupation of policy. The second orthodoxy was that the large non-market sector distorted the housing market, drew demand away and prevented it from working as efficiently as it would otherwise. The third was associated with the definition of public expenditure and the desirable level of such expenditure: all local authority expenditure, including housing, was counted as public expenditure and the convention was, essentially, to count any capital expenditure in full in the year it was incurred, rather than to count the annual costs of servicing the debt (as was more usual elsewhere in Europe). This convention operated alongside a situation where the enormous tax reliefs made use of by home owners were not counted as public expenditure. Nor were the discounts offered in association with the sale of council houses subject to any robust value-for-money examination at this stage; when they were, some 20 years later, they were reduced, and the Treasury view at that stage implied that they had previously been set at a level above that needed to achieve the desired outcome in terms of numbers of sales (see Jones and Murie, 2006; Marsh *et al.*, 2003). Although investments by councils and, say, building societies had the same economic effects (or the former were equally or more economically or socially effective), the public-expenditure orthodoxy determined against public-sector activity.

The fourth orthodoxy was that housing was a 'welfare' or 'social policy' activity rather than an economic one. This reflected the standard economic view that housing was not important in the dynamic of economic growth and housing provision responded to patterns of economic growth determined by the key factors of production – patterns of investment in housing were an output from the economy rather than an input, and attempts to assert a greater importance for housing in the economy were dismissed by the economics establishment. Finally, the fifth orthodoxy was that, apart from some limited and manageable pockets, the housing problem was largely solved. This view had developed during the 1970s as a result of the evidence of reduced unfitness and disrepair, overcrowding and sharing and the fact that the number of dwellings exceeded the number of households (albeit not all of these dwellings were in the right places or were available for use).

For some economists there was already over-investment in housing – council housing had been built to too high a standard and this made the financing and need for subsidy problematic and there was also an overall surplus of housing.

These orthodoxies can partly be identified in the Secretary of State for the Environment's accounts, in 1980 and 1981, of the decision-making process related to housing public expenditure. He referred to a range of discussions about what money was available for housing in the context of the public-expenditure constraint which the government had to introduce and about the question 'What could the government afford to devote to this field of social policy?' He also referred to 'starting from a situation where the Treasury would know . . . that we have the largest crude surplus of housing stock in our history' (quoted in Malpass and Murie, 1990; pp. 104–5). At this stage government had so far withdrawn from housing policy that it had no projections of housing demand, no targets for housing supply, no strategy to address housing need and only policies to deregulate and privatise. Local authorities' capital programmes were squeezed and their new construction activity effectively terminated; their management and maintenance expenditures were also so far constrained that the backlog of disrepair and the need for reinvestment in an ageing housing stock became chronic. The drivers of housing policy had shifted from local authorities to the private sector and there had been a centralisation or nationalisation of public policy (Murie, 1985).

Government's view had been that council activity had crowded the private sector out of the market and that once the public sector stepped aside the private sector would step in and expand activity; the market would begin to respond to demand, and filtering or trickle-down processes would mean that all households would benefit. John Biffen as a Treasury Minister in 1979 had expressed the view that housing 'can, in the main, be better provided by the private sector' (quoted in Malpass and Murie, 1990, p. 131) and in 1988 Nicholas Ridley as Secretary of State for the Environment indicated that local authorities' role in housing would be to 'act as facilitators to ensure that the markets work, that house-builders, private landlords and associations meet the full range of housing needs . . . ' (quoted in Malpass and Murie, 1990, p. 119) There had been a marked shift from the language of the comprehensive housing authority to that of the enabler. The state's role was at long arm's length, the unshackled market would work and the frameworks utilised by economists would be sufficient to explain what was happening.

One response to the public expenditure orthodoxy was for enterprising housing associations, and then the Housing Corporation, to develop a private-finance model that left them as more attractive routes for investment than local authorities. I initially resisted by the Treasury, this formula came to be welcomed by government under the Housing Act, 1988. Although the Housing Corporation and housing associations' contribution was continually under attack and by no means filled the gap left by the reduction in local authority activity, the rebranding of housing associations as Registered Social Landlords – operating outside the public-expenditure collar and accessing private-sector loans to enhance the impact of government funding for them – provided the basis for the associations to escape from the constraints that continued to impair the council sector. While the expansion of housing associations can be presented as facilitating demunici-palisation, it undoubtedly also offered an alternative to a 'true' privatisation, which would have involved the transfer of stock to private landlords, who could dispose of stock and manage and maintain properties without regulation, leaving tenants protected only through the courts.

Privatisation and deregulation had changed the architecture of housing policy. Central government and the Housing Corporation were increasingly driving public policy; and housing associations and private-sector agencies and professions were growing in importance while local authorities presided over a diminishing activity. The ambition of a comprehensive housing policy had given way to discussion of enabling roles for local authorities and contracting out. In this environment a strong theme in the academic literature was that, once local govern-ment's role in housing had been emasculated, housing policy had become largely peripheral. There were accounts both of the mechanisms used by government to withdraw from housing (especially through the right to buy, stock transfer and changed housing finance measures) and of why it had proved so easy for govern-ment to withdraw from a key part of welfare-state provision (see Cole and Furbey, 1994; Forrest and Murie, 1990).

Housing after privatisation

The housing system that emerged from the period of active deregulation and privatisation was very different than at earlier stages. The social rented sector in England had declined from its peak of 31 per cent in 1979 to 17 per cent in 2007. Between 1980 and 2007 some 1.75 million dwellings (34 per cent) of the council-housing stock was sold to sitting tenants under the right to buy. Other sales to sitting tenants, sales of vacant dwellings and sales to housing associations bring the figure of sales of local authority dwellings over the period to over three million – some 60 per cent of the stock (Jones and Murie, 2006). While some local authorities had continued to be creative and innovative there was a sustained demunicipalisation of housing provision – although it was not as dramatic as in central and eastern Europe and still leaves both England and Britain with a social rented sector that is large by European standards. The owner-occupied sector was dominant, although its growth faltered when right-to-buy sales fell away after 2004 and investment in private renting increased. The private rented sector was small (some 12 per cent compared with 90 per cent in 1914) and there was no certainty that its small expansion since the 1980s would continue (Chapter 7).

The alternative to private-sector housing had changed from high-quality, high-demand council housing to social renting that was more identifiable by its social role but also owned and managed by a diverse set of organisations. By March 2006, 140 local authorities in England had transferred some or all of their stock to housing associations and by October 2008 local authorities had transferred 1,097,921 dwellings. The housing-association sector was on course to become larger than the municipal sector by the end of 2009. Housing associations had the financial strength and organisational capacity to be major players in regeneration and development. A relatively modern, municipal tenure that housed a broad mix of income groups at favourable, non-market rents had been transformed into an older, poorer-quality sector. Spending on management and maintenance was constrained and deficit subsidy arrangements pushed rents up to levels that were not needed to meet historic costs and in many local authorities generated surpluses that were repaid to the Treasury. This social rented stock was owned and managed by housing associations and local authorities and strongly associated with low-income households. The narrowing of the social base (or residualisation) of the council sector had been evident since the mid-1960s with the decline of private renting and growth of home ownership, and the right to buy and other privatisation processes further speeded the decline in the size of the sector and the departure of more affluent tenants (see Murie, 2006). This left the social rented sector as a weak competitor with other tenures.

The analysis completed by Feinstein *et al*. (2008) indicates that the council-housing provision of the immediate postwar period proved advantageous for those who lived in it and had broken the cycle of poverty; but the changed social rented housing product available to later cohorts was damaged, failed to break the cycle of poverty and was more likely to reinforce it. It may be argued that this outcome had more or less been predicted in research which drew attention to residualisation (for example, Forrest and Murie, 1983, 1986; Murie, 1977, 1983). The policies pursued by successive governments had weakened council housing and encouraged tenants who could afford to buy to do so, and the consequence would be a concentration of deprivation in the remaining social rented sector and the lower strata of the private sector. Such concerns were either directly denied or ignored, and a series of programmes (including the Priority Estates Project and Estate Action) were seen as sufficient to deal with what were presented as localised pockets of poverty and failures of management. The wider problems were later 'discovered' and the failures of 'deprived estates' and their workless tenants were used to further attack social rented housing and the security it afforded.

The social rented sector continued to be highly differentiated. While much of the best council housing had been sold under the right to buy, the sector still comprised many houses with gardens, and the worst multi-storey estates, often depicted in the media to typify council housing, remained a minority. At the same time it is evident that the problems with the worst social rented estates were associated with more than the poor local management and allocation policies repeatedly stressed by Power (1987) and others: they were often affected by declining local economies, poor design of dwellings, blocks and estates, and by physical obsolescence. However well managed some of these estates were, they remained the least attractive in the area. In these cases management initiatives, including those associated with PEP, signally failed to remedy key problems (Foster and Hope, 1993; Glennerster and Turner, 1993). Significant demolition, rebuilding and redesign were a necessary addition to better management and a hallmark of many of the more effective strategies to make such estates attractive to live on (Tunstall and Coulter, 2006).

While social rented housing disproportionately housed the poorest sections of the community, the images of tenure polarisation (Stephens *et al.*, 2005) were misleading and problematised social housing. It is not true that all of the poor were in social rented housing and that home ownership was the preserve of the affluent and the rich. While the social base of council and housing-association housing narrowed, the home-ownership sector housed more than half of the poor households as well as the more affluent (Burrows, 2003; Lee and Murie 1997, 2002). Levels of housing satisfaction among home owners in lower council-tax bands were very similar to those among social rented tenants in the same bands – and both were very much lower than the levels associated with home ownership in the highest bands (Murie, 1997, 1998).

As the home-ownership sector developed such a dominant role, so the term 'home ownership' ceased to be a useful analytic category. Divisions within the home-ownership sector were greater than those between parts of home ownership and other tenures. Earlier accounts of home ownership in England tended to distinguish between, for example, affluent suburban owners and inner-city home ownership, but by 2007 differentiation within the market had grown. Increasing affordability problems, house-price inflation and a growing gap between the prices of the most and least expensive quartiles of houses had become a feature of home ownership. In effect home ownership operated within distinctive submarkets, with a stratified mass urban housing market distinct from a positional or elite-status urban housing market. There were enormous variations of price across very short distances or even in adjacent neighbourhoods and related to different types of dwellings and different features of the neighbourhood.

The expectation that reduced public-sector house-building would result in greater private-sector construction proved wrong. New construction in England in 1979 was 209,000 dwellings, and this figure had not been reached again by 2008, when the advent of the credit crunch further reduced building activity below any levels seen in peacetime since 1924. The new politics of urban housing involved central and local government as planners and enablers, rather than as procurers of buildings. It placed considerable reliance on making the provision of affordable housing a condition in the grant of planning permission for private residential development. It gave the initiative to developers, planners and the architectural establishment but did not leave them unconstrained. Opposition to building in the green belt and on greenfield land meant that the easiest option was to build high-density, brownfield and inner urban housing that limited change elsewhere. It took pressure off greenfield sites and avoided the political opposition to development in other parts of the country (Murie and Rowlands, 2007). But it was not generally the ideal option for developers and meant a considerable growth in apartments, which had not previously been a significant part of the built environment in England, except in London.

A failing market?

The contention of this chapter is that the post-privatisation experiment in market-based housing provision failed and that the state was rediscovering housing policy well before the credit crunch sucked it further into the housing market in 2008. The overall picture emerging from the era of privatisation and deregulation is of a stretched, more fragmented and more stratified housing market. Some of this was associated with differential levels of private investment in properties of different types, sizes and locations and some was more directly to do with the effects of policy: tenure transfers and subsequent investment and the neglect of management and maintenance in parts of the market. The housing provision system in place at the turn of the millennium exhibited a number of serious deficiencies. Some of these related to the fragmentation and stratification of the market and its implications for social exclusion and cohesion; but more importantly the housing market's functioning was out of step with ideas about economic competitiveness, both locally and nationally.

As the government more and more enthusiastically embraced home ownership and private renting, so the inflation of house prices became the focus of comment. The decade leading up to 2007 saw a stream of media and research reports highlighting rising house prices and their impact on different sections of the community. An affordability crisis was seen to exist across much of the UK. Rapid house price inflation was sustained through to 2007 when relatively small increases in interest rates and, more importantly, the international credit crisis emanating from the USA, brought it to a halt. Up to that point low interest rates, the experience of the appreciation of property values and the favourable record of investment in housing compared with investment in pensions, the stock exchange and other locations fuelled over-consumption. Lenders in the deregulated system were also willing to lend on demand and borrow on wholesale markets to back their lending, rather than link the availability of lending with the flow of funds from individual savers as in the past. Households were willing to invest more of their income in housing, and this, and the willingness of lenders to lend, contributed to house-price inflation. The growth in prices was highest in buoyant economic areas and where housing was of better quality or was regarded as a good investment.

The consequence of a continuing emphasis on market provision, deregulation of financial institutions, much greater income inequality and differential ability to borrow and to spend was increased social and spatial inequality. A larger, more differentiated home ownership sector was the predictable consequence of a succession of policies operating in an economy based on unequal reward systems. However, the discussions of affordability problems (including those in the Barker reviews of 2003, 2004 and 2006) were remarkably unwilling to refer either to the practices of lenders, or to income inequality and differential propensities to invest in housing among different income groups, as underlying causes of house-price inflation. They preferred to build models based on demographic and occupational characteristics but taking a restricted view that earnings equated with the resources that were mobilised for house purchase and that the proportion of income that households would invest in housing was unaffected by income level. Although a residual income argument suggested that the lowest income groups have little left for housing expenditure once they have paid for other basic needs, affordability models generally assumed that, irrespective of income level, the same proportion of income was invested in housing. The real error in this may be to ignore the willingness of successively higher income groups to commit, not just the larger sums associated with the same proportion of their income but increasing proportions of their income, to purchasing both first and other homes.

Much of the debate on affordability sought to demonstrate the impossibility of ordinary households meeting the thresholds required to buy properties. And yet these thresholds only existed because people had paid such prices. Perhaps the research community was too preoccupied with first time buyers, people on average incomes and dwellings with average (or lowest quartile) prices. As a way of opening debate the approach was constructive but as a basis for precise measurement, modelling or estimating the new supply needed to reduce house price inflation (especially in particular places and markets) it was inadequate. It should have given as much attention to households with their various sources of income and borrowing, and to higher income households, able to buy one or more properties at inflated prices and exacerbate the affordability problem for others. It should have addressed the overall structure of house prices and the identification of different sub markets at local and sub-regional levels. It should also have given more attention to the possibility that increased supply of certain types of housing in certain markets would draw in increased investment in housing or displace investment from other markets – in either case the increased supply would not generate reduction in prices where the increase in supply occurred.

Rediscovering housing policy

In the early years following the election of the New Labour government in 1997 there were very limited changes to housing policy. The spending plans of the previous government were retained and there was no significant shift in policy direction. Housing policy stepped up a gear following the publication of a Green paper in 2000 (DETR and DSS, 2000) but there were striking continuities with earlier policy-stock transfers and the right to buy continued to increase and it was still reasonable to assume that the role of the state was permanently diminished. The introduction of the Decent Homes programme represented a serious attempt to address the accumulated problems of disrepair and under-investment in the existing social housing stock. It broadened the concept of fitness to refer to a reasonable state of repair, modern facilities and thermal comfort. However the investment required to achieve this improvement in the council stock was most easily made available by accessing private finance through stock transfer. Equally importantly the Decent Homes Standard referred to the dwelling rather than the estate and had limitations in addressing the problems associated with multi storey blocks and the least attractive estates and properties. In some cases even after individual properties were brought up to the Decent Homes Standard, they remained in the least attractive stratum of the local market and as candidates for further regeneration and renewal.

The first real break with previous housing policy came with the sustainable communities plan (ODPM, 2003), which reflected concerns over the impact of housing and affordability on economic performance and international competitiveness. Housing was no longer seen as an area of social policy with little direct impact on the economy but had been rehabilitated as a crucial area for economic policy. The focus of policy was on housing supply and new targets to deal with population growth in the south of England. From this point onwards there was repeated reference to the damaging effect of affordability problems on the performance of the British economy and a series of reviews, commissioned by the Treasury, identified the need to increase housing supply (Barker, 2003, 2004, 2006). The Barker reviews asserted that a substantial increase in house building would be required to achieve long-term stability in the housing market, with house price increases held to a low and pre-determined level. The main mechanism was to address the failings of the planning system and bring more land forward for housing development by the private sector. While the planning system was largely to blame for failures of the market to build more (and to this extent there was still a view that too much intervention by the state was a problem) the reduction in public sector activity was identified as having left a gap in provision that was not easily filled. Existing levels of building were insufficient and an increase of between 70,000 and 120,000 units per annum in England was needed to reduce affordability problems (representing an increase of 40 per cent or more on existing rates of building). Additional funds would be needed to deliver additional social housing to meet projected future needs; however much of the increase in affordable housing would be achieved through the continuing use of S106 planning agreements – as the private sector built more this mechanism would generate more affordable housing. Although there were reservations about the quality, density, size and type of housing that had been coming forward through this route there was complete confidence that it offered a reliable basis for the expansion of housing supply, including affordable housing.

By 2007 a new government led by Gordon Brown placed housing at the top of its agenda. For the first time in many years, the Housing Minister, although still not a Cabinet member, would attend the Cabinet. The Barker reviews, carried out for Brown when he was Chancellor of the Exchequer, remained the touchstone for policy and emphasis was placed on delivering overall housing targets and increasing the supply of social housing. A new Housing Green Paper (DCLG, 2007) and new legislation was prepared. The Housing and Regeneration Act 2008 was designed to improve the supply and quality of housing in England, to secure the regeneration or development of land and infrastructure and to support in other ways the creation, regeneration or development of communities in England. The Act established a new Homes and Communities Agency with an enlarged budget of some £5 billion per year, to replace the Housing Corporation and English Partnerships and to take in parts of Communities and Local Government. It would spearhead Government's objectives in relation to housing supply and be better equipped to be involved with regeneration and act as a catalyst for community regeneration. At the same time the creation of a separate Tenants Services Authority meant the end of the co-location of investment and regulation within one agency (the Housing Corporation) and promised a more effective and objective approach to regulation (see Murie, 2008).

It is against this background that there has been a break in continuity in the housing market occasioned by the credit crunch and commencing in the latter part of 2007. No doubt there will be plenty of analysis of this in subsequent years but the sharp falls in construction activity, in the number of transactions in the housing market and in house prices in 2008 and the turmoil in the banking sector meant that lenders would no longer lend on demand or lend sums that represented such high proportions of property value. The collapse and subsequent nationalisation of the Northern Rock Bank and a later, more extended 'nationalisation' of other banks signalled an unprecedented new phase of state intervention related to the operation of the housing market. While the interventions in banking related to the wider operation of the economy and may be seen as short term emergency measures they had become necessary because of problems in housing and they were connected with the lending available for house purchase, the decline in market transactions and new building and increasing levels of repossessions. The credit crunch created problems for government, for housing associations and for individual households. The collapse of new private sector construction in itself meant that housing supply targets would not be met, but it also meant that the private-sector-led model (the reliance on planning gain and Section 106 agreements for the delivery of affordable housing) had failed. It drew government and its agencies into advocacy and persuasion of lenders to limit the impact of the credit crunch, emergency measures including a mortgage rescue package and bringing forward planned public sector investment. In effect government having already revived its concern with housing supply was now drawn in to a much wider range of interventions – not a return to the old comprehensive housing policy but driving further away from a limited enabling role.

The rediscovery of housing policy outlined above demonstrated that the deregulated, market based system emerging from the 1990s did not provide a sustainable solution that would mean that government could leave housing to the market. Government introduced new legislation, increased expenditure programmes and entered a new phase of active intervention in the housing market. The focus of government, more than 30 years ago, was upon meeting housing needs as part of the traditional redistributive approach associated with the postwar welfare state. In rediscovering housing policy government's concern was principally with the impact of housing on competitiveness and this raised questions related to the nature and role of different housing tenures. The question became more urgent with the added concerns associated with the credit crunch. A stigmatised, ghettoised, social housing sector playing a residual role and contributing to social division is seen to undermine agendas concerned with the international competitiveness of cities and regions. At the same time the problems of the private sector – from affordability to repossession, lack of access and inadequate levels of investment in new supply – were seen as having the same effect. Both the UK economy and agendas around social cohesion and exclusion were not being well served by housing.

At the same time the owner occupied market has changed dramatically. There are clear divisions within home ownership related to differences in the types of property that are owned, the rights and responsibilities associated with ownership; leaseholder and freeholder owners, the value of the property, its location and the extent to which it provides access to a range of other services: including schools. The significance of housing is no longer simply as a source of shelter but relates to access to other services and to the accumulation of wealth. In this sense the housing market is driven by demand from households with increasingly different incomes. As a result of this the home ownership sector is fragmenting into high status and elite sectors and lower status, low accumulation sectors. The privatised council estate does not provide the same opportunities for asset appreciation as the privately owned property in an exclusive, affluent suburb. Properties in new city centre developments equally provide different packages of opportunities and advantages.

Policy debate has begun to give more attention to differences within tenures and about places and wealth inequalities. The competition for housing is competition within home ownership and the consequence is increasing stratification within the home ownership sector. There is also considerable stretching of market values as income inequalities translate into a willingness to pay premiums to obtain high status housing or housing that provides unique or privileged access to particular facilities including schools and access to the countryside.

Alongside all of this, new expressions of demand for private rented housing are not just from people who want to be tenants but more critically are from people who want to own more than one property. Increasing income inequality generated in the 1980s has translated into increasing wealth inequality and differences in the capacity to buy not just one property but to buy more than one. This links to government's encouragement of individual asset building and the development of an asset based welfare state to supersede the postwar settlement (see Groves *et al.*, 2007). The development of the buy to let and second home markets in Britain is an important feature of the maturation of the private market in an era of considerable income inequality. The ability of some people to buy two or more dwellings competes with the ability of other households to buy one dwelling. Some households are squeezed out of buying one dwelling and become tenants, not by choice but by necessity. The complication apparent here is that the modernisation of tenure responding to the needs of capital includes the desire of affluent individuals to buy investment homes.

Rediscovering rented housing

In this context the future for housing and the rented sector has continued to be contested. The collapse of the private-sector-led model has arguably left a policy vacuum. Government has had to abandon its 'target' to increase housing supply and to rely on planning measures to generate new affordable housing. Further creativity in developing new pathways to 'affordable' home ownership or to encourage the growth of private renting also appeared to be working against the direction of the market and the likely longer term reluctance to revert to the lending practices (especially related to sub-prime lending) that had contributed to problems. In this context government had brought forward funds to enable more social rented housing to be built and looked to the financial and organisational capacity of local authorities and housing associations to limit the damage done and maintain some momentum in addressing housing problems. But even here the picture was not straightforward. Local authorities had run down their housing construction and mortgage lending activities over previous years and their expertise and capacity had been affected. The capacity of some housing associations had also been damaged by the higher cost and reduced availability of loans from the private sector and by problems related to the value of holdings of land and unsold market or shared equity housing. Nevertheless there was potential for further growth of rented housing using housing associations and local authorities.

In this environment, however, there was no consensus over the rented sector. The collapse of the private-sector-led model had left something of a policy void.

The market would clearly not provide but government and others were not sure where to turn next and appeared reluctant to break with the policies of privatisation and deregulation. Neither the Hills (2007) nor Cave (2007) reviews, both commissioned by Government to set the direction for social rented housing, had set an ambitious agenda for the renaissance of rented housing. They had set out a future scenario of a residual role for the social rented sector and lighter touch regulation designed to attract private builders into social housing. Hills's analysis of the social rented sector presented rationing, rents and subsidy as the crucial determinants for the way in which social housing operated rather than quality and consumer choice of dwelling. He presented the character of the sector as determined by the bureaucratic rationing of access to it and household decisions about moving home and about employment were shaped by the nature of the subsidy system and by the fact that rents in the sector were below market levels. This approach constructed a discourse in which lack of social mix and problems of worklessness were associated with rationing, rents and subsidy. The response from the then housing minister encouraged the diversion into a debate on worklessness that suggested making security of tenure conditional upon efforts to find employment or undertake training. Although research commissioned to explore the issue (see Fletcher *et al.*, 2008) did not support the thesis that worklessness was encouraged by tenancy arrangements in the social rented sector, the discourse in relation to the social rented sector continued to start from a negative position. The Chartered Institute of Housing fuelled the discussion in 2008 by proposing reduced security for tenants in the sector but neither its proposals nor those it appeared to have built on (see Dwelly and Cowans *et al.*, 2006) were based on any robust evidence or analysis. At the same time the Conservative party's 'think-tank' followed the same route by suggesting that in the future tenants who were in work should have a preferential opportunity to buy their property (see CSJ, 2008). In spite of the changes of the previous quarter century and the concern about residualisation and concentration of deprivation at neighbourhood level, the prospect was of more of the same – an approach that would further stigmatise places and people. In spite of the failure of the private-sector-led model to deliver the quantity and type of housing needed, these proposals were to dig deeper, eroding the securities of tenure that had been part of the package of rights previously associated with the right to buy and altering the basis of the latter from one related to years of paying rent to one based on employment status.

At this stage the dominant direction of thinking by government and others continued to be about enabling social tenants to move to home ownership (see e.g. ODPM, 2005). New approaches to making social home purchase more accessible and a continuing emphasis upon affordable solutions for first-time buyers sounded like more of the same rather than any radical shift in policy. The Hills review set out where social housing could fit within a system predominantly based upon market provision and asset appreciation. It offered an agenda to ensure that the quality of social housing was adequate for a minor tenure seen as a safety net and providing a springboard to home ownership, rather than a viable and sustainable alternative in its own right. All of the proposals were built on an orthodoxy that saw social renting as a sector of last resort and a stepping-stone to other preferable tenures. They amounted to no more than a reassertion of the policies of the previous 30 years – with little learning about the consequences of pursuing such an approach. Indeed, they involved a further deregulation both through a direct attack on security of tenure and because the prospect was of an increased role for the deregulated private rented sector in housing those with the lowest incomes and employability. The social rented sector as envisaged would only house the poorest households but would also be too small to accommodate all of those who might reasonably be seen as qualifying for it.

If this becomes an account of a dominant orthodoxy and a professional and policy community bankrupt of ideas, it is important to recognise alternatives. Elsewhere in debates about, for example, education or health, government has argued that public services should be as good as or better than their private alternatives – and so there should be a real choice between different providers. In housing this approach resonates not only with debates about social mobility but also about regeneration of neighbourhoods and stable opportunities to build family life. It means seeking to restructure the social rented sector in order to redress its residual status by enhancing its quality and desirability and encouraging those in the sector and in work to stay. The renewal or regeneration of the least desirable estates and the full involvement of existing tenants in that process becomes a key part of the agenda and part of the expansion of the sector taking advantage of opportunities to achieve environmental and energy efficiency and to contribute to wider economic regeneration.

Rather than maintain a drive to make tenants become home owners there is a case for creating a tenure where some tenants, who could technically afford to move out, would choose to stay because the dwelling and service they receive is as good as or better than they would obtain in the market. This is a much more ambitious agenda than the residual approach where the departure of tenants can be seen as a sign of success. It is also a more ambitious agenda than that associated with better local management – as the evidence suggests this is necessary but not sufficient to create a rented sector that works. Regeneration and reshaping of estates as well as substantial capital investment is needed in most cases. And this is likely to involve significant demolition and rebuilding – with the need to address how this can work for local communities and not be dismissed with no reference to context, resources or process. It also sets a competitive challenge for a private rented sector that still has too many shortcomings in terms of dwelling quality (including failures to meet the decent homes standard) and service delivery and, unless it is brought within a regulatory framework, is unlikely to serve the poorest households well.

But the rebuilding of a rented sector of choice raises questions about wider policy. It is unlikely to be achieved where the rented properties that are a sustainable asset in building a tenure of choice are periodically sold with substantial discounts. Arguably the tenure could withstand sales at close to market values if the receipts from such sales were used to acquire equally attractive properties. This brings the financing of rented housing back to centre stage. The reconstruction of a viable rented sector of choice presents challenges for financing and longer-term perspectives on asset management to the fore. The orthodoxies about market pricing and means tested assistance with rent have not worked well in terms either of direct public expenditure or creating sustainable housing and neighbourhoods and the advantages of alternatives should not be dismissed without further consideration.

Conclusions

This chapter has discussed features of housing in England after an era of privatisation and deregulation. In spite of a view that housing had ceased to be a major area for government policy, the opposite has been the case. Even before the credit crunch further reduced output, new private housing construction failed to fill the gap left by reduced public investment and there was more concern with the economic dimensions and consequences of housing market development, affordability problems and the failure of the deregulated system to deliver the quantity of housing needed.

This chapter has argued that, against the expectations of policy makers in the 1980s, there has been a rediscovery of housing policy. This has not meant a reversion to the comprehensive policies of the 1970s. Although some local authorities may begin to play more active roles the changes since the 1970s mean that local authorities and local government as a whole will not recapture previous roles. Some of the credit crunch interventions may not continue in place over the long term. Nevertheless the lessons from before the credit crunch as well as those during it indicate that housing associations and the new government agencies set up in 2008 are likely to continue to have an active role in housing.

The concern about the impact of housing on the economy and the renewed interest in housing affordability and supply meant the abandonment of some of the orthodoxies of the earlier period. Government's involvement in housing is no longer seen simply as a hangover from the postwar welfare state settlement and as an aspect of social policy. Rather it has been rehabilitated as a key element in economic policy, affecting the competitiveness of cities and regions and, through that, of the national economy. Nor is the orthodoxy that the housing problem was largely solved still supported. However, other orthodoxies remain in place. The overwhelming preference of the British electorate for home ownership continues to dominate the thinking of government and others and to leave it struggling to engineer new pathways to home ownership, and at times leaves it more inclined to rescue struggling home owners than tenants. Although the non-market sector is now very much smaller than in the past, the view that this distorts the housing market continues to exist. The orthodoxy associated with the definition of public expenditure and the desirable level of such expenditure also appears unassailable. Unfortunately a new orthodoxy appears to have been forming in the debates around the future of social housing in recent years: that the way social rented housing is allocated, the rent regime associated with it and security of tenure contribute to worklessness and the problems associated with 'estates'. This emerging orthodoxy, added to the others, appears to mean that, rather than the rediscovery of housing policy leading to a radical rethinking, the vessels making the most noise argue for more of the same – a further weakening of the planning system, conditional tenancies and confirming the safety net and springboard role of the social rented sector – and leads automatically to criticism of whichever organisations are involved in providing non-market housing. The orthodoxies crowd out any tangible evidence that would challenge them.

The rediscovery of housing policy has, however, resulted in a reinvigoration of the regulation of, and investment in, affordable housing. Government's agencies operating in the housing field and working with local authorities and housing associations were strengthened in 2008 and this could enable a new era of public investment in housing and regeneration. While there has been a decline of state housing and a growth of home ownership the social rented sector remains large by European standards and this leaves England with social landlords that have considerable organisational and financial strength. Their share of the market is testament to a strong interventionist tradition, closer to other European neighbours than to 'Anglo-Saxon' comparators.

It makes sense in the next phase of policy to pay less attention to American models either of finance or renewal and instead to build alternatives that complement home ownership by providing secure housing and building on the different financing and organisational models that are achievable within a rented sector. In a situation where the private sector fails to overcome shortages, the processes of filtering or trickle-down, which have been doubtful at the best of times, certainly will not work to meet the needs of lower-income households. In the different context of today the rediscovery of housing policy would not be expected to recreate the same rented sectors as in the past. However, the provision of high-quality housing, directly targeted at those who are in housing need, has proved in the past to be the most effective mechanism for delivering housing that assisted in social mobility and improved the life chances of those living in it. It is the residual nature of social renting that has generated problems rather than anything intrinsic to rented housing provided outside the market. There is an opportunity to develop a more ambitious agenda for rented housing as more than a safety net and stepping stone to home ownership and ensure that it is more than a source of problems and a contributor to worklessness. A new generation of rented housing could be an important vehicle for investment and regeneration and for environmental and neighbourhood improvement. It would also provide long-term stable housing for those who would choose to rent if there was a different but competitive offer when compared with what was available to them what was on offer were to bear a reasonable relationship to what was in the private sector.

References

Barker, K. (2003) *Review of Housing Supply: Interim Report.* London: HMSO.

Barker, K. (2004) *Review of Housing Supply, Delivering Stability: Securing our Future Housing Needs: Final Report – Recommendations.* London: HMSO.

Barker, K. (2006) *Barker Review of Land Use Planning: Final Report.* London: HMSO.

Bassett, K. and Short, J. (1980) *Housing and Residential Structure: Alternative Approaches.* London: Routledge & Kegan Paul.

Bowley, M. (1945) *Housing and the State 1919–1944.* London: George Allen & Unwin.

Burrows, R. (2003) 'How the other half lives? An exploratory analysis of the relationship between poverty and home ownership in Britain'. *Urban Studies,* 40(7), 223–42.

Cave, M. (2007) *Every Tenant Matters: A Review of Social Housing Regulation.* Wetherby: Communities and Local Government.

Centre for Social Justice (2008) *Housing Poverty,* London: CSJ.

Cole, I. and Furbey, R. (1994) *The Eclipse of Council Housing.* London: Routledge.

DCLG (2007) *Homes for the Future: More Affordable, More Sustainable.* HMSO Cm 7191.

DETR and DSS (2000) *Quality and Choice: A Decent Home for All.* The Housing Green Paper. London: DETR, DSS.

Dwelly, T. and Cowans, J. (eds) (2006) *Rethinking Social Housing.* London: The Smith Institute.

Feinstein, L., Lupton, R., Hammond, C., Mujtaba, T., Salter, E. and Sorhaindo, A. (2008) *The Public Value of Social Housing: A Longitudinal Analysis of the Relationship between Housing and Life Chances.* London: Smith Institute.

Fletcher D. R., Gore, T., Reeve, K. and Robinson, D. (2008) *Social Housing and Worklessness: Qualitative Research Findings. Department for Work and Pensions* Research Report No 521. London: HMSO.

Forrest, R. and Murie, A. (1983) 'Residualisation and council housing: Aspects of the changing social relations of housing tenure'. *Journal of Social Policy,* 12(4), 453–68.

Forrest, R. and Murie, A. (1986) 'Marginalisation and subsidised individualism – The sale of council houses in the restructuring of the British welfare state', *International Journal for Urban and Regional Research*, 10(1), 46–65.

Forrest, R. and Murie, A. (1990) *Selling the Welfare State* (2nd edition) London: Routledge.

Foster, J. and Hope, T. (1993) *Housing, Community and Crime: The Impact of the Priority Estates Project*. London: HMSO.

Glennerster, H. and Turner, T. (1993) *Estate Based Housing Management: An Evaluation*. London: HMSO.

Groves, R., Murie, A. and Watson, C. (2007) *Housing and the New Welfare State: Perspectives from East Asia and Europe*. Aldershot: Ashgate.

Harloe, M. (1995) *The People's Home? Social Rented Housing in Europe and America*. Oxford: Blackwell.

Henderson, J. and Karn, V. (1987) *Race, Class and State Housing*. London: Gower.

Hills, J. (2007) *Ends and Means: The Future Roles of Social Housing in England*. London: Centre for Analysis of Social Exclusion, London School of Economics and Political Science.

Holmans, A. E. (1987) *Housing Policy in Britain*. London: Croom Helm.

Jones, C. and Murie, A. (2006) *The Right to Buy*. Oxford: Blackwell.

Kemeny, J. (1981) *The Myth of Home Ownership*. London: Routledge and Kegan Paul.

—— (1995) *From Public Housing to the Social Market*. London: Routledge.

Lambert, J., Paris, C. and Blackaby, B. (1978) *Housing Policy and the State*. London: Macmillan.

Lee, P. and Murie, A. (1997) *Poverty, Housing Tenure and Social Exclusion*. Bristol: The Policy Press.

Lee, P. and Murie, A. (2002) 'The Poor City: national and local perspectives on changes in residential patterns in the British City' in Marcuse, P. and van Kempen, R. (eds) *Of States and Cities: A Partitioning of Urban Space*. Oxford: Oxford University Press.

Malpass, P. (1990) *Reshaping Housing Policy: Subsidies, Rents and Residualisation*. London: Routledge.

Malpass, P. (2000) *Housing Associations and Housing Policy: A Historical Perspective*. Basingstoke: Macmillan.

Malpass, P. (2008) 'Housing and the new welfare state: Wobbly pillar or cornerstone?' *Housing Studies*, 23(1), 1–20.

Malpass, P. and Murie, A. (1990) *Housing Policy and Practice* (3rd edition). Basingstoke: Macmillan.

Malpass, P. and Murie, A. (1999) *Housing Policy and Practice* (5th edition). Basingstoke: Macmillan.

Marsh, A. *et al.* (2003) *The Impact of the 1999 Changes to the RTB Discount*, London: HMSO.

Merrett, S. (1979) *State Housing in Britain.* London: Routledge & Kegan Paul.

Mullins, D. and Murie, A. (2006) *Housing Policy in the UK.* Basingstoke: Palgrave Macmillan.

Murie, A. (1977) 'Council House Sales Mean Poor Law Housing', *Roof,* 2(2), 46–9.

Murie, A. (1983) *Housing Inequality and Deprivation.* London: Heinemann.

Murie, A. (1985) 'Housing' in Loughlin, M., Gelfand, D. and Young, K. (eds) *Half a Century of Municipal Decline?* Allen & Unwin, 187–201.

Murie, A. (1997) *The Housing Divide in British Social Attitudes : The 14th Report,* R. Jones, *et al.,* (eds). Ashgate, 137–50.

Murie, A. (1998) *Attitudes to Housing in England in 1996,* University of Birmingham.

Murie, A. (2006) 'Moving with the Times, Changing Frameworks for Housing Research and Policy' in Malpass, P. and Cairncross, L. (eds) *Building on the Past.* Bristol: Policy Press.

Murie, A. (2008) *Moving Homes: The Housing Corporation 1964–2008.* London: Politico's.

Murie, A. and Rowlands, R. (2007) 'The New Politics of Urban Housing', *Environment and Planning C*: Government and Policy Vol. 25.

Murie, A., Niner, P. and Watson, C. (1976) *Housing Policy and the Housing System.* London: Allen & Unwin.

ODPM (2003) *Sustainable Communities: Building for the Future.* London: ODPM.

ODPM (2005) *HomeBuy – Expanding The Opportunity To Own.* London: ODPM.

Power, A. (1987) *Property Before People.* London: Allen & Unwin.

Rex, J. and Moore, R. (1967) *Race, Community and Conflict.* Oxford: Oxford University Press.

Stephens, M., Whitehead, C. and Munro, M. (2005) *Lessons From The Past, Challenges For The Future For Housing Policy: An Evaluation Of English Housing Policy 1975–2000.* London: Office of Deputy Prime Minister.

Tunstall, R. and Coulter, A. (2006) *Twenty-five Years On Twenty Estates: Turning the Tide?* York: Joseph Rowntree Foundation.

13 Conclusions and questions about the future

Chris Paris

This book has been written during a turbulent period in the history of housing in the UK as in much of the developed world. All of the chapters in this book have been substantially reconsidered and revised over the last year to reflect current concerns about the credit crunch, widespread instability in housing markets and continuing debates about government policy responses, both generally to the economy and specifically relating to housing markets and provision. The contributing authors all conclude, to greater or lesser degrees, with a sense of uncertainty about future directions of change in the housing system, housing policy and the wider socio-economic circumstances within which housing issues are embedded.

Just as the benefit of hindsight enables us to see the 1970s as a crucial period in the history of housing provision and policy in the UK, so there is now a sense that we may be living through the end of *another* era. The 1970s marked the decisive turn away from the broad post-war consensus regarding two key priorities of replacing the slums and adding to overall supply. The last 30 years are characterised in this book as a period of government withdrawal from direct housing provision, deregulation of many elements of housing markets and finance, and the promotion of home ownership almost at all costs. There have been booms and recessions between the early 1970s and 2007–8, but the recent past may come to be seen as the high water mark of the tide of rampant deregulated pro-market policies. The contributors to this book seem to agree that we are probably moving into a different phase of housing history, though it is too early to know quite what that is going to look like. For example, in Chapter 7 Kemp considers what implications the credit crunch may have for the future of private renting. He suggests that, whatever happens, the future of the sector will be more secure than it was in the 1970s, and it will undoubtedly be *different*.

The next section of this chapter provides an overview of the structure and contents of the book before attempting to answer the key questions posed in the first chapter regarding the transformation of housing provision and housing policy over the last 30 or so years. Some questions take longer than others to answer, and the answers are more clear-cut for some questions than for others. But these differences in my answers are inevitable given the greater intractability of some issues than others and the extent of agreement and disagreement between the authors of the other chapters in this book.

This chapter concludes with a review of some of the agreements and differences between the contributors to this book in terms of their analyses and interpretation of housing provision, housing markets and related public policies over the last 30 to 40 years.

Overview

Most of the chapters in this book accept the premise of the opening two chapters that the 1970s marked a pivotal period in the history of housing provision and housing policies in the UK. The first two chapters set the scene, with Malpass and Rowlands providing an overview of the background to the 1970s, 'a tumultuous decade of political and economic turmoil both domestically and internationally'. Watson and Niner see the 1970s as a turning point in the housing system and policies, but more as the culmination of developments that had already begun *plus* some key economic and other changes, not as a sudden switch away from well-established policies and practices.

Chapters 3 and 4 review the role of the right to buy in transforming council housing from the early 1980s. The two chapters together provide a clear overview of the background, dimensions and consequences of the introduction of the RTB, though with different emphases and orientations. In Chapter 3, Forrest describes council housing as a 'social escalator' and argues that the success of the RBT largely depended on the *success* of council housing. In Chapter 4, Jones highlights the magnitude of the impact of RTB in terms of reducing the size of the council sector and increasing home ownership. Both chapters also highlight some unanticipated outcomes of the RTB, especially the growth of private renting in former council houses.

In Chapter 5, Mullins and Pawson review the growth and effects of stock transfer, conceptualised as a form of 're-nationalisation' rather than 'privatisation' because central agencies can manage relationships with housing associations, and direct them towards preferred outcomes, without interference from local authorities. In Chapter 6, Malpass also identifies demunicipalisation as a central strand in government support for housing associations, especially the strong sponsorship by the Conservatives in the 1980s. Malpass reviews current debates about the future of housing associations and sees the cave report and agrees with Mullins and Pawson that stock transfer to housing associations to date may be seen as an *alternative* to full privatisation. They also agree that the future of housing associations is uncertain, though Malpass anticipates future privatisation of some larger associations.

Elements of private market housing provision and related public policies are reviewed in Chapters 7, 8 and 9. The transformation of private renting since the early 1970s is examined by Kemp in Chapter 7. He argues that a mix of factors led to the resurgence of private renting and that the rise of BTL investment from the late 1990s was an industry initiative and *not* led by policy. Williams reviews changing home ownership markets since the 1970s in Chapter 8 and relates growing but differentiated home ownership to overall changes in wealth and inequality. He suggests that the Brown government's aim to increase the proportion of households owning their own homes cannot succeed and suggests that we face a downturn 'with no immediate sense of when the market will settle or where it will settle'. He anticipates a new phase in terms of regulation and lending practices. Bramley examines questions relating to meeting the demand for new housing in Chapter 9, reflecting on the changing roles of national and local government in relation to new housing supply, including the retreat from direct promotion to reliance on regulation through planning. He identifies a 'rediscovery' of the issue of housing supply and emphasises the centrality of *political* debates and differences regarding housing supply, especially in relation to the 'problems of policy implementation in a complex and decentralised system'.

The final two substantive chapters focus on current policy debates and issues especially regarding regeneration and sustainable communities. Lee uses the concept of 're-scaling' to capture the sense of taking a wider spatial perspective than narrowly focussing on poor neighbourhoods, often council housing estates, by locating local circumstances to wider national and regional processes of economic restructuring. He reviews some aspects of the Sustainable Communities Plan and concludes his analysis of regeneration policy by emphasising a new approach, or, one might suggest, a new rhetoric, about the centrality of economics to regeneration. Rowlands takes up some of the same issues in Chapter 11, through a critique of the conceptual basis for terms utilised in current UK government policies regarding 'sustainable communities' and housing 'mix'. When combined with the equally vague term 'sustainable', it is hard to disagree with Robinson's (2008) suggestion that such policy discourse amounts to little more than 'contrived ambiguity': nice-sounding but analytically empty phrases that appear to convey concern and strong principles but are actually vacuous (and/or specious).

As was noted in Chapter 1, the chapters in this book have varying geographical foci, especially regarding public policies relating to housing provision: some mainly or solely discuss developments in England (Malpass on housing associations, Bramley on the supply of new housing, Lee on regeneration and Rowlands on sustainable communities). Others make some reference to Scotland and/or

Wales (Watson and Niner on the 1970s, Kemp on private renting and Williams on home ownership) but there is no reference to Northern Ireland apart from some commentary in the first chapter. Mullins and Pawson, for example, discuss stock transfer from councils to other non-profit landlords without any reference to the transfer of council stock to the Northern Ireland Housing Executive in the early 1970s and the subsequent *lack* of stock transfer of Housing Executive stock to non-state non-profit landlords. Yet their own argument about stock transfer being more about control and demunicipalisation rather than privatisation can be *strengthened* by reference to the Northern Ireland case: housing functions had *already* been demunicipalised and other political issues had much higher prominence (Paris, 2001).

A closer examination of the Northern Ireland case more generally throws some of the other analyses in this book into sharper relief, as the Housing Executive continued to undertake redevelopment and new building much longer than any other part of the UK. A much more permissive planning regime, albeit changing during recent years, allied with strong pro-development ethos across all major local political parties, facilitated a much faster increase in new housing construction after the mid-1990s in response to growing demand boosted by local demographic and economic factors. Despite new production booming to record levels in 2006–7, however, house prices also rose strongly after the mid-1990s, with a dramatic surge in 2005–7. The situation was more dramatic in the Republic of Ireland: house prices and new house building *both* increased even more strongly between 1996 and 2006, and then, after early 2007, housing output *and* prices both fell at the same time. Thus any expectation that an increase in supply will necessarily lead to a reduction in prices needs to be taken with a very large pinch of salt, especially in the hot-house region of South-East England. Clearly, as Forrest emphasises in Chapter 3, the complexity of socio-economic phenomena means that we should avoid using simplistic cause–effect models of policy impact.

Key questions about the transformation of the housing system since the 1970s

In the first chapter of this book, Malpass and Rowlands pose six key questions about the transformation of housing markets and housing policy since the 1970s:

- How much is the process driven by policy and how much by other factors?
- How are tenures changing their meanings and roles in the overall housing system?
- How far will residualisation proceed, or has it begun to level out?
- Is tenure becoming less important than locality in some parts of the housing system?

- How are people affected by when and where they enter housing, and are some cohorts significantly advantaged or disadvantaged?
- What lessons can be learned from the past, and what do they imply for the future?

The rest of this concluding chapter is structured around these questions and sets out to answer them, mainly on the basis of the evidence and arguments in the other contributions in this book. Some other evidence and arguments are also introduced, although this may break one of the rules about 'conclusions', namely that no additional material should be introduced that has not already been examined in the preceding body of material in the paper, monograph or book. This chapter, however, has never been conceptualised simply as summarising and responding – rather, it provides me with an opportunity to set out my own considered view of housing, markets and policy over the last 35 years.

The role of policy in the transformation of the housing system

The short answer is that the transformation of the housing system has been driven by *combinations* of policy and other factors: in Chapter 8 Williams shows that the growth of owner occupation was driven by the combined effects of policy-led deregulation and market-driven changes in lending practices. A longer answer involves an appreciation that there have been many and diverse combinations of factors; combinations have changed over time; and their outcomes often differ from the aspirations of policy makers and implementers and the preferences of individuals, households and organisations.

The inherent complexity of socio-economic phenomena and their changes over time, as Forrest argues in Chapter 3, cautions against the use of simplistic cause–effect models of policy impact. Some chapters in this book review housing system changes that are almost entirely due to policy initiatives, although some outcomes were unanticipated or perverse. In other instances, however, changes were initiated entirely from market processes or other non-state actions, and were subsequently incorporated into policy.

Kemp shows that policy *directly* affected changes in private renting, especially deregulation and the BES, but that outcomes were *also* affected by the housing slump of 1989–93. The growth of BTL investment, however, was initiated by the finance industry, *not* government policy. Malpass argues that the use of private finance to supplement government grants was initiated by housing associations (albeit encouraged by the Housing Corporation); it became government policy *later* and appears to be an excellent example of a policy *following* rather than leading change. The same is true of stock transfer. We also have examples of simple policy failure, where none of the policy's objectives were achieved: especially Housing Investment Trusts, discussed by Kemp in Chapter 7.

The move away from construction subsidies for local authorities ('bricks and mortar') to consumption subsidies in the form of housing benefit (whether payable directly to landlords or to tenants) is identified by contributors to this book as a crucial policy-led driver of transformation in the housing system. Thus, as elsewhere, the introduction of housing allowances moved the focus of housing policy away from 'shelter' towards income support and distribution (Heidenheimer *et al.*, 1990).

Some changes occurred *within* the structures and organisations responsible for public policy, including the creation of new devolved national assemblies. Contributors to this book emphasise the fragmentation of governance at a local level, following centralisation of power and demunicipalisation of housing policy functions. Policies now must be implemented through numerous agencies, including non-government agencies, so there is greater scope for implementation failure. In Chapter 9 Bramley emphasised the loss of *agency*, conceptualised as a combination of organisations and power, to develop and implement housing policies; thus central government may want to increase overall housing production but it has to face up to complex political opposition and intransigence from local authorities in affluent areas of southern England.

Many non-government institutions and organisations also have policies relating to housing and they actively pursue their own interests, especially the Council for Mortgage Lenders. As housing association development has come to rely heavily on private finance, so governments have been reluctant to review housing benefit because this underpins the business case that housing associations make in securing finance. Professional associations and non-profit organisations are also active in housing policy debates in pursuit of the further prosperity of their industry sectors, especially the Chartered Institute of Housing and the National Housing Federation: both were insignificant in the mid-1970s.

Bourne (1990) suggested that 'non-housing policies' may have greater impacts on housing provision than public policies explicitly relating to housing: Lee's chapter in this book testifies to the impact of non-policy economic change and non-housing policies on the fortunes of deprived neighbourhoods.

Heidenheimer e*t al.* (1990) suggest that policy can best be conceptualised as a 'string of decisions that add up to a fairly consistent body of behaviour sanctioned by governmental authority'. Malpass sees the rise of housing associations 'as incremental and opportunistic' but suggests that governments had strategic *principles*, to rely on markets as much as possible for housing provision; hence his expectation that some housing associations could become for-profit market organisations.

Apart from Kemp's discussion of factors affecting demand for private rental accommodation, contributors to the book have not explored demographic changes since the 1970s as drivers of the changing housing system, yet Murie *et al.* (1976) identified 'households' as a core component of the housing system. This issue is complex, because some demographic changes and aspects of housing are highly inter-related. Many of these changes represent *personal choices* of millions of individuals regarding their living arrangements, fertility and familial associations (though such decisions may reflect a context within which assumptions, attitudes and behaviour reflect life in an established welfare state). Nonetheless, whilst not driven by housing policy, demographic changes have had major impacts on the housing system since the 1970s; for example, falling birth rates (until very recently), decline in marriage rates, growth of single parenthood, the transformation of household structures – all amounting to the often-exaggerated 'death of the family'. The UK has had both population growth *and* falling average household size for 40 years: thus about 30 per cent of the growth of household numbers in Northern Ireland between 1971 and 2001 was due to changing household composition and falling average household size (Paris *et al.*, 2004). The recent migrant surge into the UK clearly boosted demand for private rental housing, at least in the short term, and appears to be a factor in the recent up-turn of birth rates as well as changing ethnic compositions in many localities.

The changing meanings and roles of tenures within the housing system

The chapters by Jones and Forrest show how the meaning and role of council housing has changed since the 1970s. It was a differentiated sector, with attractive homes in suburban estates, newer but less popular high-rise housing and, in the early 1970s, older slum housing which had been acquired for clearance. The desirable housing estates in Birmingham, for example, were typically represented by Labour councillors, many of whom were powerful in council politics. These were the council homes that Forrest describes as social escalators and that Rex and Moore (1967) described as a 'prize'. Most were acquired under the right to buy, and many of their 1970s occupants' jobs, for example in the car factory at Longbridge, no longer exist. But much 1970s council housing was less popular: I recall campaigning in local elections and advising tenants in high-rise council housing that they should vote Labour if they ever wanted a transfer to the more popular low-rise estates (for Conservatives would sell them all off!). It would be quite wrong to imagine that *all* council housing was popular.

The two related processes of council house sales and growth of housing associations during the 1980s and 1990s resulted in changes to the relative desirability of the remaining council housing – increasingly in high-rise or other high-density forms – *and* the loss of the organised-labour aristocracy that once represented many council housing areas. In addition, and not discussed in this book, there were changes in the allocation of council housing. The end of slum clearance removed one stream of entrants and the 1977 Homeless Persons Act marked the beginning of 'needs-based' allocations leading to increasing numbers of homeless households, a growing proportion of sole parents and, by the 1990s, growing levels of applications from single homeless people. The possibility that homelessness legislation would be a pivotal factor influencing the mix of entrants into council housing was *not* anticipated at the time; rather it was seen as a way to ensure that families were not split up by involuntary homelessness.

The council sector was shrinking but housing associations were growing in the 1980s and 1990s. A new concept emerged in the UK during the 1980s: the idea of 'social' housing. This term was not used in the UK during the 1970s and did not appear at all in *Housing Policy and the Housing System* (Murie *et al.*, 1976) when housing associations were only minor players in UK housing. Their development into the major players was not foreseen by contemporary commentators. The creation of 'social housing' came about partly through the growing appreciation of the diversity of forms of non-profit rental housing provision across the EU. The term may also have been used strategically by housing association representatives to distance themselves from those Conservative politicians in the 1980s who wanted to use associations as a way of reviving private renting.

The term social housing is now widely used to refer to all forms of non-profit housing provision, but many private landlords also accommodate tenants in receipt of housing benefit, thus providing similar or even *more* desirable services than councils or housing associations. Housing associations and private landlords differ in terms of legal status and regulatory regimes, and private landlords have a profit motive. But the career aspirations and remuneration objectives of housing association managers may not be motivated purely by altruism and we may come increasingly to consider that many private landlords provide a form of 'social housing'. Murie suggests in this book that living in social rented housing is increasingly likely to reinforce poverty rather than helping lower income households break out of poverty. Some tenants in receipt of housing benefit, however, may choose to rent from private landlords in preference to life in a more stigmatised estate.

Continued expansion of home ownership, fuelled partly by the right to buy but also by growing affluence, made the remaining council housing appear ever less desirable. As Forrest *et al.* (1990) emphasised, home ownership is a highly *differentiated* sector. Few affluent home owners in the Home Counties have anything in common with struggling owners of run-down older housing in poor estates in Liverpool or Paisley. Differences derive from class, income and wealth, as ever, not the trivial fact that they can be classified together within the one tenure. During the 1990s, moreover, there was growth in the level of *outright* home ownership, especially among younger home owners, identifiable from the 2001 census at a time when housing commentators were concerned about a declining number of first time buyers and growing affordability problems for low income households.

Private renting, as Kemp shows in Chapter 7, has changed enormously since the 1970s, and this change may have been least expected at that time. It is no longer a dingy residual sector, with rent-controlled tenancies and decrepit older housing. The growth of BTL investment and demand from young single house-holds, as well as students and mobile workers, means 'goodbye Rachman, hullo yuppies!' One of the more beneficial consequences of the credit crunch, however, has been the drying up of the once prolific self-congratulatory newspaper articles by in-house writers discussing their successful BTL investments (names are omitted for legal reasons, but they know who they are!)

How far will residualisation proceed – or has it already levelled out?

Residualisation is not a thing, it is a concept designed to capture the changing nature of social housing: both as a process of change in the stock and socio-eco-nomic and demographic characteristics of tenants. I find it extremely hard to envisage any reversal of residualisation within the UK council housing, though some public housing remains more popular than others. In Northern Ireland, slum clearance and new build occurred later than in GB, and public sector housing is generally low rise and of good quality, so it retains a wider basis of support and a more desirable image than in many other parts of the UK.

The term 'residualisation' was used initially with reference to council housing but increasingly is also appropriate for much housing association stock, though this remains more variable in quality than the remaining council stock. The loss of stock from councils in future now appears more likely to be through transfers to housing associations than through right-to-buy sales, and there is little prospect at present of surging growth of social housing provision of any kind.

Residualisation is not explored much in this book, but on reflection I am struck by the idea that it may not really be a tenure issue at all. The departure of the labour aristocracy from the council sector marked the final abandonment of Labour's commitment to council housing. Social housing is increasingly the tenure of immigrants and an alienated and disorganised underclass. So, as Forrest and Murie (1990) suggested, it is the *people* who are residual – or in current policy terms 'socially excluded' – and they happen to be living in social housing as a result of what types of lowest-cost rental accommodation were available at the time. In other countries with no social housing they would be renting from private landlords, often perhaps in over-crowded multi-occupied buildings, or they would be on the streets.

The relative importance of tenure and locality in parts of the housing system

There are many different scales of locality: street, neighbourhood, suburb, towns, re-gions and countries. Although there is evidence that there are greater concentrations of poverty and social exclusion in areas of social housing, neither owner occupation nor private renting is homogeneous – there are many variations by class and income, bundled together in specific localities. Affluent but mobile tenants live next door to affluent home owners with little evident social friction. Thus tenure and locality are both highly differentiated categories, so it is impossible to give any single answer to this question.

The key questions thus become *whose* tenure and in *which* localities. As with the consideration of the changed nature and meaning of tenure, so with regard to locality we can conclude that what is at issue is changing class structures and polarisation of wealth and income distribution, with growth both of super-rich and underclass – not tenure.

It is precisely the complexity of these issues, and the opacity of much of the policy jargon, especially recycled and re-badged area-based approaches, that both Lee and Rowlands are addressing in their chapters in this book. It is logically just about impossible to deal consistently across space in the face of diverse local combinations of physical housing conditions and socio-economic relations. Ethnic diversity and other bases of social differentiation only add further complexity and layers of sensitivity to any policy development and implementation.

The significance of cohort effects

There is a simple answer: yes, people have been *massively* affected by when and where they enter housing; and some cohorts have been significantly more advantaged or disadvantaged than others. There were enormous changes in terms of patterns of housing conditions, tenures and costs throughout the twentieth century. The impact of wars on the development of the housing system was noted by Malpass and Rowlands in Chapter 1. Rent control in the private sector, introduced during the First World War, had long-term effects for access to private renting by subsequent cohorts. That war, as well as other social conflicts, led to the rise of council housing in the 1920s and delayed slum clearance until the 1930s. The Second World War brought greater physical damage to the housing stock, and post-war shortages ran through to prolong the rise of new housing construction, thus contributing to the long drawn-out process of slum clearance and redevelopment, which was only just coming to an end when the seminal *Housing Policy and the Housing System* was published in 1976. Again, we see how path dependency developed over long periods.

Newly formed households in 1975 had a completely different range of opportunities and constraints than those forming some 30 years earlier or later. In the 1970s there was very little opportunity to rent privately, apart from poor-quality older housing, often in decaying, subdivided, multi-occupied dwellings owned by 'pariah' landlords (Rex and Moore, 1967). Access to mortgages to buy a home was tightly controlled, and available mainly from building societies rather than banks. For those households able to save and buy a home, however, mortgage interest tax relief meant that home ownership could be both affordable and also a way of gaining a prized asset. There was a large and diverse council housing stock, but waiting lists were often very long and applicants' choices were often very limited (Lambert *et al.*, 1978).

There was a step-change in housing opportunities after 1980, particularly benefiting many households that were already well housed. The disposal of council housing through the right to buy provided once-off opportunities for existing council tenants during the 1980s but reduced the pool of available council housing for subsequent applicants. This also had the unanticipated outcome of subsequent growth of private renting within what had previously been wholly council estates.

By 2005 there was an ample supply of opportunities in a 'new' private rental sector, though rents may have been high for some prospective tenants. Many local authorities no longer had *any* housing, though they still had statutory responsibility to deal with homelessness; but in some areas there was a good stock of other 'social housing', though most households with members in the paid labour force would have been reluctant to apply. House prices in some areas had reached dizzying heights, but even households on the average manual wage could dream of home ownership, provided they had dual incomes: mortgage finance was plentiful and barely rationed at all – prospective purchasers were able to borrow four or five times their annual incomes at 100 or even 110 per cent of property valuations. Some commentators were concerned about the growing gap between incomes and house prices and suggested that a correction was becoming increasingly likely, but nobody took much notice at the time.

Moving to 2008, we see a turbulent environment for new entrants to the housing system. House prices are falling, so affordability may improve, but mortgage finance is as severely rationed as it was in 1975, although now by banks rather than building societies. Meanwhile, however, growing outright owner-occupation and income polarisation are having new inter-generational effects through inheritance.

Lessons from the past, implications for the future

This question leaves us with most room to disagree and debate. A couple of years ago we might have argued that a key lesson was that policies which went with the grain of market and social change were more likely to succeed – however such 'success' may be measured. The current finance and housing market crisis, however, cautions against such a view, as greater resistance to market trends might have resulted in less dramatic outcomes. Indeed, if there is a lesson, it is that unfettered and unregulated free market entrepreneurship, in globally interconnected markets and economies can result in chaotic outcomes: after the plunderers have departed the scene with their outrageous 'performance' payments, millions of ordinary decent folk have lost their savings, pensions and homes.

Bramley suggests the current crisis in housing markets has changed both the economic context and also the political mood; thus 'the high era of free-market liberalism and the belief in the unbounded benefits of unregulated free markets has run its course'. Thus he predicts a period of greater regulation and more tightly constrained lending practices. Williams also expects to see increased regulation and more conservative lending practices. Lee also concludes 'that we have entered a new phase of policy development' but notes an apparent contradiction between growing acceptance of the qualitative concept of social exclusion and an accompanying emphasis on positivist methodologies to 'predict and provide' for future planned housing needs.

But only history will tell us, at some stage in the future, whether the current crisis has been structural or merely cyclical. We came to realise pretty quickly that 'the end of history' had not happened in the wider world, so it is possible that the end of recent housing history in the UK also may not happen. In other words, after a suitable pause for reflection, once the current housing market malaise has departed the scene, we may return to much the same in terms of owner-occupation at all costs, close down the remaining public housing sector and, as usual, prioritise market processes above public intervention. This book certainly demonstrates the significance of path dependency and long-term prioritisation of market provision of housing, wherever and whenever possible. As chapter authors have shown, however, it can be very difficult to accomplish desired policy outcomes in a much more fragmented system of decision-making and implementation than in the 1970s.

But then again, Williams believes that there is 'no immediate sense of when the market will settle or where it will settle' and suggests that such settlement 'could be up to two to three years away and with prices, on average, at least 25 per cent down from the peak and possibly closer to 30 per cent down'. He describes the government's recent housing market package in England as 'a useful coordinated exercise' but expects only a very limited impact 'in terms of easing the downturn or stimulating a recovery'.

Much contemporary policy jargon is impenetrable by rational thought, as Rowlands showed clearly and as Lee also demonstrated in his chapter. 'Regeneration' is an especially good example; it is a metaphor implying something organic and natural to do with re-growth, but in almost every case such policies are about *changing* places. They often result in the replacement of one set of residents with another group and can be drivers of gentrification. Perhaps one lesson, therefore, is to attempt greater clarity in articulating what policies are for. However, I can only agree with Rowlands' critique of ideas relating to 'sustainable communities' and Robinson's (2008) description of much contemporary policy double-speak as 'contrived ambiguity'. The result of combining ambiguous words into compound expressions simply multiplies and compounds ambiguity and vacuity. So the term 'mixed communities' can mean anything that you want it to mean and be at any scale or type of mixing: class, ethnicity, tenure and religion (as in Northern Ireland where religious identification is a metaphor for the two separate communities). The idea of 'mix' is typically presented as self-evidently desirable, but in practice mixing is precisely what many people do *not* want; thus they buy into particular places to avoid mixing with undesirable others.

What are the futures for various tenures? Most of the preceding chapters indicate uncertainty rather than clear directions of change. Will there be a re-growth of council housing, perhaps under a new logo and with new circumstances? Will housing associations continue to grow or will some become fully fledged private corporations? How will regulation across all housing sectors be developed and implemented? Will the BTL boom in retrospect be seen as the BTL bubble? Such questions may be seen as rather quaint, when considered in retrospect by another generation of housing researchers around the year 2035. By that time, any of the current authors in this book who are still alive will probably have retired – unless such a notion also has become anachronistic!

Conclusions – or maybe just some questions

The contributors to this book have chronicled major changes in the housing system in the UK since the 1970s, within a wider international context of the shift from Fordism to post-Fordism, the globalisation of production and consumption, the emergence of new developing economies, economic restructuring and labour market transformations and transformation of capital and finance markets.

Housing policy moved during the 1970s away from an emphasis on new building and replacement of slum housing towards a focus on improving the existing stock and freeing the market by privatisation and deregulation. The longer-term effects of wars and processes of recovery were over. Thus as Harloe (1985) and Malpass and Rowlands in this book argue, public policy in the UK returned to its long-term basis of assuming that housing is primarily a market good rather than an element of the welfare state, albeit within a changed, wider milieu. We have gone from the long post-war recovery and boom through cycles of boom and recession: the current period is merely the latest down-turn – almost certainly *not* the cataclysmic end of capitalism!

There has been both change and continuity in urban and regional planning priorities and practices, including a structural policy shift in the state's approach to housing conditions. Slum clearance ceased and policy switched to house and neighbourhood 'improvement', initially with the aid of grants. There has been long-term continuity in strategic metropolitan regional planning, the 'containment of urban England' (Hall *et al.*, 1973) has continued unabated, with powerful NIMBY (Not In My Back Yard) and BANANA (Build Absolutely Nothing

Anywhere Near Anything) lobbies opposing any attempts to develop more housing outside established built-up areas.

We conclude amid uncertainty. The credit crunch appears by the end of 2008 to have had major implications for housing with a substantial decline in house building, widespread evidence of falling house prices and great uncertainty over the future directions for social housing, or even what that term may come to mean in future. It may be best simply to end by reflecting on Watson and Niner's suggestion in Chapter 2 that wise governments and academic commentators should 'view many housing problems as more of a moving target than problems capable of outright solution'.

References

Bourne, L. (1990) Introduction to van Vliet, W. (ed.) *International Handbook of Housing Policies and Practices*, New York: Greenwood Press.

Forrest, R. and Murie, A. (1990) *Selling the Welfare State*, 2nd edition, London: Routledge.

Forrest, R., Murie, A. and Williams, P. (1990) *Home Ownership: Differentiation and Fragmentation*, London: Unwin Hyman.

Hall, P., Thomas, R., Gracey, H. and Drewett, R. (1973) *The Containment of Urban England*, 2 volumes, London: Allen & Unwin.

Harloe, M. (1985) *The People's Home? Social Rented Housing in Europe and America*, Oxford: Blackwell.

Heidenheimer, A., Heclo, C. and Teich Adams, C. (1990) *Comparative Public Policy: The Politics of Social Choice in America, Europe, and Japan*, 3rd edition, New York: St Martin's Press.

Lambert, J., Paris, C. and Blackaby, R. (1978) *Housing Policy and the State*, London: Macmillan.

Murie A., Niner, P. and Watson, C. (1976) *Housing Policy and the Housing System*, London: Allen and Unwin.

Paris, C. (ed). (2001) *Housing in Northern Ireland*, Coventry: Chartered Institute of Housing.

Paris, C., Holmans, A. and Lloyd, K. (2004) *Demographic Trends and Future Housing Need in Northern Ireland*, Belfast: Northern Ireland Housing Executive.

Rex, J. and Moore, R. (1967) *Race, Community and Conflict*, Oxford: Oxford University Press.

Robinson, D. (2008) 'Housing and cohesion in England', presentation to the HAS Conference, York, http://www.york.ac.uk/inst/chp/hsa/spring08/conferencepapers.htm, accessed 19 December 2009.

Index

Index